THE LIFE AND WRITINGS OF ALEXANDRE DUMAS

ALEXANDRE DUMAS PÈRE.

THE
LIFE AND WRITINGS
OF
ALEXANDRE DUMAS
(1802-1870)

BY

HARRY A. SPURR

AUTHOR OF "A COCKNEY IN ARCADIA," ETC.

WITH MANY ILLUSTRATIONS

University Press of the Pacific
Honolulu, Hawaii

The Life and Writings of Alexandre Dumas
(1802-1870)

by
Harry A. Spurr

ISBN: 1-4102-0508-8

Copyright © 2003 by University Press of the Pacific

Reprinted from the 1902 edition

University Press of the Pacific
Honolulu, Hawaii
http://www.universitypressofthepacific.com

All rights reserved, including the right to reproduce this book, or portions thereof, in any form.

In order to make original editions of historical works available to scholars at an economical price, this facsimile of the original edition of 1902 is reproduced from the best available copy and has been digitally enhanced to improve legibility, but the text remains unaltered to retain historical authenticity.

This Book,

THE OUTCOME OF MANY YEARS OF LOVING STUDY

IS RESPECTFULLY DEDICATED

TO

MADAME DUMAS *fils*,

IN GRATEFUL RECOGNITION OF HER

SYMPATHY AND HELP.

PREFACE

THE centenary of the birth of Alexandre Dumas *père* occurred in July of this year. As no satisfactory " Life " of the great Frenchman exists in English, this was thought an appropriate moment for giving the public, with whom his romances are so popular, an account of Dumas's life, character, and writings, which should be both interesting to the ordinary reader, and trustworthy as a book of reference. The author has endeavoured to tell the general reader—" the man in the public library "— who Dumas was, what he did, which books he did write and which he did not write, and finally, what his *confrères* and the great critics have said of him.

One or two points may be dealt with here, by way of anticipating obvious criticism. The first relates to the omission from the following pages of the spiteful libels of MM. " de Mirecourt," de Cassagnac, etc. It is almost impossible at this date for any one, particularly an Englishman, to take the circumstantial allegations of these gentlemen and refute them in detail. It is now over sixty years since they were made: they had their source in admitted enmity, and their medium was equally contemptible. Dumas ignored them; his colleagues in the higher ranks of literature discredited them; his enemies accepted them willingly, without demanding proof. "M. de Mirecourt" was sentenced to imprisonment for publishing his statements; but their improbability is still stronger proof of their falseness. When Dumas's "collaborators" denied the allegations made "on their behalf," "M. de Mirecourt" impudently accused them of having allowed Dumas to dictate their denials; when he "proved" Dumas's illiteracy, by an anecdote in which he cited M. Maquet in support, that gentleman promptly gave the libeller the lie!

We make no apology for dwelling on this point, for the charges of this M. Jacquot have been accepted almost universally as the truth. Quérard cites the gentleman with obvious complacency; Larousse in his "Dictionnaire" quotes him constantly, and Mr Fitzgerald condemns the man's testimony almost as often as he makes use of it. Mr Henley's article in Chambers's "Encyclopædia" is probably the only biographical account of Dumas which is trustworthy. That in the ninth edition of the "Encyclopædia Britannica" is by Mr Fitzgerald.

Of M. Quérard, who in his "Supercheries" proves to his own satisfaction that with one or two insignificant exceptions Dumas never wrote anything at all, it is sufficient to point out that he considered

PREFACE

that author as merely "a clever arranger of the thoughts of others." When a new edition of the "Supercheries" was issued, the *exposés* of M. Quérard, which stopped at 1848, were not continued, and the editors formally expressed their regret that the great writer had received such treatment from the critic. They further hinted that only a determination to use the material of the first edition of the work in its entirety prevented them from dealing with M. Quérard's accusations.

We have referred to Mr Fitzgerald. His "Life and Adventures of Alexander Dumas" was written shortly after the novelist's death, is now forgotten, and is probably out of print. This relieves us from the necessity of saying more than that Mr Lang in his "Essays in Little," Mr Brander Matthews in his "French Novelists," Mr W. H. Pollock in the *Nineteenth Century*, Mr A. B. Walkley in "Playhouse Impressions," and others, have all condemned the book as being inaccurate and unworthy of the subject and the writer. A great change has taken place in the literary estimation of Dumas during the past thirty years; and it is our aim to convey this desirable revolution in opinion to the mind of the ordinary reader.

Consistent with the declaration made above, we have ignored the charges brought against Dumas with reference to his attitude toward Louis Philippe

The ex-employee of the Duke of Orleans is accused of having alternately abused and fawned upon that dignitary when he became king. We prefer to take the responsibility of suppressing the allegations respecting this episode in Dumas's career as utterly at variance with his practice and his nature.

Another omission requires explanation. We have dealt with the plays of Dumas, so far as they affected his career, in Part I.; we have touched on them in general terms in other portions of the book; but have refrained from dealing with them at all extensively. The general reader of the English-speaking public does not know Dumas's plays, and has had no opportunity of seeing them or of reading them, therefore one cannot hope to interest him in them; and at the risk of throwing the subject out of its proper proportion we have omitted to treat them fully. To those who do know and appreciate him as a dramatist, we can recommend "Le Drame d'A. Dumas" by M. H. Parigot, published by Calmann-Lévy.

There is a general confusion in books of reference concerning the year of Dumas's birth. As Glinel shows, by reproducing the certificate of birth, the author was born in 1802.

The author has tried to make his book as accurate as possible, but the task has been difficult, as no impartial and complete biography of Dumas exists,

PREFACE

even in French. He will therefore be grateful to any critic, friendly or otherwise, who will point out any errors of fact in the text.

Note.—My thanks are due to Madame Dumas *fils* for her kind assistance; to M. D'Hauterive, her son-in-law, for similar kindness; to Mr Lang, Mr W. M. Rossetti and Mr Swinburne for courteous replies to inquiries; to Mr Robert Garnett for valuable advice and help; to M.M. Calmann-Lévy for information given; to Mr F. M. Duncan for his photographs of illustrations in the British Museum Library; and to M. E. Roch, secretary of the Villers-Cotterets Centenary Fêtes Committee.

CONTENTS

	PAGE
DEDICATION	v
PREFACE	vii
LIST OF ILLUSTRATIONS	xv

PART I.
HIS LIFE AND CHARACTER

BIRTH, MANHOOD AND EARLY SUCCESSES (1802-30)	3
THE REIGN OF DUMAS I. (1830-48)	40
WANDERINGS, DECLINE AND DEATH (1848-70)	94
CHARACTER	125

PART II.
HIS WRITINGS

HIS WRITINGS	183

PART III.
HIS GENIUS

A DEFENCE	273
A COUNTERCLAIM	309

APPENDICES

		PAGE
A. HISTORY AND FICTION: A COMPARISON	. .	351
B. CHRONOLOGY OF DUMAS'S LIFE .	. .	355
C. TABULAR ANALYSIS OF DUMAS'S WRITINGS	. .	357
D. LIST OF BOOKS CONSULTED	. .	373
INDEX	. .	377

LIST OF ILLUSTRATIONS.

	PAGE
ALEXANDRE DUMAS *père* . . .	*Frontispiece*
HOUSE IN WHICH DUMAS WAS BORN, VILLERS-COTTERETS	8
DUMAS IN 1828 (*from a drawing* BY DEVERIA) . .	30
PORTRAIT OF DUMAS, AFTER MAURIN . . .	36
DUMAS'S THEATRE, THE " HISTORIQUE " . . .	86
ALEXANDRE DUMAS *fils*	108
TITLE-PAGE OF " NOUVELLES CONTEMPORAINES " .	185
" D'ARTAGNAN " (*from the* DORÉ STATUE, PARIS) .	209
THE DUMAS MONUMENT BY DORÉ, PARIS . .	342

PART I

HIS LIFE AND CHARACTER

BIRTH, MANHOOD AND EARLY SUCCESSES (1802-30)—THE REIGN OF DUMAS I. (1830-48)—WANDERINGS, DECLINE AND DEATH (1848-70)—CHARACTER

From Birth to Manhood and Fame (1802-30)

IF, like Defoe, we were about to offer fiction in the guise of biography, instead of biography in a more or less romantic form, we should be tempted to preface the story of Dumas with one of those elaborate sub-titles in which the author of "Robinson Crusoe" delighted. It would probably run somewhat in this fashion, if we allowed ourselves to prepare one, which of course we do not:—

> "*The life and adventures of Alexandre Dumas of the World, who was both a black and a white man; a Royalist and a Republican, an aristocrat and a* sans-culotte; *who took part in three revolutions, and made three different reputations; who wrote more books than any other man living or dead, who erected two "Monte Cristos," one of which made his fortune and the other of which unmade it; who enriched the world and was poor all his life; together with an account of his exploits as dramatist, romancer, traveller, politician, wit, journalist, diplomatist, soldier, lecturer, cook, historian, poet, etc.*"

Before this Alexander entered the world he was about to conquer, much was already his own by inheritance. He was born into the atmosphere of fiery light and fierce heat which the Revolution had left behind it. He was destined to possess a good share of blue and of black blood, for his grandfather was no other than the Marquis Antoine-Alexandre Davy de la Pailleterie, a French nobleman, self-exiled to San Domingo, and his grandmother was a negro-woman, Louise-Cessette Dumas. It was a romantically ill-assorted match, full of interesting possibilities. The son of this marriage threw over parentage and aristocracy, enlisted in the French army as a private under his mother's name, and at thirty-one years of age had risen to the rank of general. Times and circumstances were both fruitful and portentous—for they were leading up to the birth of our hero.

In 1790 the swarthy young Republican Hercules, being stationed at Villers-Cotterets, a little town on the high road from Paris to Laon, fell in love with an innkeeper's daughter there, and duly married her on the 28th of November, 1792. Thus when Alexandre was born, ten years later (on the 24th July, 1802, to be exact), he was a quadroon, and dowered at birth with many of the characteristics, good and bad, of the African race—the ardent, imaginative temperament, the levity of nature, the impulsive soul—a host of qualities which were strange to the comprehension of both friends and enemies in after-life; because side by side with them were all the native characteristics of the Frenchman, existent in full vigour.

All his life Dumas was taunted with his negro descent; the caricaturists and lampooners, with execrable taste, made the crisp hair and lean calves of the quadroon the subject of innumerable gibes. "Blackwood" tells us that a person more remarkable for inquisitiveness than for correct breeding once took the liberty to question the romancer rather closely concerning his genealogical tree.

"You are a quadroon, M. Dumas?" he began.

"I am, sir," replied the author, who had sense enough not to be ashamed of a descent he could not conceal.

"And your father? ..."

"Was a mulatto."

"And your grandfather?"

"A negro," hastily answered Dumas, whose patience was waning fast—too fast for him to trouble about accuracy.

"And may I enquire what your great-grandfather was?"

"An ape, sir!" thundered the great man—"an

ape, sir. My pedigree commences where yours terminates!"

Dumas's title of Marquis was another favourite topic for the malice of his enemies. It was asserted that he was not truly "De la Pailleterie," because his grandparents were not married. Mr. Fitzgerald repeated this assertion; but M. Parigot * refutes it. "Son grandpère paternel . . . avait *épousé* une négresse Marie-Cessette (*sic*) Dumas, décédée en Amerique, à la Guinodée, en 1772." Although the legitimate holder of the title after his father's death, Dumas never but once in his life alluded publicly to it; that indiscretion was absurdly magnified, and the truth of the statement was doubted. Yet (says Janin) when M. Theodore Anne, in his researches concerning the cross of St. Louis, discovered the origin of the La Pailleteries, and proved them to be indisputably noble, Dumas said simply, "I knew it." His son for his part said, "I did not know it." Such was the pride of the father and the son. But to return.

The first of three Alexanders—Mr. A. B. Walkley has dubbed him "Alexandre the greatest" —was a true Frenchman, an ardent Republican, a brilliant soldier, and an honest man. The son, who was apt, at times, to decorate his facts with a gorgeous edge of appropriate fiction, seems to have

* Alexandre Dumas Père ("Les Grands Écrivains Français").

done no more than justice to his father, in the proud appreciations contained in his "Mémoires." Those who are incredulous respecting the wildly heroic deeds of the four Musketeers should read General Dermoncourt's account of how Dumas kept the bridge of Clausen single-handed, against the Austrians—an act which gained that hero the name of "the Horatius of the Tyrol"; or the story of that terrible night assault of the fort at Mont Cenis, when the General led three hundred soldiers up an ice-wall. "Every man who falls," said Dumas curtly, "must understand beforehand that he is a dead man,—that nothing can save him. It will be useless then to cry out—and by so doing he may give the alarm, and ruin our chances." Three men, so the son tells us, did fall; and their bodies dropped into the darkness, bounding from crag to crag. But not a cry was heard—not a moan—not a sigh!

When General Dumas's Republicanism brought him into conflict with Bonaparte's ever-increasing ambition, he turned his back on the Egyptian campaign, and set sail for France. Unhappily, the ship was obliged to put into Tarentum, and the Frenchmen were thrown into prison. The General's account of his struggle against the insidious manœuvres of his jailers, who tried to poison him with food and with medicine, is a terribly enthralling one, and inclines one to believe in heredity, for it is told with all that artless art of which the son, in after years, became such a master.

Our readers may think that we are as unconscionably tedious in getting our hero born, as Charles II. could possibly have been in accomplishing the opposite process; and we will therefore hasten to quote the following historic document—a letter written by General Dumas to his brother General, Brune:—

"I am glad to tell you that my wife gave birth yesterday morning to a fine boy, who weighs nine pounds, and is eighteen inches long. You can guess that if he continues to grow in the outer world in the same proportion as he has done in the inner, he promises to be a good size!"

But a sad, brief fatherhood was in store for the proud parent. The effects of his two years' struggle in a Neapolitan prison, against poison and persecution, began to show themselves in the soldier's constitution. He took a journey to Paris to consult a specialist, and learning his fate, set to work to secure the good-will of his comrades there on behalf of the future widow. The little three-year-old went too, rode cock-horse with the sword of Marshal Brude, whilst wearing the hat of Murat, King of Naples. At last even the boy became conscious

HOUSE WHERE DUMAS WAS BORN, VILLERS-COTTERETS.

of the shadow that had fallen on the household. "My father," he wrote in after years, "grew very weak, went out less often, more rarely mounted his horse, kept his room for longer periods, took me more sadly on his knees."

Then the broken-hearted General, refused all redress by his old colleague the Emperor, died, suffering, and in poverty, and greatly troubling for those he left behind. The widow, in spite of her prayers and tears, in spite of her husband's brilliant services to France, in spite of the intercession of soldiers as brilliant—Dumas's own friends and colleagues—failed to obtain a pension from the Emperor. Not a sou would Napoleon grant, to keep from starvation the widow of the man who had once dared to foresee and condemn the ambitious Emperor, in the "patriot," General Bonaparte.

And now there began for both widow and son a life of cruel poverty, a time of humiliation sweetened only by the affection of the mother for the son, and the son for the mother.

The widow went back to her father's house with her children, and Alexandre began his life-education. Of these early days he has gossiped very pleasantly, telling us of the three houses which he visited, that of Madame Darcourt, where he rejoiced his heart with an illustrated copy of "Buffon," and of M. Collard, who owned two treasures, a big

Bible and a little park, both of which the youthful Alexandre learnt almost by heart. For mythology, too, the boy had a childish passion; and " Robinson Crusoe " (!) gave him his geography. "And so," he writes, "when five or six years of age, I possessed these two accomplishments (reading and writing) in a superior degree, a fact which made me wondrously conceited. I can still see myself, about the height of a jack-boot, and in a little cotton jacket, taking part, with the utmost precocity, in the conversation of grown-up people, and contributing thereto my store of knowledge, profane and sacred."

The memory of these early days was always dear to our Dumas, and he loved to dwell upon them, and introduce them and reintroduce them into his books. He tell us that the places, surroundings, people and events of these days all had their influence on his writings and character, and those who care to pursue the subject will find traces of these times in " Ange Pitou," " Catherine Blum," " Conscience l'Enfant," and other books.

The descriptions of these early days, as given in the " Mémoires," are full of delicate humour and charm. Dumas tells us of the old chateau, and its park, in which he revelled, and draws a lifelike portrait of his august relative M. Deviolaine, a man who had indeed "a stern look but a gentle heart."

That gentleman's daughter, Cecilia, was one of the boy's favourite playmates. Dumas, then as always, had a great tendency to vertigo, and the mischievous girl delighted in trapping him into some such peril. Once during their rompings the youthful Alexandre fell into a pond, and ran the risk of drowning: the occasion prompted his first *mot*, which if it was not very witty, at least showed the lad's coolness and gaiety. He tells an amusing story of an adventure which befell him about this time. He and a companion were fighting outside a grocer's shop, and Dumas was unluckily pushed into a tub of honey. The grocer, who was busy at work inside, with a knife in his hand, ran after the terrified boy, who imagined that something worse than the fate of the blind mice was about to happen to him. The grocer overtook his victim, threw him down, raised his knife . . . and carefully scraped the honey off the trembling youngster's trousers.

Alexandre's first day at school was an eventful one. According to the brutal custom of the times he was subject to a series of practical jokes of a rough and painful nature. The schoolmaster found the new boy crying, and guessing the truth, punished the boys for such cruelty to a newcomer. Alexandre foresaw a warm reception outside when school was over, and his heart sank at the prospect. He determined to face the situation, since there was no help for it, and assuming a boldness which he certainly did not feel, he accosted the first boy he met and challenged him to fight. Young Dumas's impetuosity soon carried all before it; his opponent was thoroughly beaten, and ever after that little Alexandre was respected and let alone.

In due course the boy was prepared to receive his first communion, and there naturally followed for him a period of religious exaltation. He tells us that when the time came he swooned from excess of emotion. But Dumas was never one on whom religion in the narrow sense obtained any hold, and he soon recovered from this morbid state of ultra-piety. More lasting was the love of sport which he acquired in his boyhood. He was friendly with all the keepers and poachers, and —when at last he possessed a gun of his own— did a little sly shooting on his own account. His adventures at the boar-hunts and other sporting expeditions in which he was allowed to take part are told by Dumas with much gaiety and relish, and his character-sketches of his companions are drawn to the life.

Alexandre was not by any means a studious boy, and he watched with anxiety the various vain efforts made to get him into colleges set apart for the sons of officers. When a vacancy occurred in the

Seminary of Soissons, he saw himself in imagination "*un prêtre malgré lui*" and the raillery of the fair Cecilia prompted him to hide away from his mother for three days, in a bird-catcher's hut. He was forgiven, of course; and obtained some sort of teaching at the hands of two Abbés of very opposite types, the gentle, pious Grégoire, and the bluff, worldly Fortier. Three masters struggled hopelessly to instil some notion of mathematics into the boy's head. He did not possess that kind of brain at all.

These peaceful lessons were interrupted by "alarums and excursions" such as Dumas's idol Shakespeare has described. It was now 1814, and the Allies were approaching Paris. Madame Dumas fled thither out of hearing of that terrible bogey-cry, "The Cossacks!" and as a consequence her son got a sight of the young king of Rome, who, on the abdication of the Emperor, was acclaimed as his father's successor by fickle and enthusiastic Paris. The skirmishes in the streets of Villers-Cotterets are vividly described by Dumas. It was at this period, according to our author himself, that his mother laid before him the choice of being a Davy de la Pailleterie, a "Marquis," and an aristocrat, like his grandfather, or a Republican, a simple "Dumas," as his father had been. The lad did not hesitate, although the advantages of the former career, under the new monarchy of Louis XVIII., were frankly pointed out to him.

Other indications of the nature of "the child," who was to be "father of the man," were not wanting. A certain M. Oblet, one of those who strove vainly to teach the volatile Alexandre mathematics, gave his pupil an accomplishment invaluable to him throughout his life—a beautiful writing-hand.

The first indication of the boy's future career, the first promptings towards it, were afforded by the visit to Villers-Cotterets of the son of a neighbour, a youth named Auguste Lafarge, who was a clerk in Paris. This city-mouse stirred the deep but slumbering ambitions of his poor "country cousin," and when, on his departure, the young visitor left behind him an epigram, levelled against a cruel inamorata of the neighbourhood, Dumas was fired with a desire to write French verse also. However, his tutor gave him some "*bout-rimés*" to complete, which, for the moment, effectually quenched the student's ardour.

Then came the thrilling drama of the "Hundred Days." Dumas had the good fortune to see the Emperor pass through the little town of Villers-Cotterets on his way to Waterloo, and on his return from that fatal field, and his description of the two episodes is most vivid. His passionate admiration for will-power and genius made him then, as he always remained, a Bonapartist — that is an individualist—in sentiment and fiction, though a staunch Republican in practice and politics.

He has given us a pen-picture of himself at this period. "I was rather a good-looking young monkey," he says. "I had long, curling hair, which fell over my shoulders, and which did not crispen until I was fifteen. I had big blue eyes, which are still the best feature of my face, a straight nose, small and rather well-shaped, big and mobile lips, and white and rather regular teeth. Lastly, add a startlingly pale complexion, which turned darker at the time that my hair became crisp."

He was a lad of spirit, "without knowledge and without fear," and his roving, out-door life was building up his frame with the strength to face the enormous life-work before him.

At sixteen a "calf" love-affair gave a necessary "finishing touch" to Dumas's education. He was stricken with admiration for one of two somewhat disdainful damsels who came on a visit from Paris. At that time our shabby-genteel hero dressed in rather an antiquated fashion, and the girls and his rivals made sly fun of the boy. On one occasion, anxious to "show off" before the "fair" in his gala attire, the impetuous Alexandre sprang across a wide ditch. The feat was skilful, but not particularly impressive—for the jumper split his tight knee-breeches in the effort. In the end the girls bade the love-sick but *gauche* young gentleman return to his marbles! But he had learnt something, for he had loved, and suffered in pride and heart.

And now there entered upon the scene an important actor in the drama of Dumas's life. Our hero was at this time only the junior clerk of M. Mennesson, the notary, with little more than clerkly prospects and ambitions, when there came to Villers-Cotterets an elegant young aristocrat, the Vicomte Adolphe Ribbing de Leuven by name. De Leuven dazzled his young friend completely. He could make amorous verse; he had written plays, he had even read one of them, at the Gymnase Theatre, at Paris; and being admitted behind the scenes of the theatres, could talk airily and familiarly to his envious friend of Mars and of Talma.

The call to Paris — the call to London — what young and aspiring heart does not know it? The summons that was at first a whisper became to the soul of the ardent young Alexandre a call, ever louder and more imperative; and now, a day's holiday at Soissons brought Dumas into contact with Shakespeare. It was Shakespeare diluted by Ducis, it is true, but even Ducis could not entirely spoil "Hamlet;" and the young provincial, who entered the theatre ignorant of all three names, came out enraptured—dazzled—transformed. Whilst de Leuven was exciting the ambition of his friend, another comrade, Amedée de la Ponce, assisted to equip Dumas for the coming fight, by teaching him Italian, so that he might read Dante and Ariosto in the original, and German, enough to read Schiller. Better still, he gave him this priceless advice, which Dumas gratefully records:—"Be sure that there is something else in life besides pleasure, love, sport, dancing, and all the wild dreams of youth. There is Work: learn to *work*—learn, that is, to be happy."

Dumas's blood and parentage had important influences on his character; and a third factor to be remembered is the atmosphere of the times into which he was born. Even in his village seclusion, young Dumas could, as it were, feel the hot breath of Romanticism on his brow. The literary-political revolution was then commencing: a moderate "Romantic" like Casimir Delavigne was conquering Paris with his "Vêpres Siciliennes"; Béranger was thrilling France with his songs; and the popular feeling against the Bourbons—the old Republican spirit modified—expressed itself now in songs, plays, squibs and pamphlets. These Dumas read greedily, and the seed fell on fertile ground. Furthermore, de Leuven condescended to collaborate with the young clerk in some vaudevilles and other plays, and when the aristocrat returned with his father to

Paris, he carried Dumas's heart and hopes with him.

The months passed, and doleful news came from headquarters to the would-be dramatist. The Parisian managers seemed strangely blind to their own best interests. At this juncture Dumas was promoted to a clerkship with one M. Lefévre, a Crépy notary, and it was from this town that he entered, with his accustomed impetuosity, into one of those rash enterprises of which youth is so commonly guilty, and which so often appear afterwards in the light of inspirations.

A comrade named Paillet came one day to Dumas and proposed that in the absence of M. Lefévre, who was about to pay a three days' visit to Paris, they, too, should take a holiday in that city. It was one of those mad, impossible schemes which always recommended themselves to Dumas. Two clerks, with thirty-five francs between them, were to set out to do the forty or fifty miles to Paris, enjoy themselves in the city, and return—in seventy-two hours! But Dumas's ingenuity was equal to the problem. Paillet had a horse, and the two youths used it alternately. That halved the walking distance. The one on foot carried the gun, and the game that they shot on the way was to pay for their food in Paris. Whenever they sighted a keeper, one rode off with the game and gun, the other stayed behind to demonstrate his innocence, to propitiate and, if necessary, "tip" the keeper. Paillet explained to the landlord of the little hotel they patronised that they had wagered with some Englishmen to visit Paris without spending a sou: and so persuaded the landlord to supply them with food, lodging and beds, in exchange for the game. Needless to say, this plan was young Alexandre's.

At Paris the first ambition of the budding author was realised; for, thanks to his friend de Leuven, he saw Talma, the tragedian, in "Sylla," and had the overwhelming joy of being admitted into the great man's dressing-room. Dumas was duly questioned as to his profession, and had to confess, with deep humiliation, that he was "only a notary's clerk."

"You need not despair on that account," said the kindly actor. "Corneille was an attorney's clerk. Gentlemen," he went on, turning to the brilliant company, "let me present to you a future Corneille!" Then, at the young man's earnest request, Talma laid his hand on Dumas's crisp locks, saying—

"Alexandre Dumas, I baptise thee Poet, in the name of Shakespeare, of Corneille, and of Schiller! Return to the country—go back to your office, and if you have a true call, the Angel of Poetry will be sure to find you, wherever you are!"

After such a benediction, the moment when Dumas should come to close quarters with his fate in Paris was but a matter of time, and, to the ardent young man's mind, the sooner the better!

The opportunity came sooner. M. Lefévre had returned to Crépy before his truant clerk, and Dumas answered the inevitable reproof with a rash resignation. This fertile brain had already begun to grow its first crop of ideas. The notary's clerk resolved to attack Paris at once.

He could scarcely have chosen a more inopportune moment, for his mother's resources had dwindled to a capital of 253 francs. Nevertheless, Dumas contrived to sell some old engravings; won his coach-fare to Paris from the proprietor of the posting-house, by means of his skill at billiards; and then, armed with letters written to General Dumas by his father's old friends, Marshals Jourdan, Victor, Sebastiani, and the rest—tokens which he believed to be better than any letters of introduction—he set out for Paris. He had first knelt and prayed with his mother, who, with many fears and sighs, let him go on his audacious quest.

At this point in the life of Alexandre Dumas there is a sharp dividing-line. Until now he had been a boy, living an aimless life, without ambition and without prospects. He himself has confessed to the imperfect nature of his education, adding, "I possessed, however, all the physical advantages which a rustic life gives: I could ride any horse;

I walked a dozen leagues to dance at a ball, and was pretty smart with the foil and pistol; I could play tennis like a St Georges, and rarely missed a hare or a partridge at thirty paces." His kindly patrons had tried to make a musician, a priest, a notary, or a scholar of him; now he freed himself from all restraining influences, and began to live, think, plan, and work for himself. The change, as we shall see, worked wonders. Perhaps the phrase "for himself" is misleading; for his worst friends (and he made many) never doubted Dumas's passionate love for his mother. "I was a man, now," he writes, "for a woman depended on me. I was going to repay my mother in some degree for all the care she had lavished on me." Truly, he was a man, in two senses: he had reached the age of a man, and he acted with all a man's courage and sense of responsibility.

Of all his long and adventurous career, the story of Dumas's early struggles is the most familiar to the general reader; every sketch of his life, however short, deals with it, so that we, in turn, can be as brief as this interesting period will allow.

On his arrival in Paris Dumas went to each of his father's old comrades, and experienced the sad but inevitable disillusionment. Jourdan, Victor, Sebastiani, turned their backs on their old colleague's son; Verdier had himself been superannuated, and was poor in money and influence. General Foy, however, received Dumas kindly, but found the young provincial woefully ignorant. Nevertheless, he bade the youth write down his address. When he saw the clerk's exquisite penmanship the General cried out—

"We are saved!"

"Why?"

"You write such a good hand!"

Dumas felt profoundly humiliated. He resolved then and there to earn his living one day, not by his penmanship, but by his pen.

This skill in caligraphy obtained for the despairing young man a clerkship in the Secretary's department of the Duke of Orleans, with a salary of about fifty pounds a year. Fifty pounds a year! It was the riches of Monte Cristo! Dumas hurried home full of joy, reached Villers-Cotterets at midnight, and rushed into his mother's bedroom, shouting "Victory! Victory!" He had indeed drawn first blood!

Once installed in his modest lodgings, No. 1 Paté des Italiens, Dumas set himself to study. The days were his noble master's, and from seven till ten every evening he returned to the bureau to work; but half the night he spent reading Juvenal, Tacitus, Suetonius; or in studying geography and physiology. He also followed with a certain curiosity the theatrical productions of the period; but as he was not in sympathy with the style, the dialogue, the construction of those plays, which were of the pre-Romantic type, he felt no desire to imitate them. So steadily did he work, however, that when two months later his mother joined him, she scarcely knew her son again: he had become so serious!

Meanwhile the Romantics, like a crowd without leaders, growled and threatened inarticulately. Their growing power was greatly augmented by the stupidity of the Government, who persecuted that very moderate innovator Casimir Delavigne, and ennobled Ancelot, his Royalist rival. The year 1823 was indeed a year of revolution, literary and political. Hugo and Lamartine had already begun the attack in poetry, with the "Odes and Ballades" and the "Meditations"; Nodier had published his *genre* romances. Then came the turn of the painters; and the Salon of 1824 was full of pictures of a new type—Scheffer's "Death of Gaston de Foix," Delacroix's "Massacre of Chios," and Coigniet's "Massacre of the Innocents." Géricault, too, was at work on his famous 'Wreck of the *Medusa*."

From abroad came winds to fan the flames. Byron, who died in this year, was deeply impressing the future author of "Antony"; Scott, who was eagerly read by the men of the rising generation, had revolutionised the old ideas of romance in general, and Dumas's notions in particular; and Cooper, the now-forgotten, found in the country of Chateaubriand and Rousseau a congenial home for his poetic romances of the prairies.

All this time the young collaborators, de Leuven and Dumas, had not been idle. In spite of his content with his modest salary, young Alexandre had spent more than double that income, during the first year, and his mother's little store was almost gone. At this crisis a third person was taken into the flourishing dramatic partnership—a clever drunkard named Rousseau; and the little play which resulted—"La Chasse et l'Amour"—though rejected at the Théâtre Gymnase, was accepted at the Ambigu, and played with success in 1825. This lightened the poverty which was weighing upon the author's household, and thus emboldened, Dumas put together three little stories which he had written, and persuaded a foolish publisher to go halves with him in the risk of producing them. This little volume, "Nouvelles Contemporaines," of which we shall treat at greater length later on, was published in 1826, but was not a success. Dumas tells us variously that four and again that six copies only were sold. It was favourably reviewed, however, by Etienne Arago, and proved a species of letter-of-introduction to Buloz, when the *Revue des Deux Mondes* came into existence.

In the midst of these ever-growing interests and possibilities—for Alexandre had now the privilege of contributing (without pay) to a monthly magazine called *Le Psyche*, and was interested, along with a colleague named Lassagne, in the fortunes of a second play called "La Noce et l'Enterrement"— a blow fell upon him. News of this employee's frivolous dallying with the Muses had reached the ears of the authorities, and Lassagne was forbidden to encourage such evil practices for the future. Dumas was so alarmed at this threatened stoppage of his life-work, that he found courage to beard his superior, M. Oudard, in his den. That official, it appeared, would be pleased to permit the young clerk his literary pranks, if he strove to emulate Delavigne; but Dumas replied, with more honesty than prudence, that if he did not hope to do something in the future very different from what M. Delavigne had done, he would then and there renounce all his ambitions. This answer was treated as an impertinence by the chiefs of the bureau, and laughed at as the drollest of jokes by the rest of the staff. From this time dated the series of petty persecutions which in the end cost the youth his salary, and nearly lost him his place.

Whilst Dumas was struggling on, more or less in

the dark as to the nature and direction of his own abilities, two events of great importance happened. Louis XVIII. had died, and had been succeeded by Charles X., whose career in some respects resembled that of our James II. Charles had pledged himself on his accession to abolish the censorship; but he soon attempted to re-impose it. A political-literary agitation followed, and after a struggle the obnoxious threat was withdrawn. The other event was the arrival in Paris of Kean and an English company of Shakespearean actors. Not so long before, English players had been pelted from the pit of the Porte St Martin, but at this moment (1827) the French had been seized with Anglo-mania. Scott was being read and dramatised on all hands; Guizot was studying the British constitution, for future application to French politics, and Byron was a literary fashion. Dumas was even more prepared to welcome Shakespeare than were the majority of his fellow-Romantics. He saw "Hamlet," and it electrified him. He knew every word of the play beforehand, and strange as he found the English style of acting, he "saw light" for the first time on the path of his future. But let him speak for himself:

"Ah, this was what my soul had been seeking after: this was what I had lacked, and which had come at last! Here were actors forgetting that they were acting—here was mock life become real life, by the power of art; here was truth of speech and action, which transformed the players into human beings, with their virtues, passions, and weaknesses, instead of into cold-blooded posers, unnatural, declamatory, sententious. . . . I read—nay, devoured—not only the repertory of Shakespeare but that of every other foreign dramatic poet, and I came to recognise that in the world of the theatre everything emanates from Shakespeare, as in the real world all emanates from the sun. . . . I recognised, in short, that he was the one who had created most, after God."

"From that moment my career was decided: I felt that the special call which is sent to every man had come to me, then; I felt a confidence which has never since failed me. Nevertheless I did not disguise from myself the difficulties which such a life-work would involve. I knew that above all other professions this one demanded deep and special study, and that, to operate with success upon living life, I should first need to study 'dead nature' long and earnestly. Shakespeare, Corneille, Molière, Calderon, Goëthe, and Schiller—I laid their works before me, like bodies on the surgeon's table, and with scalpel in hand, long nights through, I probed them to the heart to discover the secret of their life. I saw by what admirable mechanism these authors set the nerves and muscles of their creatures moving and working, and noted with what skill they clothed and re-clothed with different flesh that framework which was always the same."

Dumas had translated the "Fiesco" of Schiller, and vainly attempted to dramatise Scott with Soulié, but Shakespeare filled his heart and brain with new thoughts, greater ambitions. No sooner had the English actors gone than the Salon opened, and the young author, paying an early visit, was immediately impressed by a picture representing the murder of Monaldeschi by order of Queen Christine of Sweden. Dumas seized upon the incident then and there as a subject for a poetic drama; he found the details of the tragedy in an article in the "Biographie Michaud," and set to work.

"Christine" was soon written. It was only half-classical in style, for although it observed some of the "unities," it was thoroughly romantic in form. "What, then, was to be done with the bastard infant, born outside the pale of the Institute and the Academy?" Dumas asked himself. The Comédie Française, a State-endowed theatre, ruled by the Government and a committee of its actors, and bound by tradition to the classic school of Corneille and Racine, would not be likely to tolerate any suspicion of vulgarity, in the shape of plays cast in the mould of Shakespeare. But this very system of national control enables young writers to obtain, by right, at least a hearing. There was, Dumas learnt, an official examiner of plays, who would probably be a year before he got down to "Christine," so great were his arrears of work; but there was the commissary, Baron Taylor, open to give attention to more favoured candidates. Dumas succeeded in obtaining an appointment with the Baron, though it was for seven in the morning—the only time the overworked official could spare. Very droll is the young dramatist's account of Baron Taylor in his bath, groaning whilst a merciless poet read every line of a five-act tragedy to him. At the end of the reading the commissary was frozen and cross, and poor Dumas offered to come again; but the kindly Baron encouraged him to begin his own play, and became quite enthusiastic at the end. Thanks to Taylor's exertions, the trembling author read the play before the brilliant staff of the Française; he was applauded loudly, and the play was accepted with acclamation, subject to revision. It is worthy of remark that Dumas, hurrying home to delight his sorrowing mother with the news, lost the MS. on the way,—and rewrote it that night. He knew every line of it by heart!

The gentleman appointed on behalf of the Comédie Française to consider "Christine" was of the classic school, and he smilingly bade the young iconoclast go back to his desk—and stay there. Yet again the play was read, and once more set aside for revision; and this time Dumas took the opportunity of remodelling and entirely altering the motive of the play.

Poor "Christine"! No sooner was she clad in her new robe, than bureaucratic and social intrigues forced Dumas to consent to the indefinite postponement of its production, in favour of another version of the subject by a more influential writer. But he was far from being daunted, and a chance occurrence set him on the road to success by another path.

One day the office cupboard from which Dumas usually got his writing-paper was locked, and he was obliged to go into another office to fetch some. As he passed through the room his eyes fell on a book which was lying on a desk. It was a volume of Anquetil, open at the passage which describes the Duke de Guise's jealousy of St Mégrin, and the trick which he played upon the Duchess in consequence. Guise gave her a dose of what he called "poison," but which turned out to be harmless soup. The incident seemed so dramatic that it excited Dumas's interest, and he sought for and read the story of the murder of St Mégrin, and of Bussy d'Amboise in the "Mémoires d'Estoile." From

DUMAS IN 1828. FROM A DRAWING BY DEVERIA.

these, he tells us, he constructed his play of "Henri Trois et sa Cour."

"I was then twenty-five years of age," he writes; "'Henri Trois' was my second serious work. Let a conscientious critic take it and submit it to the most searching examination—he will find in the matter of style everything to censure; in the matter of plot, nothing. I have written fifty dramas since, and none of them is more skilfully constructed." These are bold words, and would be boastful if good critics did not confirm them.

The young author's superiors were equally busy during this time. They piled the work upon him for fear that he should use a minute of their time in writing his "trashy" dramas; they took away his salary, and if Dumas had not been able to borrow from Lafitte, the famous banker and politician, he and his mother would have starved. Finally, the Duke of Orleans withheld from our author the customary yearly bonus given to his staff. But for all that, "Henri Trois" was written, was read privately, and greeted with enthusiasm—was read before the Comédie Française, and accepted by acclamation.

Soon the news got about that a new play—a play which would revolutionise the French stage—had been written by an obscure young man, and little by little the public excitement grew. The production was fixed for February 10th, 1829, and rehearsals went forward more or less smoothly. Firmin (the leading actor since Talma's death) and Mdlle. Mars were to play the chief parts, and Dumas was full of joy and hope and pride, when news came to him that his mother was dying.

Madame Dumas had never possessed the buoyant spirits, the hopeful temperament, the love of daring which characterised her quadroon son. She would probably have borne the anxieties which his ambitions caused her—for she loved him and believed in him—if her friends and neighbours had not aggravated her trouble with their croaking, spiteful tongues. On the eve of the production of her son's play, the poor widow, coming away after a more or less trying interview of this nature, fell down in an apoplectic fit. Alexandre, struck with despair, rendered his mother all the help which devotion and intelligence could give, but the fateful night came, and found her still unconscious and in danger.

Of all "first nights" on record, probably that of "Henri III." was the most eventful and strange. As an epoch-making event, as a triumph, it was greater even than "Hernani" a year later, and "Antony," which afterwards made such a sensational *début*. The accounts of those who witnessed this *première* have assured us that the author's description does the scene no more than justice.

"I passed the whole day by my mother's bedside," he says. "She was still unconscious. At a quarter to eight I left her, and entered my box as the curtain rose."

"The first act was received complacently, although the exposition of the plot was long, stiff and tedious. As the curtain fell I ran out to revisit my mother."

"On my return I had just time to cast a glance round the auditorium. Those who were present will recollect what a magnificent *coup d'œil* it presented. The first tier was crowded with men resplendent with the Orders of five or six countries on their breasts; the whole aristocracy was massed together in the boxes, and the ladies glistened with diamonds."

"The second act, containing the sarbacane episode, about which I had been so nervous, passed without opposition, and the curtain fell in the midst of applause."

"From the third act, to the close the play was no longer a success: it was a growing delirium. Everyone applauded, even the women; and amongst them Madame Malibran, leaning far out of a box and clinging with both hands to a column to keep herself from falling." . . .

Then, when Firmin came forward to name the author, the enthusiasm was so unanimous that the Duke of Orleans himself rose and listened, standing, to the announcement of his talented employee's name. That night Dumas received an effusive letter of congratulation, from the very official who had deprived him of his salary!

Next morning the successful young playwright's room was crowded with bouquets, which he proudly placed on his mother's bed. Dumas had sold the manuscript of his play for 6,000 francs, and repaid Lafitte, when news came that "Henri Trois" was suspended by the Minister of the Interior. Happily, Dumas straightway obtained a revocation of the order, but during the interim the young author could scarcely be said to breathe!

He began immediately to pay for his success. An anonymous attack in one of the papers brought a challenge from the fiery young author, and—greater honour still!—seven "classical" playwrights drew up a pompous address to the King, imploring him to save the national theatre from "despicable mountebanks," and to keep to the orthodox writers—that is, themselves. Happily Charles X. replied simply, that he had only his place in the pit, as other Frenchmen had, and could not interfere.

About this time Nodier, of whom we have spoken, was holding his *salon* at the Arsenal, and Dumas had the good fortune to be admitted to that brilliant literary circle. Nodier's daughter, Marie Mennessier-Nodier. tells in her recollections of her father an amusing story of Dumas's first introduction to the Arsenal. The librarian was constantly pestered by poorer literary brethren, who called to sponge on him. Therefore, when one day Marie begged her father to receive a handsome young "man of letters" who had called, the wary bibliophile flatly refused. Dumas laughed, went away, and—called again. Marie was much taken with the gay, good-looking young fellow, and Nodier at last grumblingly consented to see him, preparing as he spoke to part with a score or two of francs. He received Dumas, first with distrust, then with surprise, chatted with him animatedly, and parted with him as unwillingly as he had greeted him. Needless to say, money was not mentioned!

Nodier gave the young writer more than money: he gave him a social life, and a literary encouragement and education which was invaluable. Here the young author met Hugo, De Vigny, Sainte Beuve, De Musset, and others almost as brilliant but less known. Thenceforth a place was kept for the witty young writer at the famous Sunday dinners of the Arsenal, and here in due course, "little Alexandre" was brought. The friendship between the two men remained close, affectionate and unalterable, until the elder man's death.

Fame now came swiftly to the author of the first great romantic play. Dumas was appointed assistant-librarian to the Duke of Orleans, under Delavigne, at the princely salary of £100 a year! The author of "Henri Trois" was the lion of Paris for the winter of 1829; Deveria made an engraving of him; David of Angers a medallion. "Nothing was wanting to my glory," says Dumas frankly,—"not even that little shade of the ridiculous which always accompanies literary reputations." Wild stories were repeated in "classic" circles, of the triumphant orgies of the Romantics,—how they had danced about a bust of Racine, crying exultantly that they had "done for him"; how they were calling for the heads of the Academicians on chargers, and so forth. No wonder the Seven appealed to the King!

"Henri Trois," indeed, was a revelation and a revolution. It was a romance drawn from French history; its characters were real in origin, and true to life in their words and deeds; instead of dull declamatory couplets, and a tawdry, meaningless plot, the audience was enthralled by the rapid, merciless development of a story of human passion. The love of St Mégrin for the Duchess of Guise, the Duke's jealousy of St Mégrin, both private and political, the vivid picture of Henri III. and his mignons and the everyday life of the French court—the series of dramatic scenes which develop the intrigue, until St Mégrin goes to the assigna-

ALEXANDRE DUMAS. FROM A LITHOGRAPH BY DELPACH OF A DRAWING BY MAURIR.

tion which Guise forces his wife to make—all this was so novel, so congenial, so startling, that for the moment Paris talked of nothing else.

Our author, with characteristic tact, determined to follow up this success with another as soon as he possibly could. He withdrew "Christine" from the Comédie Française, where it was receiving lukewarm treatment, and took it to the Odéon. He had reconstructed the play, "to make it more modern and more dramatic"; and for this purpose had taken coach to Havre and back, working out the remodelled play in his brain, to the jolting of coach!

But this time the "classicists" were not to be taken by surprise. The play was forbidden: then, when the mandate was withdrawn and the rehearsals went forward, an opposition was organised. Fortunately the young "romantics" rallied round Dumas; his friendly rival Soulié brought in a number of his workmen to form a claque, and the forces were about equal. On March 30th, 1830, the battle of the Odéon was fought. The theatre resounded alternately with applause and "hissing"; roars of delight and of disgust succeeded each other. This terrible battle lasted seven hours. "Ten times overthrown, the play sprang to its feet after each reverse, and at two in the morning it finished, having thrown the public, panting, thrilled and terrified, on its knees!"

Yet the success of "Christine" was still undecided when the curtain fell, and Dumas and his backers retired to supper, jubilant but exhausted. The author had seen that many parts of the dialogue urgently required to be altered or omitted, and had arranged that the revisions should be sent to the actors next morning; but how was it possible for the host of that joyous company to find the time to do the work? Hugo and Alfred de Vigny grasped the situation, and came to the rescue. Bidding Dumas entertain his guests, they retired to another room and wrought at the play for the rest of the night, and at dawn walked away, arm-in-arm, leaving the revised MS. on the mantelpiece in the room where the revellers were snoring.

With the change consequent on his achievement of fame and (in a less degree) of fortune, Dumas closed a chapter in his life which had an important influence on his future. When he first took lodgings in Paris, he was not quite twenty-one. He lived in a garret, dreamed of fame, and was happy, like Béranger's hero—

"Dans une grenier, qu'on est bien à vingt ans!"

The handsome lad had for neighbour one Madame Marie-Catherine Lebay, a young and pretty seamstress, amicably separated from her husband. She brightened the life of the young playwright with her cheerful society, and the pair fell in love. When Madame Dumas followed her son to Paris, he found her rooms elsewhere, and Alexandre Dumas *fils* was born of this intimacy, in 1824. When worldly temptations came upon the vain young genius he separated from his mistress, and little by little lost sight of her. Although the object of jealous rivalry and of a struggle for possession between father and mother, and although alternately under the control of each, the younger Dumas grew up to love his two parents, so strangely different in nature and position, with almost equal affection. As long as the father possessed a franc the son was welcome to it, and this affection was repaid to the full in the last sad days of the elder man's life.

What Dumas might have been, had he remained true to his first love, we can only conjecture. That it would have been for the good of his genius, his happiness, and his success, those who have read the story of this sweet and able woman's life cannot doubt. Although at first there was a bitterness between them after the separation, she remained through life proud of the success of her famous lover, and during the last years was reconciled to him. Her death in 1868 was one of the sorrows of the old Dumas, when he himself was nearing his end.

The Reign of Dumas I (1830-1848)

The successful young dramatist was preparing to visit Algiers, which had just been captured by the French, and which, (with that instinct which he developed in later years, Dumas was anxious to explore and exploit), when the Revolution of July 1830 broke out.

It is not our intention to describe the political crisis which led to the downfall of Charles X., and the accession of the younger branch of the Bourbons in the person of Louis Philippe, Duke of Orleans, but sufficient must be told to explain the part which our hero played in the strange tragic-farce.

Charles X. had done much, during his brief reign, to rouse the old revolutionary spirit by his autocratic measures. On the 25th July 1830, he caused the famous "Ordonnances" to be issued, "putting an end to the freedom of the press, already largely curtailed, appointing a new mode of election, and dissolving the recently-elected chamber." Once more Paris saw the old familiar barricades rise in a single night; faded flags were brought forth, old watch-words were revived, and old veterans reappeared; the roll of the drums, and the thrilling notes of the "Marseillaise" resounded once more in the streets of the city. The revolutionaries, to which party the son of the General Dumas belonged, hoped to see a second Republic rise out of the ruins of the discredited monarchy, and the story of "the days of July" is told in Dumas's "Mémoires," by himself as an eye-witness. M. Parigot, commenting on this description, in his study of our author, says:—

"If you have any desire to breathe a little of the atmosphere which heated all brains at that moment you need only read 'the three days of July' in Volume VI. There the different means are described, as well as the concentration of sentiments, which united to make the throne of Charles X. totter. Turn over the leaves of Louis Blanc and compare. Dumas is a magician for demonstrating the picturesque. The ever-growing enthusiasm which cut the streets into barricades, uprooted the trees on the boulevards and burnt the guard-house of the Exchange, to the cry of 'Vive la Charte!'; the indecision of journalists and politicians, the discontent of the public, who wished to 'avenge Waterloo in the streets of Paris'; the excitement of the young collegians, Lafayette domiciled at the Town Hall—and along with all this the opposition which was beginning against the Provisional Government—all is painted with the exactitude of an eye-witness who has a fine sense of spectacular effect. And, moreover, Dumas was one who had the courage to lash the 'comfortable middle-classes' for their politic opportunism. They kept securely indoors, during the fray, but were quite ready to take advantage of the popular movement, after the danger. He denounced the timorous and underhand conduct of these people, and the work of reaction which they insidiously accomplished, even at the moment when the people were triumphing."

Alexandre's share in the Revolution was chiefly confined to two exploits—the saving of precious military relics, during the sacking of the artillery-museum, and the fetching of the powder from Soissons. This latter episode, though it had no very important bearing on the fate of the revolution, was a brilliant *coup* in its way, worthy of the son of Napoleon's brave general, and of the creator of D'Artagnan.

Charles X. had fled from Paris in the first days of the tumult, but remained outside the city at Saint Cloud, with an imposing army, awaiting the turn of events, and in particular the action of his representatives in Paris. Dumas heard Lafayette (who was informally the Minister of War of the insurgents) remark that if the King advanced on Paris the revolutionaries would have no powder wherewith to defend themselves; and he at once offered to go to Soissons, a town some sixty miles away, and in his native department, where, as he knew, a powder-magazine was located, and to bring the ammunition back. His wild proposal was laughed at; but by his persistence Dumas obtained an order for the powder, and a recommendation to the people of Soissons; and with these credentials (which he boldly took upon himself to strengthen by interpolation) he prepared for his daring expedition.

The bold young "red" posted for Soissons on the afternoon of July 30th, with a comrade named Bard. On the way, as one of the postillions refused to keep his horses up to the pace of the young adventurer's impatience, Dumas fired a blank cartridge at the man, who fell from the horse in affright. Young Alexandre promptly donned the posting-boots and took the coach forward himself. At his own beloved Villers-Cotterets the hero halted and supped hastily, in the midst of enthusiastic fellow-townsmen; and having recruited a young friend named Hutin, whose mother lived in Soissons and who was a native of the place, the party drove forward and entered the gates of that town at one o'clock in the morning.

All the rest of the night Madame Hutin and her household worked to make a tricolour, which was to float from the flagstaff of the cathedral that morning. Bard and Hutin set out to smuggle the flag into the church, to overpower the sacristan and exchange the Bourbon white for republican red-white-and-blue; and Dumas himself lingered about a small pavilion at the Fort St Jean, which was used as a magazine, until he saw the tricolour floating where a minute before the Royalist flag had waved. Then he climbed the wall of the pavilion, and dropping into the garden, confronted with his gun two soldiers who were peacefully hoeing the beds, and announced his errand. After a parley the three guardians of the magazine agreed to remain indoors, and behave as neutrals, until some decisive order came from headquarters, and Dumas went off to accomplish the second and more difficult part of his enterprise.

Commandant Liniers, in charge of the depôt at Soissons, found himself that morning confronted by a swarthy and very earnest young man with a gun, who demanded the ammunition in his keeping. He scoffed at the youth and his written order, and denied that there was any quantity of powder in the magazine. Dumas retired to assure himself of the truth or untruth of this statement, and on his return found that Liniers was reinforced by three other officers, and therefore still more scornful and incredulous.

Dumas did not hesitate, for he saw that he must act promptly, or he was lost. "I had gone too far to withdraw," he says; "I was almost alone, in the midst of officials hostile to the new government. It was a question of life or death for me." He pulled out a pair of double-barrelled pistols, and swore that unless he received an order for the powder in five seconds, he would blow out the brains of the whole party! At this critical moment the commandant's wife, who had evidently got wind of the affair, rushed in, and flung herself into the midst of the company, imploring her husband to yield. Liniers was now willing to give way, if his "face" could be "saved." Dumas took the hint, sent for two or three of his comrades to assemble in the court outside, threw open the window, and bade them fire when he gave the signal. Liniers sat down and wrote the order.

Then followed denials and delays on the part of the mayor and other authorities. At last Dumas in anger broke open the magazine himself, procured carts and loaded them with the powder, and at five o'clock the adventurous little band were on their way back to Paris. At nine next morning Dumas delivered his precious convoy, so daringly procured, at the "rebel" headquarters, the Hôtel de Ville.

But even while the young Dumas was "bluffing" the Soissons garrison so gloriously, the cause of Republicanism was being betrayed. Between the alternatives of Charles X. and an elected President a compromise was made; and the Duke of Orleans, having abandoned his King and promised all things democratic, entered Paris, and was presently chosen lieutenant-general of the kingdom, and then "monarch by the will of the people." A "moderate" party, who believed in constitutional government, acting with the very best intentions, had given away in reality all that their "extremist" allies had fought and died for; and Louis Philippe began to reign, the revolution having made a distinction without a difference. The new ruler, all affability, congratulated his employee on his return from Soissons, saying, "You have just written your best drama!"

The affair of Soissons, and the excited state of public affairs unsettled our susceptible Dumas. Charles X. had taken refuge in England, but there had been for a moment a fear that he might flee to La Vendée, the Royalist provinces, and let loose upon France the horrors of civil war. Dumas, knowing that the late king had renounced the throne in favour of his grandson "Henri V." (the Comte de Chambord) whose mother, the Duchesse de Berri, was a woman of much courage and determination, suggested that to prevent the possibility of any future rising, a national guard should be organised in the Royalist department, and that he should be sent as a special commissioner to consult the responsible officials upon the subject. Lafayette gave Dumas the required mandate, and on August 10th he set out.

Except that by his intercession a poor wretch of a coiner was saved from the galleys, Dumas did nothing notable during his six weeks in La Vendée; and when on his return Louis Philippe sent for him, the envoy declared very frankly that it was useless to attempt to organise the national guard in La Vendée; but that if the West were opened up, by means of high-roads, so that communication between all parts of it might be rapid and easy, this would decrease the chances of a second outbreak of guerilla-warfare. The "poet" prophesied—so he tells us —another, though a less serious, La Vendée, if occasion offered. Indeed, only two years later, the Duchesse de Berri aroused the "Chouans" once more and created a little Vendéan rising on behalf of her son.

But the King did not like the prophecy.

"You are a poet: write poetry, and leave politics to kings and ministers," he said with a frown.

"Sire," answered Dumas, "the ancients called their poets 'seers.'"

The young author was dismissed from the Royal presence, and sent in his resignation forthwith.

The dramatist in Dumas was still subservient

to the would-be politician, when he wrote his next play "Napoléon," which, if we may believe the "Mémoires," was produced under novel and comic circumstances. For some time Harel, the manager of the Odéon theatre, had been pressing Dumas to write him a play on this subject; but the young republican could not give his mind to desk-work, and moreover, the theme did not appeal to him. One night, after a *première* at the Odéon, Dumas and several other guests went to sup with Harel, and after the feast Mademoiselle Georges led the unsuspecting playwright into another room, "to show him something." On their return Dumas found that the guests had disappeared, and the smiling Harel informed his coy young author that he was a prisoner. Dumas was startled, but took his imprisonment in good part. He was fed sumptuously and treated like a lord; all the books which he required to consult were at his elbow, and in eight days this enormous play was ready. Its author confesses frankly that it is a bad piece of work; but under the circumstances the blame can scarcely be laid upon him, for with him the quality of his work depended entirely upon his inspiration, which in turn was a matter of his own initiative.

One of the causes of the failure of "Napoléon" as a work of stagecraft was possibly the author's preoccupation, for his mind was full of the prospects

ALEXANDRE DUMAS

of his famous play, "Antony." To the bulk of British admirers of Dumas the very title will be strange; but in France our dramatist was better known, for generations, as the author of "Antony," than as the writer of any romance or play whatever. He tells us that the idea of the drama came to him at the time when "Christine" was temporarily forbidden.

"One day I was pacing the boulevards . . . I stopped suddenly, and said to myself, 'A man who, when surprised by the husband of his mistress, should kill her, saying that she had resisted him, and who should die on the scaffold in consequence, would save the honour of that woman, and expiate his crime.' The idea of 'Antony' was found: six weeks afterwards the play was written."

"When I was writing 'Antony,'" says Dumas elsewhere, "I was in love with a woman of whom I was terribly jealous: jealous because she was in the position of Adèle (in the play) in that she had a husband, an officer in the army. . . . Read 'Antony': he will tell you what I suffered then."

M. Parigot, in his study " Le Drame d'Alexandre Dumas," throws further light on this subject. A number of unpublished letters from the lover to the lady were placed in the critic's hands, and he has quoted from them exhaustively. The "Adèle" appears to have been one Melanie

W——, to whom Dumas was presented (as he tells us in "Le Testament de M. Chauvelin") at the house of her father-in-law, the bibliophile Villenave, in 1827. The conquest of a lady of position and of some pretentions to learning evidently flattered the young man's vanity—"there was something of the air of Villers-Cotterets about him still"—and the young lover vowed, cursed, adored, despaired, and rhapsodised for three years. Then "Antony" was written; the intimacy had unconsciously fulfilled its purpose, and came to an end accordingly. Meanwhile this amorous heart, overflowing with passion, had found opportunity to fall in love with another Melanie (the mother of Marie-Alexandre Dumas), with Marie Dorval, and others. The need for love had for the time possessed this ardent nature as with a fever.

It was of this experiment-in-love, in which he took himself and his passion in such tragic earnest, that Dumas was thinking when he wrote these verses, with which he prefaced "Antony":—

> Que de fois tu m'as dit, aux heures du délire,
>   Quand mon front tout à coup devenait soucieux:
> "Sur ta bouche pourquoi cet effrayant sourire?
>   Pourquoi ces larmes dans tes yeux?"
>
> Pourquoi? C'est que mon cœur, au milieu des délices,
>   D'un souvenir jaloux constamment oppressé,
> Froid au bonheur présent, va chercher ses supplices,
>   Dans l'avenir et le passé.

Jusque dans tes baisers je retrouve des peines ;
   Tu m'accables d'amour : l'amour, je m'en souviens,
Pour la première fois s'est glissé dans tes veines,
   Sous d'autres baisers que les miens.

Du feu des voluptés vainement tu m'enivres ;
   Combien pour un beau jour de tristes lendemains !
Ces charmes qu'à mes mains en palpitant tu livres,
   Palpiteront sous d'autre mains.

Et je ne pourrai pas, dans ma fureur jalouse,
   De l'infidélité te réserver le prix !
Quelques mots à l'autel t'ont faite son épouse,
   Et te sauvent de mon mépris.

Car ces mots pour toujours ont vendu tes caresses,
   L'amour ne les doit plus donner ni recevoir ;
L'usages des époux a réglé les tendresses
   Et leurs baisers sont un devoir !

Malheur ? Malheur à moi que le ciel en ce monde
   A jeté comme un hôte à ses lois étranger !
A moi qui ne sais pas dans ma douleur profonde
   Souffrir longtemps sans me venger.

Malheur ! Car une voix qui n'a rien de la terre
   M'a dit " Pour ton bonheur c'est sa mort qu'il te faut ; "
Et cette voix m'a fait comprendre le mystère
   Et du meurtre et de l'échafaud.

Viens, donc, Ange du Mal, dont la voix me convie !
   Car il est des instants où, si je te voyais,
Je pourrais pour son sang t'abandonner ma vie,
   Et mon âme . . . si j'y croyais !

Years after, in his " Mémoires," Dumas confessed that the verses were poor, the sentiment was affected, and the blasphemy was a wanton one—prompted, his son has shrewdly suggested, by the rhyme.

Once set at liberty by the tyrannical Harel, Dumas hastened to the Comédie Française, where "Antony" had been accepted and placed in rehearsal. But Mars and Firmin, the leading actor and actress of the national theatre at that time, were accustomed to more orthodox rôles than those of the weak, fascinated Adèle, and Antony, the masterful Ishmael-of-society; and the Comédie Française itself, as our author confesses, was not the frame for such a picture. The two artists, losing faith in their parts, hinted as much to the author, Firmin with diffidence, Mars with a bold pretext. Dumas astonished them by demanding the manuscript from the prompter, and walking out of the theatre.

It so happened that M. Crosnier, of the Porte St Martin, had received Hugo's "Marion Delorme," when that poet had also abandoned the stifling atmosphere of the Française to breathe freer air elsewhere. The young dramatist, although profoundly discouraged concerning the merits of his latest born, went forthwith to Marie Dorval, the leading lady of the Porte St Martin, a clever actress, ready-witted, naive, and full of nervous energy. He read the play to her, and her trained and receptive intelligence at once saw the possibilities of the piece. She shut the young author into a room, to spend the night in rewriting the last act, which did not appeal to her in its original form; and next day negotiations began. The play was duly read to the manager of the Porte St Martin and accepted; but it was something of a blow to the author's vanity when M. Crosnier politely struggled with slumber during the third act, slept comfortably in the fourth, and snored unrestrainedly through the fifth!

At length the night of "Antony's" birth arrived, and the miserable infant, which had now been waiting two years for its delivery, had given its parent much anxiety. For once Dumas had lost that magnificent confidence in himself which aided him so powerfully in his career.

But if the moment for producing the play was inopportune—appearing as it did in the midst of distracting political ferment—the social atmosphere was charged with a feverish electricity, which the story of "Antony" attracted irresistibly to itself. How is a social outlaw like Antony to win for himself the lovely wife of a man in high society—how is he to break through, and persuade her to break through, all the bars to self-abandonment which society has erected? By will-power— by the strength of an unscrupulous individuality! For such a story of power and passion the Parisian of that day was fully ripe.

As the play progressed, the emotion of the

audience mounted to a painful height. The first act ended in applause; and the second was as warmly received. In the midst of the play the author, unconsciously copying Goldsmith, rushed out for a time and paced the boulevards, unable to face his fate. The startling climax to the third act took away the breath; and for a moment the fate of the play hung in suspense: then the theatre shook with a rushing storm of applause. The curtain fell on the fourth act amid frenzied "bravos." "A hundred francs," cried the excited author to the scene-shifters, "if the curtain goes up again before they stop applauding!" And the fifth act actually commenced before the audience had finished acclaiming the fourth.

We have already indicated the *dénouement* of "Antony." That "hero," surprised by the husband, stabs Adèle, and throws the dagger at the wronged man's feet, saying, "She resisted me; and I killed her!"[1]

[1] Dumas tells a story respecting this famous "tag" which we cannot omit. At a revival of the play, some years later, the prompter, through ignorance, rang down the curtain immediately Antony had stabbed Adèle. The public, furious at being cheated of the famous line, clamoured "*Le dénouement! le dénouement!*" Bocage sulked in his dressing-room, and would not return; but Marie Dorval good-naturedly remained on the stage, and the curtain was rung up again, in the hope that Antony would feel obliged to return.

Adèle was discovered, dead, in her chair. There was a silence. At last Dorval rose slowly, and coming down to the footlights, remarked pleasantly, "Gentlemen, I resisted him, and he killed me." Then she made her best bow, and retired, amidst frantic applause.

The curtain down, the audience in a fury of impatience demanded a sight of the author. Calls and recalls followed. Dumas, in rushing behind the scenes from his box, took a short cut through the corridors; he was recognised, and chased by a crowd of young enthusiasts, and his coat was torn to ribbons.

"Antony" excited much enthusiasm and opposition. It was a daring, provocative play, destined to set the fashion in French society dramas for the rest of the century. When it was about to be revived, three years later, this time at the Comédie Française, one of the many journals hostile to Dumas attacked "Antony" for its immorality. The denunciation came from such a powerful quarter that Thiers, who had arranged not only for the revival, but for new plays from its author's pen, was forced to forbid the performance. Dumas went to law, and obtained £400 damages, and an order that the piece should be produced within a certain time.

But even "Antony" failed to bring its author fortune, so greatly were the public preoccupied by things political; and to avoid the unsettling atmosphere of Paris, Dumas went for a holiday to Trouville, which in those days was a quiet and charming little Normandy seaside village. As usual with him, Dumas's holiday meant a different working-place, for here he was busy evolving his most poetical play, "Charles VII.," inspired, as he acknowledges, by De Musset's "Marrons au feu," and by "The Cid" and "Andromaque." Here also one M. Beudin came to him with the prologue of a play which afterwards became "Richard Darlington."

It was on our author's return from Trouville, to witness the first night of Hugo's "Marion Delorme," that Dumas encountered a kind friend who told him that he was too late, and informed him of the comparative failure of the play. The critic-friend was astounded to hear a detailed and eloquent eulogy of "Marion" from the lips of the author of "Christine."

When Dumas had finished, the critic shrugged his shoulders with an air of profound amazement. "A *confrère!*" he said. Further words failed him.

"Charles VII.," like "Henri Trois" and "Antony," was, in spite of its historical setting, a play of the times—a challenge to the old social régime; a part of the romantic movement; a powerful plea for individuality. This Dumas himself declared, in the lines which he prefixed to his "Comme je devins auteur dramatique" (the first draft of his "Mémoires") in 1833—

> "Un jour on connaîtra quelle lutte obstinée
> A fait sous mon genou plier la destinée ;
> A quelle source amère en mon âme j'ai pris
> Tout ce qu'elle contient de haine et de mépris :
> Quel orage peut faire, en passant sur la tête,
> Qu'on prenne pour le jour l'éclair d'un tempête,

> Et ce que l'homme souffre en ses convulsions,
> Quand au volcan du cœur grondent les passions.
> Je ne cacherai plus où ma plume fidèle
> A trouvé d'Antony le type et le modèle,
> Et je dirai tout haut à quels foyers brûlants
> Yaquoub[1] et Saint Mégrin puisèrent leurs élans...."

"Charles VII." was a failure, or at best a *succès d'estime*. Dumas *fils* has told us how sadly he and his father walked homeward after the play; for the tragedy had contained its author's most conscious and most literary attempt at poetry; and all his many successes in life never compensated Dumas for the fact that he was not in the strict sense of the word a poet, and could not disguise the fact from himself.

"Charles VII." was of the school of "Christine," and was the result of Dumas's occasional yearnings after a classical reputation; but the drama-proper was his more congenial *métier*. "Richard Darlington," a legitimate son of "Antony," was successfully produced, and became one of its author's favourite plays. In spite of this Dumas, who on this occasion had collaborators, refused to allow his name to be announced, even as part-author. Unfortunately "Richard Darlington" will be read by English people—if it is read at all—with more amusement than respect; for the scene is laid in England, and the details of our social life which it offers have all the piquancy of novelty, and discount the dramatic strength of the play.

[1] The "hero" of "Charles VII."

An incident which we find in the "Mémoires" gives us an interesting insight into the author's skill and knowledge of stage-craft. Whilst Dumas was busy writing "Richard Darlington" with Goubaud, he stopped short at one point, unable to advance. It was at the crisis when the ambitious Richard, anxious to get rid of Jenny, his plebeian wife, so that he may marry into higher society, determines to make away with her. Someone is coming up the stairs; if the existence of this wife is discovered by the newcomer, all Darlington's plans will be overthrown. The only obvious resource is to throw Jenny out of the window into the rushing torrent below. This is where the skilled dramatist discovers and resolves a problem of stage-management. It would revolt the audience to see a woman struggling for life every inch of the way to that window; it would make them laugh, if the husband, in lifting his victim to hurl her to death, should expose her ankles.

At length the idea came, and Dumas like Columbus with the egg, broke the end, and made it stand, thus:

Darlington threatens Jenny; she rushes towards the balcony, crying for help. He follows her, closing the folding doors of the recess behind them. "A cry pierces the silence. Richard strikes the doors with his fist, they fly open and disclose him on the balcony, pale, wiping the sweat from his brow, and alone.

Jenny has disappeared—*Voilà tout!*"

It was at this period of his fortunes, when he was writing with Anicet Bourgeois "Teresa," which he describes as "one of my worst," and "Angèle," which he considered one of his best plays, that Dumas gave his famous ball. As he wished to invite three hundred guests, and had only four rooms in which to receive them, he hired another suite from his landlord. Three days before the eventful night, Dumas turned ten of the foremost painters of France into these empty rooms to decorate them, and as the great men were all friends of the young author, this was at once an economy, an attraction, and a novelty. With the same object of saving expense, Dumas took some friends out of town, and they shot their own game for the feast.

It was a brilliant affair, for it was a costume ball, and all Bohemia-in-Paris gathered in the little rooms, which by midnight were crowded with dazzling dresses, and filled with laughter and music. Here, among others, came Lafayette, Rossini, De Musset, Sue, Lemaître, Mars, Georges, Dejazet and Delacroix—who had painted the panel allotted to him in two or three hours! M. Tissot, of the Academy, went "made up" as a sick man, whereupon Jadin followed him as a long-faced, funereal-looking undertaker, and dogged the other's footsteps, croaking out lugubriously every other minute, "I'm waiting for you! I'm waiting for you!" The party broke up at nine in the morning, with a wild galop in the street.

And now events conspired to work an important change in Dumas's life. So far, the author of "Antony," under the influence of Goëthe and Byron, had "posed" in his writings, as a Manfred or a Mephistopheles; and with folded arms and cynic laugh had affected to deny, and disdain, the virtues and pleasures of the world. But one day Dumas wrote a begging-letter for his friend Lassailly, who, on reading the note, turned to its author with a stupefied air.

"Well," he said, "this is comical!"

"What is?"

"Why, you have wit!"

"Why shouldn't I? Envious fellow!"

"Well, you're probably the first man of five feet nine who has ever been witty!"

Dumas has himself defined and described his own gaiety. "Some folk," he says, "are gay because they're well, or have a good digestion, or have nothing to worry about—that is the ordinary gaiety. But mine is invariable gaiety, which shines through disturbing influences, through troubles, through danger itself."

The young writer had been unconscious of the

existence of this unfashionable quality; but it was destined to show itself henceforth — first in his books of travel, and afterwards in his comedies and romances; and, in short, more or less in everything he wrote or spoke.

Dumas's gaiety does not, perhaps, appear in his first romance—if we can call it so—of "Isabel de Bavière." Four of his friends had previously scraped together a little money, and started the world-famous *Revue des Deux Mondes*, and Dumas agreed to assist the new-born with his pen. The "Histoire des Ducs de Bourgoyne" of Barante made a powerful impression upon him at this time, "finishing," he says, "the work begun by Scott." Still, the young author did not feel strong enough to write an entirely original romance; and he therefore put into a picturesque form, and into dialogue, selected scenes from Barante, which he first called "Scènes Historiques," and which proved a great success in the pages of the *Revue*. This decided the ambitious author to write forthwith the history of France from the days of Charles VI. to his own. It is hardly credible—and yet Dumas confesses to it—his ignorance of history at this period was so profound that he was studying it by the aid of poetic tags!—

> "En l'an quatre-cent-vingt, Pharamond, premier roi,
> Est connu seulement par la salique loi." . . .

The novelist was delivered from this school-book thraldom by a more learned friend, and introduced to Thierry's " Conquête des Normands." History became a passion with him, and the days of that tremendous historic-romance-cycle grew nearer and nearer.

In 1832 the cholera swept over Paris, emptying the theatres, filling the cemeteries, and carrying terror everywhere. Nevertheless it could not daunt our author's new-found gaiety: he wrote the dialogue of one of his wittiest plays—"Le Mari de la Veuve"—for an actress who was about to take a benefit, and who begged from Dumas some novelty to put on the bills. Every night a group of friends forgathered in Dumas's rooms. "We chatted; sometimes Hugo decided to recite us some of his poetry; Liszt thumped hard on a wretched piano, and the evening passed by without one of us thinking any more of the cholera than if it had been at Pekin."

But one evening, immediately after Dumas had watched his joyous friends depart, he himself was seized with the cholera. For five or six days he was prostrate and in great danger, but his wonderful physique withstood the attack of the terrible disease. The first person to greet him in his convalescence was Harel, the manager of the Odéon. The cholera, he cheerfully declared, had "gone away without even making its expenses," and he pressed the fever-ridden author to set about a new play. This was destined to be "La Tour de Nesle." The plot of that drama was common property; from Villon's day all French readers had known of the vile Queen Marguerite of Burgundy, of her foul, nightly revels in the terrible Tower, and of the bodies which were found in the Seine next morning. It may be added that there is not a horror, or an incredible incident in the play, which history has not only justified, but asserted.

The authorship of the play led to a long and acrimonious dispute, which is best described in the words of Mr Walter Herries Pollock:

"It seems to me that no one who devotes a moderate attention to his dramatic works can reasonably doubt that in the celebrated quarrel about the play called the 'Tour de Nesle,' right was on the side of Dumas. This quarrel is worth some attention. The story takes up some four chapters of Dumas's 'Mémoires'; but briefly, the main facts were these:

"Harel, the great theatrical manager, had received a play in manuscript from a young author named Gaillardet. He thought there was capital stuff in it; but as it was written it was quite unfitted for stage representation on account of the author's inexperience. Jules Janin had tried to do something with it, and had failed. Harel then came to Dumas, who, according to his own account, which I for one believe, entirely remodelled it, and made of it one of the most impressive melodramas ever put on the stage. He had previously written a somewhat imprudently self-effacing letter to the young author, who, instead of being grateful, was furious at having, as he said, a collaborator thrust upon him, and ended by writing to the papers to assert that he was the sole author of the piece.

"The matter went through all kinds of intricacies into which it would be tedious to go; but the last word which ought to be said about it is found in a letter written by Gaillardet in 1861 to the manager of the Porte St Martin theatre. The letter runs thus:

"'A judgment of the courts in 1832 decreed that the "Tour de Nesle" should be printed and announced under my name alone; and this was done up to the date of its being forbidden by the censorship in 1851.

"'Now that you are going to put it on the stage again, I give you permission—nay, more, I beg you—to join to my name that of Alexandre Dumas, my collaborator. I wish to prove to him that I have forgotten our old quarrel, and that I remember only our later pleasant relations, and the great share which his incomparable talent had in the success of the "Tour de Nesle."'"

The success of the drama, indeed, equalled that of "Antony." Yet, although Dumas was determined that Gaillardet should receive the sole credit of the play, a quarrel developed—for which Harel's unscrupulous behaviour as the go-between was responsible—and a duel was fought, fortunately with no serious results.

But no sooner was our ardent hero out of this scrape than he got into another. There was a Republican riot during the funeral of General Lamarque, a devoted servant of France and of Napoleon. Dumas took part in the riot; and next day he read, in a legitimist paper, that he had been taken with arms in his hand, summarily court-martialled, and shot!

"The news," says Dumas, "was of so authentic a nature, the details of my execution were so circumstantial, the information came from such an infallible source, that I experienced a moment's doubt. I felt myself all over!" Nodier wrote to say that he had heard of Dumas's death, and expressed a hope that it would not prevent him from dining with a few friends on the morrow. The other replied that he was not at all sure whether he was living or not, but that either in body or in spirit he would come to dinner. He added that, as he had eaten nothing for six weeks there would probably be more of his spirit than his body present.

But if he had not been shot, and if the cholera had failed to kill him, Dumas was still in some danger. One of the king's aides-de-camp gave the literary politician a hint that the question of his arrest was being considered, and advised a temporary absence from Paris. Accordingly Dumas set out in July, 1832 for Switzerland.

This tour, the account of which delighted the public by its freshness, gaiety and picturesque style, possessed one or two notable features. With true journalistic instinct Dumas called on Chateaubriand, the self-exiled Royalist poet, and chatted to him of politics; he interviewed Jacques Balmat, and heard from the lips of the guide his narrative of the first ascent of Mont Blanc; and he wrote the famous fable of the "bear-beefsteak," which he pretended to have eaten at a certain inn. Thenceforth travellers by the score stopped at that inn and called for bear-steak, and the unhappy landlord, quite unable to satisfy the guests either with his explanations or with the required dish, went nearly mad, and cursed the very name of Dumas.

The most interesting portion of the "Impressions de Voyage en Suisse," from a serious point of view, is the account of Dumas's interview at Arenenburg with Hortense Bonaparte, ex-Queen of Holland, and mother of Louis Napoleon, afterwards Napoleon III. The young Republican philosopher did not hold out any hopes to the royal exile of a restoration by force, or by the power of the Napoleonic tradition alone. In reply to a request from the queen for advice as to the means by which one of her family might re-establish the dynasty, Dumas replied:

"I would say to him, obtain the revocation of your exile; buy a home in France; cause yourself to be elected deputy; and try by force of your talent to secure a majority in the chamber, and make use of it to overthrow Louis Philippe, and get yourself chosen king in his stead." Sixteen years later Louis Napoleon followed this advice pretty closely, and his success is a matter of history.

The Swiss holiday was followed by a brief visit to England in 1833, and a tour in the South of France, which was much more lengthy. The following year Dumas started for Italy, with his friend Jadin, and "Mylord," the bull-dog. He was arrested at Naples as a dangerous "red," and it was only when he produced papers proving that he was entrusted with a private mission by the French Government that he was released. In November of the following year the traveller was privileged to have an interview with Pope Gregory XVI.—after which he was arrested a second time!

The next year or two passed in the most delightful way; Dumas enjoyed himself like a schoolboy in holiday-time, sailing round Sicily, exploiting

Naples and Florence, and "earning his keep" by writing most entertaining accounts of his adventures.

On his return "Catherine Howard," "Don Juan" and "Kean" were produced in successive years. "Kean," as played by Frederick Lemaître, made a strong impression on Heine and others, but in spite of its English *milieu*, the play is so French in spirit as to appeal most to our sense of humour. Thackeray, who was visiting Paris about this period, was terribly shocked by the naive and earnest irreverence of "Don Juan" and "Caligula." In his "Paris Sketch-book" he has denounced them both, in that bluff "damn-everything-that-isn't-English" style, so cheap, yet so dear to the public.

Dumas had been on familiar terms with the young Duke of Chartres, who succeeded to the title of "Duke of Orleans" (which corresponded to our "Prince of Wales"), when his father obtained the throne. In 1836 our author had stayed with the prince at Compiègne, and when the heir was married in 1837, and fêtes were held at Versailles in honour of the occasion, four crosses of the Legion of Honour were placed at the disposal of the young prince. Dumas received one of them—a knight's cross. Seven years before, on the morrow of "Christine," Louis Philippe himself, at his son's request, had asked for the cross for his young employee from Charles X., but had been refused. Dumas's name was on this occasion removed from the list by the King's own order; upon which Hugo, who was about to receive an officer's cross, declined the promotion indignantly. The offending name was accordingly re-entered on the list, and the two friends went to the fête together, and left it arm-in-arm. But Alexandre felt that the honour came too late. Instead of fastening it to his button-hole, he put it in his fob.

By this time Dumas had become so famous that, with his artless vanity, his outspoken ways, and his unbusiness-like methods, he had earned a host of enemies, mockers, detractors, denunciators and the like. His "Caligula" failed, although it was produced at the Comédie Française in the most costly fashion; and its author discovered that the leader of the claque (or organised gang of applauders) had been bribed by a number of actors, who were not performing in the play, to do all he could to damn the piece!

In 1838 Dumas suffered the great misfortune of his life. His mother, to whom he had been so passionately attached, died suddenly. Friends brought him the news that Madame Dumas had been seized with a second apoplectic stroke. The first attack, eight years before, had partly disabled the sufferer, and this one proved almost immediately fatal. The dying woman was able to open her eyes and look on her son once more—and that was all. With a choking heart Dumas sent word of the event to his young patron, and an hour later the kindly duke was at the street door in his carriage. The mourner ran out, at this sign of friendly sympathy, and kneeling at the prince's feet, burst into tears. There was remorse mingled with grief in this passion of regret for the life that was passing away in the room above, for although Alexandre had usually visited his mother constantly, and shown her every loving mark of affection, there had also been periods of absence and neglect, which now he regretted only too keenly.

At the foot of the sketch of his dead mother, which Duval drew, Dumas wrote these lines—

> "Oh, mon Dieu! Dans ce monde où toute bouche nie,
> Où chacun foule aux pieds les Tables de la Loi,
> Vous m'avez entendu, pendant son agonie,
> Prier à deux genoux, le cœur ardent de foi.
> Vous m'avez vu, mon Dieu, sur la funèbre route,
> Où la mort me courbait devant un crucifix,
> Et vous avez compté les pleurs qui, goutte à goutte,
> Ruisselaient de mes yeux aux pieds de Votre Fils.
> Je demandais, mon Dieu, que moins vite ravie,
> Vous retardiez l'instant de son dernier adieu :
> Pour racheter ses jours je vous offrais ma vie ;
> Vous n'avez pas voulu : soyez béni, mon Dieu !"[1]

[1] ("Oh, my God, in this world, where all men deny Thee, where the feet of men spurn the Tables of Thy Laws, Thou hast heard me, as I

It was in the next few years that Dumas, in the interval of travels and foreign residence, wrote the three comedies which seem destined to outlive his dramas, and to prove in the future the sole support of his reputation as a playwright. These were " Mademoiselle de Belle-Isle," " Un Mariage sous Louis Quinze," and " Les Demoiselles de St Cyr." These plays, which sparkle with wit and are alive with interest, are still in the repertoire of the Comédie Française. The " Mariage" was "commanded" by the responsible Minister (fancy the Home Secretary ordering a play from Mr Grundy for the Lyceum!), was written in Italy, and sent in to the theatre. On the author's return, his enemies in the company told him gleefully that the comedy had been rejected. Dumas quietly produced the Minister's letter, and informed the dismayed actors that they had no option but to play it, whether they liked it or they didn't. Tableau!

Dumas now led a roving life. In 1838 he had visited Belgium and the Rhine; two years later

knelt at her feet, throughout her agony, praying, with a heart full of faith. Thou hast seen me, oh God, go with her on that last sad journey, when Death's hand bowed my back and bent my gaze on the crucifix, and Thou didst count the tears that one by one streamed from my eyes on the feet of Thy Son. I asked, oh God, that Thou wouldst delay for a while, however brief, the last parting of mother and son. To purchase life for her I would have sold my own. It was not Thy will: be Thou blest, oh my God!")

he went to Italy, returning there in 1841 and again in 1842. In 1840 he married Mdlle. Ida Ferrier, a fascinating woman but a second-rate actress, who appeared in her husband's tragedy-drama "Caligula," and other subsequent plays. The marriage was a very ill-advised one, and finally extravagance and irreconcilable differences of character combined caused the lady to leave her husband and go to live in Florence. She never returned to France, and died in Italy in 1859.

The "Comtesse Dash," an intimate friend of Dumas and his wife, has given us, if not the real excuse for his "immorality," at least the true explanation of it:

"A woman who would have loved him enough to love him as he wished to be loved (she writes in her "Mémoires d'Autres"), a woman who would have had the tact to close her eyes to his pranks, and make home comfortable, so that he could invite his friends there; and above all, who *would not have disturbed him in his work*—that woman would have been perfectly and eternally happy with him."

The character of Madame Dumas has been clearly drawn for us by the same pen. "Ida" was a beautiful woman of mediocre abilities and with a jealous, narrow and contemptible nature. She tolerated little Marie, Dumas's daughter, but hated young Alexandre, because of the love his father bore him. The two were obliged to meet by stealth, for the young man was not allowed in the house. As the actress "Mademoiselle Ferrier" forced Dumas to give her parts to which her talents were not equal; as a mistress she was furiously jealous of every other woman, and played practical jokes of doubtful taste on the master. Dumas bore patiently with her extravagance, her constant interruption of his work, and the daily quarrel which seemed necessary to her existence; but soon after the pair were married the connection came to its inevitable end.

Whilst Dumas was staying at the Villa Palmieri at Florence, early in 1842, old Jerome Bonaparte suggested that the author should take the young Prince Napoleon, who was just returning from Wurtemburg, for a cruise, with the object of "teaching him France." The nephew of the great Emperor naturally desired to visit both Elba and Corsica; and it was during this trip that the travellers espied from the mainland of Elba, the insignificant islet of Monte Cristo. Curiosity prompted them to visit it, and Dumas was so much struck by the appearance of the picturesque little spot that he resolved to use its name as the title of his forthcoming romance.

It was one of Dumas's laughing complaints that Scribe was considered a "moral" writer, whilst he himself was looked upon as immoral. Therefore, when the opportunity came to him to play a practical joke on his *confrère* he could not resist.

Whilst Dumas was staying in Florence about this time an actor-friend of his, named Doligny, came to him and asked permission to play some of his best-known dramas. The author gave his consent willingly, but warned the actor that the authorities would refuse him permission to perform. When Doligny returned he confessed that his friend was right—the censor had rejected the plays by "that immoral writer"—but Dumas came to the rescue. He took Doligny with him to the office of a friendly printer, and ordered new covers for the four plays in question. It was very simple:—

In place of "Richard Darlington, by A. Dumas," was printed "Ambition, or the Executioner's Son, by Eugène Scribe."

In place of "Angèle, by A. Dumas," was printed "A Ladder of Petticoats, by Eugène Scribe."

Instead of "Antony, by A. Dumas," was printed "Love's Victim, by Eugène Scribe."

"Instead of "La Tour de Nesle, by MM. Gaillardet and A. Dumas," was printed "Adultery Punished, by Eugène Scribe."

The old plays with the new coats—if we may believe Dumas—duly passed the censor without comment; the public found the plays masterpieces of improving literature, and the grand-duke applauded them furiously!

In July of the same year Dumas heard of the sudden and shocking death of the young Duke of Orleans, who was thrown from his carriage, through his horses taking fright, and mortally injured. Full of grief, the author hurried post-haste to Paris, and arrived just in time for the funeral ceremonies, and the interment at Dreux. His sorrow for the promising young prince, of which there is no reason for doubting the sincerity, was artless and unrestrained, and afforded his enemies ample scope for mockery.

Dumas, like most French authors, had a desire to be judged Immortal whilst he lived, and had already more than once put himself forward for election to the Academy, and in particular to the seat vacant by the death of his old colleague and rival Casimir Delavigne, the author of "Louis XI." But in 1843, as on previous occasions, he was rejected by the Forty, whose orthodoxy was shocked by the audacious methods of this wicked "Romantic." On one occasion Hugo would have nominated Dumas for a vacant chair, but there were only thirteen Academicians present and twenty-one votes were necessary for election. Dumas consoled himself with the fact that he occupied the "forty-first fauteuil" in good company, and recollecting the treatment which the Academy had meted out to great Frenchmen, from Corneille and Molière, downward. Repulsed once more, he returned to Florence, saying to himself, "Je demande à être le *quarantième*, mais il paraît qu'on me faire faire *quarantaine!*" ("I ask to be made the fortieth, but it appears they wish to keep me in quarantine!")

The year 1844 was one of the great years in the life of Dumas. "Les Trois Mousquetaires" and "Monte Cristo" both appeared at that time, and were welcomed enthusiastically by the public. During their progress in *feuilleton* form, people had discussed the sayings and doings of D'Artagnan or Dantès as if the men were alive, and known to everybody—as, indeed, they were. Villemessant tells us how he woke his wife in the night to tell her of the escape in the sack from the Chateau d'If; and Gautier has described amusingly enough the grip which the two books obtained on the imagination of the Parisian public. Dumas had achieved a second fame.

In his preface to "Les Trois Mousquetaires," Alexandre Dumas *fils* has left us a charming picture of his father at the time these great romances were written. Their author was then working in some modest lodgings, overlooking the courtyard of the house (No. 22 Rue de Rivoli), his rooms plainly furnished with a big white-wood table, a sofa, two chairs, a few books on the mantelpiece, and an iron bedstead, where he slept for a few hours when the evening's work was prolonged into the night. "It was there," adds the son, addressing his father in apostrophe, "that you sought refuge, to be undisturbed by the importunate, and all the parasites who incessantly besieged that door which you did not close half often enough. Clothed in your *pantalons à pied* and shirt sleeves, your arms bare to the shoulder, your collar unfastened, you sat down to work at seven in the morning and you kept at it until seven at night, when I came to dine with you.

"Sometimes I found your lunch untouched, on the little table by your side, where the servant had placed it. You had forgotten to eat it. Then, whilst we dined and dined well, on the dishes which you yourself had prepared, you recounted to me, by way of relaxation, all that your characters had done during the day, and rejoiced in the thought of what they were going to do, on the morrow. This lasted for some months.

"Ah, those happy days! We were both of an age: you were forty-two, and I was twenty!"

Fiorentino declares that Dumas, being accustomed to fill his twenty sheets a day, finished " Monte

Cristo," in his presence, on the fifteenth page. Not wishing to depart from his rule, the romancer took a fresh sheet, wrote at the top "Les Trois Mousquetaires," and completed five sheets of the new story before finishing for the day!

It will be readily understood that with his *bonhomie* and contagious wit Dumas's social popularity was enormous. Villemessant, whose stories of "the master" were always amusing and sometimes trustworthy, tells us

"When he spoke, the most celebrated guests were silent, in order to listen to him; when he entered a salon, the wit of the men and the beauty of the women—all that makes for the joy of life—were eclipsed by the glory of this one man. He was really the King of Paris, sovereign by virtue of intelligence and wit—the only man for a whole century, who had made himself adored by all classes of society."

Janin relates that on the occasion of the Duke of Montpensier's wedding with the Infanta of Spain a grand fête was given at Madrid. An old diplomat, arriving late, was astonished to see there a man dressed simply in black, and a perfect stranger, to whom the greatest lords of Spain were listening with all their ears, forgetting the queen and the royal bridal pair in their enjoyment. He asked who the attraction was.

"*Pardieu*," answered his friend, "that's Alexandre Dumas—who else do you think it would be?"

A certain Parisian named M. Pitre-Chevalier, being a sort of Lyon-Hunter, was (so Villemessant declares) anxious to obtain the presence of all the social celebrities at his salons, and made unheard-of efforts to secure the lion of the hour for one of his evenings. Dumas chose his salons, as he chose his theatre, or the newspaper for his *feuilletons*, and when it was known in Paris "Dumas will be at So-and-so's to-night!" society attacked the lucky host's house as if it had been the doors of a theatre, on the night of a *première*; all the company stood up as he entered, and his journey towards his host was a sort of triumphal procession. Pitre-Chevalier had his way; but the next day the gossips of the boulevards talked of nothing but Dumas's latest *mot*. Asked by a friend whether he had enjoyed the evening with M. Lyon-Hunter, Dumas replied,

"Well, I should have been very bored, if it hadn't been for—myself!"

At one of these soirées Dumas was wearing the ribbon of a certain order, having recently been made a commandant, and an envious friend remarked upon it.

"My dear fellow," he said, "that cordon is a wretched colour! One would think it was your woollen vest that was showing!"

"Oh no, my dear d'E——," replied Dumas with a smile, "you're mistaken; it's not a bad colour: it is exactly the shade of the sour grapes in the fable."

Gozlan one day asked Dumas why a certain *bête noir* of his had received the Legion of Honour.

"Don't you know?" answered the author, looking wise, and as if he had some State secret to reveal.

"Certainly I don't know—*you* don't know either!"

"Ah, but I do, though!"

"Then,—tell me!"

"They've given him a cross—because—he hadn't one!"

This is as severe as Mark Twain's comment that "few escape that distinction."

Writing furiously at his romances, our author exiled himself from society as much as possible, and for that purpose retired to some rented rooms in the "Henry IV." pavilion at St Germain; but even there he was constantly disturbed by friends, parasites and duns, and in despair found it necessary to move further afield. Driven from St Germain, he discovered between that town and Marly a site which seemed to him to be an ideal one for a quiet, unpretentious house, which should be his own—he was tired of living in other peoples' houses. He arranged with an architect for a two- or three-roomed cottage, where he could work in peace. But as he discussed the plans, the love of splendour with which his African descent had cursed or blessed him, came uppermost, and at the tempting suggestions of others his ideas expanded at such a pace that from a few hundred francs, Dumas found himself paying—or owing—tens of thousands. In July he gave a breakfast on the site of the future palace, inviting his guests to meet him there, three years later, to see his new home. As Mr Fitzgerald says, "this was like one of the dramatic appointments given in 'Monte Cristo.'"

From this period in particular, dated that system of collaboration which lasted for some years, and of which so much too much has been made. The editors who urged this ardent, *insouciant* worker to undertake twice or three times as much as any ordinary mortal could produce, were the first to attack him, either for non-fulfilment of contract, or for his "workshop" methods, as they were pleased to call them.

Inevitably Dumas, in the full blaze of success, was the butt of the envious, for envy is the shadow thrown by the sun of fame. A young gentleman of the name of Jacquot (who, like a kitchen-rogue, dubbed himself "Eugène de Mirecourt"), choosing to consider himself offended by the great man, brought before the "Société des Gens de Lettres," a resolution levelled at our author (during his absence), condemning him for keeping "a literary factory"; for "setting up as a *coryphée* of shame"; and for "laying his hand on Reputation, that white-winged maiden, dragging her through the mire, and violating her before the public gaze," with much more to the same effect. Unfortunately Dumas himself, calling in unexpectedly, interrupted the back-biting process; and when he left, after a fierce encounter with his circle of enemies, they passed a mild, emasculated resolution which, coming from so unimportant a body, had little effect.

Theodore de Banville, in his "Odes Funambulesques," has some amusing but quite untranslatable verse on this episode. Dumas is passing by, when a "mirecourt" darts out of the crowd, and abuses the great man in the foulest manner. After the thing has exhausted its bag of spleen, Dumas replies.

> Docile au mirecourt, il lui laissa tout dire,
> Pencha son front rêveur . . . puis, avec un sourire,
> Fit : '*As-tu déjeûné*, Jacquot?'[1]

Thwarted thus, Jacquot published his venomous pamphlet, "Maison Dumas et Cie," by which he got little credit or profit. There was a half-truth in this lie, and if it had been told with moderation and in a friendly and appreciative way, it might

[1] Dumas politely allowed the mirecourt to say its say; then inclined his thoughtful brow towards the creature and asked with a smile, "Hast thou lunched to-day, Jacquot?"

have had a salutary effect. As it was, both the squib and the motive for it were alike contemptible. One of the "workmen" attacked challenged the slanderer, who, at the instance of Dumas, was sentenced to fifteen days' imprisonment. Dumas *fils* took up his father's cause, and challenged Jacquot also; but that gentleman, with characteristic cowardice, shirked the encounter. Yet this contractor for the gutter press of Paris had not written in vain; for most subsequent biographies of Dumas, whether in English or in French, seem to have been founded on Jacquot's statements, and to be actuated by his spirit.

In 1846 the Duke of Montpensier, younger brother of the ill-fated Orleans, was betrothed by Louis Philippe to the Infanta of Spain, and set out for Madrid, for the wedding. The French Government invited Dumas to accompany the prince and act as official histriographer on this important occasion. Further, he was instructed to go forward to Algiers, and, in his gay, informative and incisive way, to "teach" France all about its new colony. A friendship had sprung up between the young Duke and Dumas, and the arrangement was a pleasant one for all parties. The writer, his vanity flattered by the commission, accepted, although at the very shortest notice, and without for a moment considering the consequences to himself.

The Royal party arrived at Madrid in October; the wedding duly took place, and Dumas received the cordon of Charles III. on the occasion of the auspicious ceremony. In due course he visited Tangiers, in the State vessel *Le Véloce*, called at Gibraltar, crossed again to Tetuan, and took an honourable share in the delivery of some Frenchmen, captured by the Moors. Although he did not make a long stay at Algiers — where Marshal Bugeaud failed to meet him as arranged — Dumas sailed on to Tunis and the site of ancient Carthage, and duly embodied his adventures in two series of "impressions" — "De Paris à Cadix," and "Le Véloce."

All this was wormwood to Dumas's enemies in Paris, and they were numerous and influential. On his return his travels were made the subject of a savage attack on the Government and their envoy, in the press, and in the Chamber of Deputies. Now, although M. Salvandy had expressly charged Dumas with the mission to Algiers, and although M. Guizot, the Foreign Minister, had given the author special instructions, as well as a passport, placing him under national protection, the ministers made a discreditable attempt to explain away their connection with "ce monsieur," as he was insolently called, and to pacify their enemies at the expense of Dumas's reputation. It is pleasant, by way of contrast, to read Madame de Girardin's warm and generous defence of our author, and her scorn of the "gentlemen," who had insulted the man of genius. For, when Dumas and Maquet sent challenges to the deputies who had abused them, those gentlemen sheltered themselves behind their public position and would not "come out and fight."

The following year was a busy one for the returned "envoy," for no less than seven newspapers combined to sue him for arrears of work due. One in particular had a genuine grievance; for the impulsive writer, in order to follow the fortunes of the young Montpensier, had left what is known in English as "The Memoirs of a Physician" in a state of startling incompleteness. The trial was an amusing one, for the culprit conducted his own defence, and proved himself as vivacious in dialogue with his tongue as with his pen. After three days' hearing the court ordered the defendant to resume the "Memoirs" within a month, and pay £4 a day for any delay beyond that time. He was threatened with imprisonment if the arrears of fines became too great; and in addition was fined £120 for each of the seven journals. Needless to say, nothing more was heard of the fines, and the whole affair was naturally a splendid testimony to the author's popularity.

Dumas the playwright had for some time been

embroiled with the theatres, and in particular with the Comédie Française—he gives an amusing account of his "Odyssey" at the Française in the "Souvenirs Dramatiques";—and now that fame and fortune had come to him he determined, with his usual magnificence of ideas, to have not only his own chateau, but also his own theatre, where no jealousies should come between his genius and the success of his plays. The young Duke of Montpensier secured for the dramatist a patent for the new theatre, which was to be called the "Thèâtre Montpensier"; the Hôtel Foulon, on the Boulevard du Temple, was bought and pulled down, and in its place the new theatre rose—a splendid building costing over £30,000, decorated most artistically and dedicated by its founder to the dramatic art of Europe. Unfortunately for Dumas, the Duke—at the instance of his father, Louis Philippe, it is said—withdrew this permission for the use of his name, and accordingly the new playhouse was christened the "Historique." On the 21st of February 1847 the first performance was given; the duke and his suite being present. The play chosen was a dramatised version of "La Reine Margot."

There is an anecdote told in this connection, which is truly illustrative of the characters of prince and author respectively. When, after the Revolution of '48, the Duke went into exile, his box was religiously

THE "THEATRE HISTORIQUE," BOULEVARD DE TEMPLE, PARIS.

kept vacant for him for a whole year, although he had long since ceased to pay for it. Dumas learnt later that the Duke, when he received his tickets, was wont to burst out laughing at the quixotic manager's "buffoonery"; and the proprietor then decided that the box should be devoted to public use in future, remarking that the yearly rent of a box was too high a price to pay for the privilege of making a prince laugh.

In July of this year Dumas, according to his pledge, gave a magnificent reception to six hundred guests, as a house-warming for his new palace of "Monte Cristo." The scheme had rapidly outgrown the first modest plan, and had been developed on the most lavish scale. "A beautiful building, half-chateau, half-villa, had risen in the meantime," says Fitzgerald, "embowered in trees, and in the centre of a wild garden. Its white stone walls were covered with exquisite traceries and sculptures copied from those of Jean Goujon at the Louvre, and executed by Choistat, conspicuous in the centre being Dumas's arms, with the motto '*J'aime qui m'aime*.' Inside, the walls were decorated from designs by Klagmann; while the 'Arabian chamber,' after the pattern of the Alhambra, was a marvel of Eastern gorgeousness and decoration. The gardens were charming, all leafy and shaded. On the little island in the lake rose an exquisite little Norman building, intended as a sort of kiosk, covered with exquisite carvings, the designs being by Mansson, a decorator of great eminence. Blended with the sound of falling waters—for an artificial torrent had been contrived, that tumbled over rocks as artificially arranged—was heard the chattering of monkeys, and the screaming of parrots, while huge barbaric dogs of strange shapes and colour ranged through the groves. Such was 'Monte Cristo,' which was now the talk of Paris."

Here Dumas's hospitality was princely, unlimited. "At his Abbotsford 'Monte Cristo,'" Mr Lang reminds us, "the gates were open to everybody but bailiffs. His dog asked other dogs to come and stay; twelve came, making thirteen in all. The old butler wanted to turn them adrift, and Dumas consented and repented.

"'Michel,' he said, 'there are some expenses which a man's social position and the character which he has had the ill-luck to receive from heaven force upon him. I don't believe these dogs ruin me. Let them bide. But, in the interests of their own good luck, see that they are not thirteen, an unfortunate number!'

"'Monsieur, I'll drive one of them away.'

"'No, no, Michel; let a fourteenth come. . . . These dogs cost me some £3 a month,' said

Dumas. 'A dinner to five or six friends would cost thrice as much, and, when they went home, they would say my wine was good, but certainly that my books were bad.'"

The owner himself retired to the pavilion to work, whilst his parasites enjoyed the unbounded hospitality of the establishment, and roamed at will throughout the splendid mansion. It will readily be understood that under the irresistible influence of this man, St Germain became a new place; it was filled with life and gaiety. Dumas rented the local theatre, hired a company of actors, and produced the translation of "Hamlet," for which Meurice and himself were responsible. Indeed, so transformed was this suburb of Paris, that Louis Philippe, we are told, wondered at the change; and wished the same process to be applied to Versailles, which was certainly dull enough. However, when it was suggested to him by Montalivet that Dumas should be brought to Versailles, the king turned his back on the maladroit courtier!

In 1847 the "reform agitation" broke out in France, and ended the following February in the downfall of the house of Orleans.[1] Louis Philippe

[1] Dumas is silent concerning this Revolution, and Vandam tells us that he never would discuss it. It is the opinion of the author of "An Englishman in Paris" that the romancer was a trifle ashamed of the Republican intriguers of that time.

fled to England; and Louis Napoleon became President of the French Republic, making himself Emperor, in 1851, by means of the infamous *coup d'état*. And from this epoch onward, the meteoric brilliance of Dumas's star began to fade.

Several causes contributed to this sudden and overwhelming change of fortune. Our author was, as Ferry says, a man of independence of character and opinion, "and this opinion manifested itself in an originality as rare as it was disinterested. When Dumas had known a prince in private life, or in exile, he broke with him as soon as he became King or Emperor,"—as in the cases of Louis Philippe and Napoleon III. " Misfortune and exile found Dumas friendly and respectful; triumph rendered him prudent, even antagonistic." Thus, when he joined with his brother "liberals" in commencing the agitation of 1847, he acted with a difference. He founded a journal (*Le Mois*) in order to give publicity to his political views; and he protested indignantly against the destruction of the statue of the Duke of Orleans (Louis Philippe's son) as a wanton and disgraceful act. He went further, and dedicated one of his books to the exiled young Montpensier; and by the time that the elections came on, Dumas had achieved the reputation of being an Orleanist!

Still, he decided to offer himself as a candidate for the Chamber of Deputies—not for his native department of the Aisne, where, in consequence of the Soissons exploit, he was considered an extreme "red"; nor for St Germain, because in the revolutionary days of February he had lost his command of the national guard there, by suggesting that he should lead his 750 comrades to Paris, *à la Marseillaise*, to the help of the people. It was suggested to him that the department of Yonne would be sure to acclaim him, and accordingly he went off to Lower Burgundy. When it was too late Dumas discovered that his chances in this district were fatally compromised because of his "Royalist sympathies"! He was mobbed, and fired at in the street. In vain he harangued a hostile crowd of three thousand Yonnais, and converted them into ardent supporters; he was not elected — perhaps because he had prophesied Prussia's conquest of France, twenty-two years later — although in his chant "Mourir pour la Patrie," which Dumas had introduced into his play of "Le Chevalier de Maison Rouge," he had given the Paris mob its "Marseillaise." (He had previously refused to write a "national anthem" to suit the Government.) Dumas was destined never to achieve a place in French politics, however ardently he desired it.

In M. Blaze de Bury's study of our author there is a witty account, which we wish we could reproduce in full, of a visit to Joigny paid by the writer, a certain M. du Chaffault, with Dumas, during the novelist's electoral campaign.

Du Chaffault, who lived at Sens, was awakened one morning, he tells us, to find a "horrible big devil" standing by his bedside. The apparition laughingly introduced himself as Alexandre Dumas, who had heard that this young man was "a good fellow," and would be of use to him at Joigny. Whilst the host hurriedly and bewilderedly dressed himself, Dumas changed his worn boots for a new pair of his young friend's, and, adds the narrator, "those he left are now in my library. I show them to visitors as the thousand-and-first volume of Alexandre Dumas." By the time they had started for Joigny the pair were like old friends, and Dumas's chat *en route* made the time fly wonderfully. At the second stage the candidate borrowed twenty francs from his new acquaintance, for the postillion, and the ingenuous young Du Chaffault duly entered in his note-book, "Alexandre Dumas, twenty francs." The same thing occurred at Joigny, where everyone came to the young man for money; and as Dumas invited everyone who accosted him to dine with them that evening, the six hundred francs which Du Chaffault had taken with him were gone by the following morning. " I returned to Sens," he says, " my heart full of joy at having seen and heard a man of genius. I still preserve the accounts I paid, which recall to me my two days passed in fairyland with 'Monte Cristo.' I regret only one thing—that I had not had the good sense to put ten thousand francs into my pocket, so that I might have prolonged this incomparable experience for a week or two."

Of course this political failure brought social consequences, but worse remained behind. The papers, being filled with public affairs, required no more *feuilletons*, and the " Thèâtre Historique," which at first had succeeded, did terribly bad business, and eventually closed its doors. It was afterwards pulled down to make room for one of the boulevards of the Second Empire. Meanwhile " Monte Cristo " required an enormous income to maintain it, and it will easily be understood that this literary " cigale," who had saved no store for the winter of misfortune, soon came to grief. He was obliged in the end to abandon the scarcely-finished palace and the newly-opened theatre to his creditors. It was a cruel blow to the great man's hopes and vanities; but he bore it well. He had reigned, like his old employer Louis Philippe, from revolution to revolution.

Wanderings, Decline and Death (1848–1870).

Dumas had not given way without a struggle. He had produced "Monte Cristo" at his ill-fated theatre, and tried the extraordinary experiment of playing it, half one night and the other half the next; and he had mortgaged his "palace" heavily. In 1849, at the Historique, he brought out his play of "Comte Hermann," the tone of which is in striking contrast with that of "Antony" and "Richard Darlington;" and its preface contains a sincere disavowal of the "criminal-passionate" themes of "twenty years before." In the same year Dumas attended the wedding of the Prince of Orange at Amsterdam; and was also summoned to a council of state, composed of playwrights and others, seven in all, to consider the question of the censorship. Unhappily, nothing came of the discussion. It was probably owing to his increasing embarrassments that when poor Marie Dorval died, during this year, her old friend was able to do little more than struggle to collect from others the necessary funds to bury her decently.

In 1851, as we have already said, the Republic fell, and buried Dumas's future in the ruins. He fled to Brussels, whither Hugo had already gone, and there, from December 1851 to January 1853, the novelist lived and worked, quietly but pleasantly, at No. 73, Rue de Waterloo. Almost every evening he was visited by a few old friends, of whom, of course, Hugo was the chief, and some of them would stay until two or three in the morning, sitting round the tea-table, chatting and laughing, whilst the host worked on above-stairs, now and then descending to exchange a word or two with his company. Here he turned out fifty volumes, for which, as he remarks, his enemies would have a task to find him the "anonymous collaborators" of whom they made so much.

At times, however, the ex-proprietor of 'Monte Cristo' would indulge in an evening's gaiety. One such gorgeous supper-party is described by Emile Deschanel in his volume of travels, "A Pied et en Wagon." From eleven till dawn the guests revelled in a never-ceasing series of delights and surprises, plays acted on a lilliputian stage by celebrated performers, Spanish singers and dancers, the gayest and most brilliant conversation—all in beautifully decorated salons, hung with the armorial escutcheons of Chateaubriand, Lamartine, Hugo, Nodier and Dumas himself. Such experiences always proved precious memories to those favoured ones who enjoyed them.

Misfortunes indeed, did not come singly to Dumas. His faithful Maquet had left him in 1851. Charles

Reade's account of this rupture is probably the most truthful, as it is the most charitable:—

"Dumas, if I understand rightly, used to treat with the publishers and managers, and settle with his collaborator. Dumas fell into arrears with him, arrears which, if his heart alone had been to be consulted, would have been paid to the centime; but unfortunately he had other creditors, who interposed with legal powers. In short, the situation was so desperate that Maquet had no course open to him but to withdraw from the connection; he did so, leaving 130,000 francs behind him—say £5,200."

In 1856-8 Maquet brought an action against Dumas, but although his share of the authorship of several of the most famous romances was declared, the court awarded him no further funds—a significant fact.

In 1853 the exile wearied to see his beloved Paris again, and as public affairs had quieted down, and as no doubt pressing invitations were issued by his friends, Dumas returned to Paris full of a new enthusiasm. At the establishment of the "Maison D'Or," in the Rue Lafitte, rooms were allotted to the great man, and a paper was issued under his editorship. This was the *Mousquetaire*, which started with the most brilliant prospects. The circulation throve exceedingly: the master slaved at his desk: and his name, and his kindly treatment of the young and aspiring, brought a group of clever young writers about him. But the paper was never managed on business principles, Dumas himself being the chief sinner in this respect; all was goodwill, confusion, gaiety and improvidence. The "staff" were innumerable; and the noise of the many journalists crowded into the little rooms of the "Maison D'Or" was alarming. Audebrand tells us that the neighbour on one side would cry to his valet, "They must be strangling some one next door!" and the neighbour on the other side would overhear the remark, and laughingly reply, "There must be a woman in labour in the house!"

In the same volume are some amusing stories of the great man's ménage—how he had a triple defence in the shape of three servants, who struggled to keep duns and beggars from their master's presence. A certain German, however, called one day, sat down on the step and would not leave; and Dumas was eventually aroused by the perpetual assaults on the door. It ended as it always did; the man was "starving" and would throw himself into the Seine if M. Dumas did not take pity on him. The great man pushed fifty francs into the beggar's hands—and found himself with only two francs with which to buy eggs for the omelette for his dinner!

Whilst the journalist worked, the dramatist was not idle. No less than four pieces were produced in 1854,—"Romulus," a one-act play, at the Comédie Française; "La Jeunesse de Louis XIV.," a comedy, full of Molière and Louis's first love Marie de Mancini (played at Brussels); "Le Marbrier," a powerful play (at the Vaudeville), and "Conscience," at the Odéon. Of the two dramas highly moral, not to say didactic, in tone, the latter was dedicated to Hugo. It was a daring act, but Dumas was as imprudent in this friendship as in all others.

To M. Blaze de Bury we are indebted for a vivid sketch of "Dumas *chez lui*," about this time, which he compares with the mournful home of Heine who was then also living in Paris:—

"You passed," he writes, "from the shades of death to the brilliant light of day; to loud voices and all the stir and bustle of a manufactory! The air was filled with voices in debate; you trampled upon *bon mots*, in the progress of your conversation. Then, in the brief intervals of silence, you heard a pen quietly, lightly, scratch the paper: it was Dumas, seated at his daily work. Without pausing in his writing, he held out his left hand to you with a smile. No tumult disturbed him; and a word thrown into the discourse here and there told you that he was taking part in it."

"Twenty times interrupted in one morning," adds

Villemessant, "twenty times he took up his work just where he had left it, to chat with a journalist, an actress or a director; he set aside a romance, to settle with a collaborator concerning the scenario of another book; but, as soon as the collaborator had gone, Dumas went back to his narrative, of which he had never for an instant lost the thread."

Abraham Hayward has quoted for us an account of Dumas's day's work, with less rhetoric but more detail. "He rises at six; before him are laid thirty-five sheets of paper of the largest size; he takes up his pen, and writes, in a hand that M. de Saint Omer would envy, till eleven. At eleven he breakfasts, always in company; and during this meal his spirits never flag. At twelve he resumes the pen, not to quit it again until six in the evening. The dinner-hour finds him as lively as at breakfast. If by any chance he has not filled the allotted number of sheets a momentary shade passes over his face: he steals away and returns two or three hours later, to enjoy the pleasures of the evening."

When the Queen visited Paris, in 1855, the actors of the Comédie Française gave a performance of the "Demoiselles de St Cyr" at Her Majesty's request, for she had seen the piece in London, and had been so pleased with it that she wished to see it again.

"Two or three days after the performance at St

Cloud," says Vandam, "I ran against Dumas in the Chaussée d'Antin.

"'Well, you ought to be pleased,' I said; 'it appears that not only has the Queen asked to see your piece, which she has already seen in London, but that she enjoyed it even better the second time than the first.'

"'Yes, it is like its author,' he replied; 'the more one knows him the more one loves him. But I know what would have amused her still more than seeing my play—to see me also! Honestly, it would have amused me too!'

"'Then why did you not ask for an audience? I am certain it would have been granted,' I remarked, because I felt convinced that Her Majesty would have been only too pleased to confer an honour upon such a man.

"'Well, I did think of it,' came the reply; 'a woman as remarkable as she is, who will probably remain the first woman of the century, ought to have met the greatest man in France! It is a pity, for she will go away without having seen the best sight in France—Alexandre, King of the world of Romance—Dumas the Ignorant!'[1] Then he roared with laughter, and went away."

[1] Dumas the professor of chemistry was called "Dumas le savant." "Donc," laughed the novelist, "Je suis Dumas l'ignorant."—Note by A. V.

The romancer was still full of energy, physical and mental. M. About, in his oration at the unveiling of the Dumas statue in 1883, told an anecdote illustrative of this, which we give in Mr Lang's words:

"He met the great man at Marseilles. Dumas picked up M. About, literally lifted him in his embrace, and carried him off to see a play which he had written in three days. The play was a success; the supper was prolonged till three in the morning. M. About was almost asleep as he walked home, but Dumas was as fresh as if he had just got out of bed.

"'Go to sleep, old man,' he said. 'I, who am only fifty-five, have three *feuilletons* to write, which must be posted to-morrow. If I have time I shall knock up a little piece for Montigny—the idea is running in my head.' So next morning M. About saw the three *feuilletons* made up for the post, and another packet addressed to M. Montigny: it was the play 'L'Invitation à la Valse,' a *chef-d'œuvre!*"[1]

The *Mousquetaire* died in 1857, but Dumas at once started another journal on the same lines, called *Monte Cristo*. This year he crossed the Channel with his son, and he has given us, in his "Causeries," an account of his brief visit *chez nous*.

The pair crossed from Calais to Dover one Mon-

---

[1] Dumas himself states that he wrote this play in London in 1833 (see "Causeries").

day night towards the close of May. On the Tuesday Dumas *père* visited Madame Tussaud's (he was curious to see the guillotine of Louis XVI. about which he had written so much), and spent an hour or so in Hyde Park. Then the party took a trip down the river to Blackwall, dined there, and returned to witness the illuminations in honour of the Queen's birthday, and to see that fascinating but saddening sight, the Haymarket at midnight. Next day the party drove down to Epsom to witness Blinkbonny's Derby. During Thursday and Friday Dumas attended Gordon-Cumming's panoramic lecture on his hunting adventures in South Africa, and had a chat with that explorer afterwards, visited the Crystal Palace, and witnessed that curious entertainment of " Lord Chief Justice Nicholson," the "*poses plastiques*" and mock-trial, at the Coal-hole. On Saturday he hurried back across the Channel to avoid the British Sunday, of which he had had a most satisfying experience during his previous visit in 1833.

The brief papers on these topics are full of gaiety and shrewd observation, and we can only regret that this prince of travellers did not "do" England on a larger scale, and make it the subject of " Impressions de Voyage" in several volumes.

When a writer of one nation attempts to reproduce the racial character of the people of another country, it is only just to be indulgent, and welcome any signs of accuracy and appreciation. Dumas was not a Chauvinist; his liberal principles and the breadth of mind which European travel gave him, guarded him against any of those hysterical outbursts to which the ordinary Frenchman is subject. True, we do not recognise social England of a century ago in " Kean " and " Richard Darlington;" and "Catherine Howard" is, as Dumas frankly confesses, a violation of history, which he only justifies on the plea that it produced some offspring—that is, that it was done with a purpose. But he has given us the most vivid account of the last days of Charles I. that romance has yet achieved; he could see something to admire in each of the two great antagonists of the Civil War; and in " San Felice " his portrait of Nelson has much in it that is judicious and true. Dumas certainly attributes the victory at Waterloo to God, and not to Wellington, in which he is foolish; he condemns the British treatment of Napoleon at St Helena, in which he is undoubtedly right. The conception of the Englishman which Dumas formed is largely that which Jules Verne has rendered familiar to the British schoolboy, and there is this to be said for it—the type has many of the best qualities which we claim for ourselves as a race. Sir John Tanlay in the " Compagnons de Jehu" may or may not be a faithful reproduction of the "aristocrat" who travelled Europe, following in the track of Byron, during the first half of the last century; but certainly he is a gentleman, and could never have been drawn by a hater of our people.

It may further be pointed out, that Dumas received his inspiration as a dramatist from Shakespeare, and as a romancer, from Scott, both of whom he fully and gratefully admired. "Whenever he met an Englishman," says Vandam, "he considered it his particular duty to make himself agreeable to him as part of the debt he owed to Shakespeare and Walter Scott." If Dumas has made fun — many may think legitimate fun—of some of our English characteristics and customs, he has at least known how to admire our beautiful women. The sight of a bevy of fair girls in Rotten Row, he tells us, caused him to realise in a flash that native quality in the heroines of Shakespeare, which until that moment he had never quite understood.

Some of the remarks in his chapters on England are worth quoting here. "The English, the least artistic and most industrial (I say 'industrial,' not 'industrious') of peoples, have almost achieved art by force of industry." ... "In Hyde Park you find the finest horses and the prettiest women in London, and therefore in the whole world. But to do the Englishmen justice, their first glance is for the horse, and, one might almost add, their first desire." ... "The English think that the bigger a thing is, the greater it is." ... "England fully deserves the title of a great nation, if power implies greatness." ... "Everything is forbidden in England on a Sunday; after having worked six days one does not rest on the seventh, there, *on s'ennuie*! London on a Sunday gives one an idea of what the kingdom of the Sleeping Beauty was like before the Princess was awakened." ... "The Englishman generally has the spleen in November. You may fancy that that is because of the fog, which commences in November and doesn't go away until May. Not at all! They have the spleen because they have been deprived of the fog for four months. You may ask me what the English make their fogs of? Of coal, I suppose, but that is a detail. It was not the good God who made the fog, it was the English."

"Posterity commences at the frontier." So said Dumas, a little sadly. "The old order" had changed, and fickle Paris, Paris of the Second Empire, turned a contemptuous shoulder on its old favourite. France had cooled down after the Revolution; analytic fiction had superseded the romantic. Partly to rest from desk-work, partly to warm his genius in the admiration of those strange lands where his works were so well known and so welcome, Dumas took to travel more and more readily. In the winter of 1858 he started for a Russian tour; and the reason for this sudden abandonment of his journal, his contracts and his friends, as given by M. Ferry, is very curious—and characteristic.

Home, the spiritualist, who was then in Paris, and with whom Dumas was at that time very friendly, introduced the author to a Russian count and countess. Home was about to marry the lady's sister—the wedding was to take place in St Petersburg—and the count and his wife persuaded the impulsive Dumas to leave Paris with them in five days, to be "best man." Such a tour had been one of the dreams of his life, and was to prove one of his pleasantest memories. He hunted wolves; he visited the prisons and prisoners of the Russian government; he crossed Ladoga, and explored Finland; he encountered a burning forest, in which his train ran a winning race with death; he saw the world-famous fair of Nijni Novgorod; he was uproariously fêted by officers at Kaliasine, who broke their leave to see him on his journey; he became the guest of a Kalmuck prince in the Caucasus, and was royally entertained in true, though somewhat terrifying, Tartar fashion; he crossed savage south Russia in a tarantass, and returned *via* Tiflis, Trebizond and Constantinople, having thoroughly enjoyed himself. And no wonder, for his name was known, and excited flattery and hospitality everywhere. He was absent ten months, and yet spent only 12,000 francs, so generous had been the welcome of his hosts throughout the Empire.

But the social miseries which he saw in the life of Russia profoundly saddened Dumas. Although the emancipation of the serfs has taken place since his day, much of the following is still too true, and was written, be it remembered, before Russia was exploited by the politicians:—

"The Russian Empire is one gigantic surface, and no one seems to care what lies below it. And what is more curious still, is, that in this land of abuses, everyone, from the Emperor to the lowest serf, desires that they should cease. But as soon as one lays hands on an abuse in Russia, what is it makes the loudest protest? The abuse which is threatened? No, that would be too clumsy!—it is the abuses which fear to be assailed in their turn, that make the great outcry!"

And this is his prophecy respecting Russia's future:—

"There is a taint of the old Tartar, or Hun, in this race of modern conquerors, and one finds it hard to reconcile their appetite for territory, with the canons of civilisation and intelligence. One day Russia will take Constantinople: it is written in the book of fate. Fair races have always been the conquering nations : the dark nationalities have had only brief periods of reactionary success. Then Russia will break, not into two parts, but into four. . . . It is impossible that an empire which to-day covers a seventh part of the globe should remain under one hand. If it grips too hard, the hand itself will break ; if it holds its prey too loosely, it will be forced to open its fingers and release its charge."

In 1859 Dumas made the acquaintance of "that charming woman," as Glinel calls her, Emilie Cordier, better known in those days as "L'Amiral," partly because she was accustomed to dress *en garçon*, and partly because she accompanied the romancer during his maritime adventures of the following year. The intimacy, indeed, lasted until 1864. If we may say so without being misunderstood, there was something paternal in the love of Dumas for the young girl, something filial in her affection for him; and yet a child was born of this *liaison*, at the close of 1860. The news of the event drew from Dumas two charming letters, which are worth quoting, not only because they are so characteristic of the man, but because very few letters from this "living pen" are extant. In his introduction to "Un Gil Blas en Californie" he laughingly proclaims himself the literary man who writes the most books and the fewest letters. On

ALEXANDRE DUMAS FILS.

the other hand many of his books—notably the "Causeries," and many of the "Impressions de Voyage"—are in the epistolary form and spirit.

The first letter is to the mother:—

"Joy and happiness to thee, my dear love of a child, for sending me the good news that my little Micaëlla has come into the world, and that her mother is going on well.

"You know, my dear little one, that I preferred a girl. I will tell you why. I love Alexandre better than Marie; I see Marie only once a year, whilst I can see Alexandre whenever I wish. So that all the love I might have had for Marie will now fall to the share of my little Micaëlla. I fancy I see her lying by the side of her little mother, whom I forbid to get up and go out before I come. I am arranging to be in Paris about the 12th—it will be impossible for me to be there sooner, in spite of my eagerness.

"If I tell thee one thing, my dear love, thou mayst well believe it true. In an hour my heart has grown bigger, to make room for this new love!

"If for the next few months thou dost not wish to be separated from thy child, we will take a little house at Ischia, in the best air and on the prettiest island in all Naples, and I will come and spend two or three days every week with you all the spring through : in short, rely on me to cherish mother and child.

"*Au revoir, ma petite cherie;* embrace for me the Donna Micaëlla,—who is no bigger than one's thumb, so Madame de C. writes. I will answer hers by the next mail, as well as your mother's, whom I embrace. *A toi et à l'enfant.*

"ALEX. DUMAS."

"To think that I have only got thy letter to-day (the 1st), and that thou wilt not get this, perhaps, before the 16th!

"*Je t'aime!*"

The second letter is to the baby:—

"MON CHER BÉBÉ,—As thy good grandmother—whom thou must love dearly, as well as thy little mother—writes me that you have need of money, I send thee 150 francs for thy new year's gift.

"I shall try to send thee also a little hamper of good things.

"There will be nothing to pay to the messenger who brings it.

"I embrace thee very tenderly.—Thy father who loves thee, "ALEX. DUMAS."

We make no apology for adding here three letters which have no strict historical value, so far as our subject is concerned, but are too characteristic of their author, with his large-heartedness, his irreverence (which it would be foolish to take *au sérieux*), and above all, his gaiety, to be omitted. The first is to Charles Nodier, and is dated September 2nd, 1836:—

"My Good Charles,—My great idler, my illustrious confrère, you who know the Past and the Present better than God himself—I don't speak of the future lest I humiliate Him too much—be good enough to tell me who originated this fatal mania of autograph-hunting of which you and I are victims. Someone has asked me this and I didn't know what to say; or rather I replied that I had my Charles, who knew everything, and that I would write to him.

"Ten lines, I beg, my good Nodier; I will come and thank you for them on Sunday next. You see that you do not get rid of me easily!

"Adieu! I reverence you as a master, I love you as a brother, and respect you as a son.

"Alex. Dumas."

The second letter, dated 1849, is to the critic and influential journalist, Jules Janin:—

"My Dear Janin,—You know of the death of poor little Maillet? We have buried her this morning. She leaves a mother and a young child.

"The mother is 87. Help us to the best of your

power—with subscriptions, theatrical benefits, etc.—to get her into a hospital for the aged.

"As for the child, if the father does not come forward I will take charge of it myself. It is only three years old, and it doesn't eat much yet. I will work an hour a day longer, and that will be all right.—*À vous,*   "ALEX. DUMAS."

The third, which is in our possession, is no more than an invitation to supper, but is interesting as giving a list of the novelist's intimate friends. It bears no date:—

"MY DEAR MÉRY,—Come to-night (Monday) and sup with me, 46 Rue Rutier, at 9.30 in the evening.

"I will take no excuse.—Yours,

        "AL. DUMAS."

Hugo.[1]	Charles.	Brohan.
Lacroix.	Toto.	De Leuven.
Janin.	Les Mélingue.	Person.
Meurice.	Les Guyons.	Moi.
Vaquerie.		

On his return from Russia, the "wandering Jew of literature," as he called himself with sad significance,

[1] The guests include Méry, the invited, a Marseilles poet-author, and intimate friend of Dumas's; Victor Hugo; Paul Lacroix, the author; Jules Janin, the critic; Paul Meurice, Dumas's collaborator; Auguste Vaquerie, the author and dramatist; Charles Hugo; Dumas *fils*; Mélingue, the comedian, and his wife; Guyons and his wife; Augustine Brohan, the actress: and Adolphe De Leuven, the friend of Dumas's youth.

soon wearied of Paris and his declining popularity. Feeling the desire to travel come over him once more, Dumas determined on a tour in the Mediterranean which should surpass all his previous explorations. In a little boat of his own, he would visit Egypt, Sparta, Athens, Corinth, the site of ancient Troy, Abydos, Constantinople! Such an experience had been one of the dreams of his life. But no sooner was the little schooner *Emma* built, no sooner had the merry party left Marseilles in April 1860 for Nice, than the whole scheme was abandoned. Dumas's hopes of pleasure, his holiday, his money, his safety even, were sacrificed without a murmur or a thought, to—vanity, his critics say. The reader shall judge for himself.

Garibaldi had just landed in Sicily, to give force and vigour to the revolt of the Italians against the rule of Ferdinand. The two men were no strangers. In January of that year the author had met the soldier at Milan, and a warm friendship had sprung up between them. But Dumas tells us that ten years before that, he had recognised Garibaldi's ability, energy and integrity.[1]

---

[1] So loudly (says Blaze de Bury) had Dumas proclaimed the skill and valour of that other "force of nature" Garibaldi, that a certain consul in Italy thought it wise to report the existence of this unknown person to headquarters. But when he confessed the source of his information, the consul was curtly forbidden to trouble his superiors with the idle talk of a romancer!

Immediately he heard the news, Dumas set sail in his little craft for Sicily, joined Garibaldi and his band of "redshirts," marched across the island with them and shared their fortunes. After his conquering journey along the north of Sicily from west to east, Garibaldi prepared to cross Messina Straits and begin his campaign on the mainland at Reggio; but he needed arms for the recruits who flocked to join him. Dumas had 50,000 francs with him—the money which was to have bought him his year of pleasure in classic lands. He sailed from Marseilles, after "running the blockade" of a Royalist ship, bought the guns with his money, and returned to Italy. At Naples he acted as Garibaldi's envoy, stimulating the agitation there, and was expelled by the king for his bold, seditious conduct. "Everywhere" (says Maxime du Camp, who was with Garibaldi's staff as a volunteer), "he gave the word of command, and worked to prepare for Italian unity."

When Garibaldi was at length master of Naples, he made Dumas the only return the author asked—gave him the appointment of "director of *beaux-arts*." This was an honorary post, involving the spending of much time and trouble; but the Frenchman had set his heart upon carrying out well and thoroughly the excavations at Pompeii, which had been neglected by the late government. He was now installed in a little plainly furnished *palazzo*, bent upon devoting all his energies to the service of archæology and the discovery of priceless art-treasures; but the Neapolitans, learning that a stranger had been appointed to—some post or other —waxed indignant. This "job," as Mr Fitzgerald elegantly calls it, excited the rabble, and Dumas, in the midst of his gaiety and his unselfish labours, was hooted and mobbed by the people for whom he had worked so hard. For a time, the ingratitude of the populace stunned him, and he was undisguisedly pained; but by degrees his spirits returned. This experience was probably still fresh in Dumas's mind when, on the occasion of Victor Emmanuel's triumphal entry into Naples, he pointed out to Du Camp that there were no Garibaldians in the procession. (As a matter of fact we know how the king had insulted the Garibaldians, and caused them to absent themselves.) "*Il faut faire le bien d'une façon abstraite, et ne jamais penser à la récompense,*" was our author's philosophic comment.

Nevertheless he stayed in Naples for four years, occasionally paying flying visits to Paris,—" to have a chat," as he laughingly tells us. But the *Indipendant*, the journal which Garibaldi had named and which Dumas conducted, so faithfully fulfilled its title, that the editor was continually in collision with Victor Emmanuel's officials, and in 1864 he returned to Paris, where the usual flattering chorus of welcome greeted him.

"He was just the same as ever," says Ferry, "big, powerful, robust, and yet so well-proportioned that he could not be accused of stoutness. His head, so firmly set upon that massive neck, was crowned with a forest of crisp, grey hair; the face, with its vivacious eyes, and mobile mouth, shone with almost perpetual gaiety. Never have good humour, cordiality, affability and contagious good spirits shown themselves in a human face with such expressive fidelity."

The summer of that year was spent at the Villa Catinat, a charming country house on the borders of lake Enghien, where our author had for neighbour his old friend Madame de Girardin. Unfortunately his parasites found him out once more, and his "Sundays" were the talk of Paris. On one occasion, when the servants, after a quarrel with Dumas's mistress, had all departed summarily, leaving the larder bare, the host, who was almost as famous a cook as a writer, discovered some rice and tomatoes, and prepared for his crowd of unsuspecting guests a regal and gigantic dish which entirely satisfied their appetites and palates.

"In 1864," the Martins tell us in their interesting book "The Stones of Paris." "the American

Minister to France, Mr John Bigelow, breakfasted with Dumas at Saint-Gratien, near Paris, where the romancer was temporarily sojourning. It was towards the close of the American Civil War, and he had a notion of going to the United States as War Correspondent for French papers, and to make another book, of course." Unhappily Dumas did not go, and the book is lost to us.

It was about this time that the famous quadroon, whose sympathies were naturally with the North in the great struggle, sent to Lincoln a large sum of money for the widows of the slain abolitionists. When acknowledging the gift, the President suggested that Dumas should send out some "mottoes' with his autograph attached. The author duly forwarded a hundred slips of paper, each with a sententious line or two and the great man's autograph. These were sold in the United States at 600 francs each.

The great writer was now growing old. He could no longer work twelve, fourteen, sixteen hours a day; and his efforts were unequal to the task of paying his way. Yet neither his dramatic instinct, nor his quixotic sense of honour failed him. The directorate of the Porte St Martin became bankrupt, and the company was left stranded. Dumas had just announced in the press that he had a play—a dramatisation of "Madame de

Chamblay" — ready for production; but not a manager in Paris deigned even to send for the manuscript of the author of "Antony." Some of the Porte St Martin company, however, being at their wits' end for employment, appealed to Dumas to give them the manuscript, as they had hired the Théâtre Ventadour, and wished to open with a new play. No sooner had he lent the drama to the poverty-stricken actors, than a representative of the Comédie Française itself, came to open negotiations with him. Dumas refused: he had given his word. The play was produced, but the hot weather and the cold critics killed it, although when revived later on, it proved a success in spite of the press.

Dumas's enemies were now gaining the upper hand of their old antagonist, and they did not spare him. He had occasion at this time to write to his old companion of the trip to Monte Cristo. One of our author's plays had been forbidden by the censor, and in France there is—or was—no limit to the extent of the censor's power. He wrote a public letter to the Emperor, pointing out that this was the seventh of his plays or books which had been thus prohibited—and that on almost every occasion it was a *revival* of the play which was condemned, and not a new play at all! The order was revoked.

Still another rôle was reserved for this Protean man—that of lecturer. Dumas was persuaded into giving a chatty, vivid talk on the paintings of his old friend Delacroix. These lectures, which were given at the "Fantaisies-Parisiens," were packed, as they deserved to be. It was probably this success which aroused one of the lecturer's sleeping ambitions, for early in the next year he engaged the "Grand-Théâtre Parisiens" in the Rue de Lyon, and produced his version of "Catherine Blum" there. But the play was a failure; Dumas's secretary, who was nominally the lessee of the building, turned out to be a rogue and embezzled the money, and the scheme came to naught.[1] In the following year, still clinging to his belief that the sons of his old patrons would inherit the tastes of their fathers, the dramatist appealed to his "unknown friends" the public, to subscribe to a species of co-operative play-house, a new "Théâtre Historique," with an eminent banker for treasurer and himself as the manager. The very slight and

---

[1] Dumas, owing his company arrears of salary, met the situation in a characteristic and ingenious way. He gave the members collectively the right to play the piece, and promised that whenever it was performed within reach of Paris, he would attend if duly notified. On one occasion the author missed his train, and did not reach the theatre till the second act. The audience, who before his arrival had been too uproarious and distracted to follow the play, insisted, as soon as their darling appeared and peace was restored, that the actors should begin all over again—which they were obliged to do!

quite inadequate response to this invitation gave the dramatist another painful shock of self-revelation.

In 1866 the war between Austria and Prussia broke out, and Dumas, his love of history and of travel both urging him, set out for Frankfort, to study the crisis presented by the growing power of Prussia in mid-Europe, and to traverse the yet-warm battlefields of the campaign. The result was " La Terreur Prussienne," in which the author, filled with disquietude, sees in Prussian predominance a menace to other nations, and to France above all.

Forced to earn money as best he could, Dumas went down to the Havre Exhibition of 1868, and lectured there, and at Caen, Rouen and other towns, on his way back. Two or three of his plays were revived about this time, but the old spirit of hostility was again shown by the critics, who managed to wound the now enfeebled playwright. To the last he was ridiculed, abused and slandered. Lamartine, for whom the romancer had always felt a warm admiration, died in 1869, worn out with the struggle against his debts and his enemies; and the news saddened Dumas, for it gave him a foreboding of his own end.

This brilliant and illustrious life was itself drawing very near to a close, amidst humiliating poverty, oblivion and suffering. Spongers and duns wrested from the failing giant every penny that was not jealously guarded for him; and care, which the gay heart had so long kept at bay, stole in and shared the old man's fireside. The father had always felt a certain timidity towards his son: the careless, improvident dupe had dreaded the reproaches of the other's more worldly wisdom. Not until the very bread was lacking, not until the pawnshop had been visited, did the older man send hint of his needs to his beloved " Alexandre." Again, when disease crept upon him, Dumas hid that fact from his son also, and it was not until the old man's daughter, taking alarm, sent physicians to see him, that the time came for Alexandre *fils* to realise the position, and assert himself.

From that moment the cares of money matters at least, were over. Dumas was taken to Finisterre, and lastly, to his son's house at Puys near Dieppe, where he remained until the last, watched over, cared for and comforted, in a manner which had long been strange to him.

But now another care haunted the great man; and day and night his clouding mind brooded upon it. Would his work live after him? One day when he could keep it to himself no longer, his anguish found voice.

" It seems to me," he said to his son, " that I am

standing on the pedestal of a monument which trembles, as though it were based on shifting sands."

"Be at peace," answered his son; "the pillar is well built, and the base will stand firm."

The dying father drew his son toward him, and the two met in a silent embrace. It was the cry of the soul doubting its own genius; the agony of doubt which seized Keats when he bade them write as his epitaph, "Here lies one whose name was writ in water."

In his introduction to "Les Trois Mousquetaires," Dumas *fils* tells this anecdote, and adds, by way of supporting his prophecy, that from 1870 to 1893 no less than 2,840,000 volumes of his father's books had been sold in France alone, not counting 80,000,000 of illustrated parts.

The dying man doubted everything. The world, he fancied, had not advanced as it had promised to do in the days of the glorious revolutions, political and social, of the mid-century. Such an age of agitation, he prophesied, would end in an era of disillusionment. And truly for France the outlook was dark, for the Prussians had overthrown Napoleon and were invading France. In his early days Dumas had seen the Prussians at the gates of Paris; in his last days he would have witnessed a like spectacle had he stayed there. But all such news was mercifully kept from him.

"One day," wrote his son, "the pen dropped from his hands, and he began to sleep." Like his own Porthos, the child of his virile brain, Dumas was struggling with all a Titan's strength against the forces of nature which weighed upon him and which were slowly crushing and stifling the life from his giant frame and his great heart. All night, and almost all the day, he slept; and if, with his old desire for work, he took pen in hand, no responsive thought nerved the fingers; the weapon with which he had once wrought such wonders fell from his nerveless fingers. Excess of labour, far more than excess of pleasure, had made the brain mute at last.

In his brief moments of light Dumas would play with his son's children, or would sit where his nurses placed him on the beach, gazing, motionless, at the sea, thinking long, long thoughts.

On the morning of December 5th, 1870, a priest was sent for. He found son and daughter on their knees by the side of the dying man. The good curé called his penitent by name, and Dumas slowly opened his eyes. He could not speak. He died that afternoon

Two years later, when the Prussians had departed, Alexandre Dumas was able to take his father home to Villers-Cotterets, where he had wished to lie. A host of distinguished authors and actors came to bid their old confrère farewell, but the simple reverence and affection shown by the dead man's old village friends was a far truer token of the love that he had won. When the train arrived with the coffin, the people were quietly waiting in the streets to greet it, and young and old pressed forward to contend with the bearers for the honour of carrying the body of their lost, dear friend. There, with the father of whom he was so proud, with the mother whom he so tenderly loved, he lies, in the little town from which he set out on the pilgrimage of life, and to which he so often looked wistfully back.

In the words of the man whom he reverenced most,

"After life's fitful fever, he sleeps well." . . .

His Character.

"The great eater, worker, earner and waster, the man of much and witty laughter, the man of great heart and, alas, of the doubtful honesty, is a figure not yet clearly set before the world," wrote R. L. Stevenson. "He still awaits a sober and yet genial portrait, but with whatever art that may be touched, and whatever indulgence, it will not be the portrait of a precisian." That is quite true, but in trying to sketch Dumas's character according to the ideal Stevenson has given us, we hope to show the "ventripotent mulatto" (as that author wrongly calls him) less black, both outwardly and inwardly, than even the admiring essayist deemed him,—for we seem to see the slimy traces of that ubiquitous snake-in-the-grass "M. de Mirecourt" in this passage from "Memories and Portraits."

Happily we cannot mistake our starting-point, for it is obviously best to commence one's journey round a character with that which is the subject's most characteristic quality, and which first strikes those who read about him or come into his literary presence. A score of Dumas's contemporaries have left us their impressions of the great impressionist, and they have one and all laid emphasis on his gaiety—a naïve heartiness and healthiness of temperament, springing from a semi-tropical nature, a magnificent constitution, an unclouded self-confidence, a kind, generous heart, and brilliant social, dramatic, and literary successes. "*Hercules bon enfant*," Maxime Du Camp called him, adding :—

"Like a giant who knows his strength and fears to take advantage of it, he was gentle. I have never seen in him—I will not say a sign of anger—but not even a movement of impatience. If ever a man was lovable, in the original sense of the word, that is 'made to be loved,' Dumas was that man. . . . He had so much wit himself that every one who was with him believed they had it too."

He seems to have created, as it were, an atmosphere of *esprit* which was breathed by all who came within its influence.

Roger de Beauvoir, the author of "L'Ecolier de Cluny," one day visited the great man's rooms in his absence, and was shown into the kitchen instead of the study. Wishing to "leave his card," he picked up his friend's account-book, and wrote this quatrain on one of the pages :—

> "Sur ce carnet, Dumas écrit,
> Jour par jour, tout ce qu'il dépense,
> Il n'y pourrait mettre, je pense
> Tout ce qu'il dépense d'esprit !"[1]

Many of the best stories told of Dumas naturally

---

[1] "In this book Dumas has writ
All that he spends from day to day ;
'Twould never hold, I dare to say,
His great expenditure of wit !"

ALEXANDRE DUMAS

relate to the theatre, of which he was such an habitué, and the drama, of which he was such a master. "Before telling one of the best of these," (says Mr W. H. Pollock), "it is necessary to remember that Pierre Corneille, the great dramatist, had a younger brother named Thomas, who had a considerable talent which was completely overshadowed by the greater genius of his brother. There was also in the height of Dumas's success another playwright—no relation of his—who bore the name of Dumas. This writer produced a play which is forgotten now, but which on the night of its production had enough success to intoxicate the author with joy. After the curtain had fallen, the obscure Dumas came into the box of the great Dumas and said:

"'Ah! after to-night people will talk of the two Dumas as they talk of the two Corneilles!'

"'H'm!' said the great man, looking at him from head to foot—'adieu, Thomas!'"

The phrase "the French Sheridan" occurs irresistibly to the mind, when one remembers the Master's wit and improvidence. There is something very like the author of the "School for Scandal" about the hero of the following story.

One evening at the Théâtre Français Dumas saw one of the audience asleep in his stall during the representation of a play by Soumet.

"See," said the dramatist to his *confrère*, "that's the effect that your plays produce!"

The next day a comedy of Dumas's was played, and the author was present. Suddenly Soumet tapped his friend's shoulder, and pointed out a gentleman asleep in the orchestra, saying in bitter-sweet accents:

"You see, my dear friend, that one falls asleep just the same when listening to your prose."

"That? Why that is the gentleman who went to sleep yesterday, and hasn't woke up yet!" retorted the other.

In spite of his social rank Dumas was just as much at home in the boulevards, with the gamins, and the populace, who loved him and whom he loved, as with the wits and peers. He was walking one day with his secretary Pifteau, and looking for a cab, when a post-office mail-omnibus rolled by.

"Stop!" he cried to the driver, "give us a lift. We're *men of letters*, too!"

The postman grinned as he whipped up his horses.

The *mots* uttered by Dumas or attributed to him were numberless. The saying "*tout passe, tout lasse, tout casse,*" is said to have been originated by him. The witty utterances in his books have all the flavour, and unexpectedness of spoken jests. " Heaven has made but one drama for man—the world," he wrote, "and during these three thousand years mankind has been hissing it." "A young man," he wrote to Béranger, "always makes his entry into public life with an old woman on his arm, and into the world of literature with an old thought in his head. One needs to have much experience before young ideas will come."

There was human truth, too, in this: "When the prodigal son returned to his father's house after three years they killed a calf; if he had not returned for six years they would have killed an ox." Again, take this passage from his "Mémoires" as a sample of the style of their contents: "I have been confessing the ridiculous weaknesses of my childhood; I shall be equally frank about those of my youth. I shall be more courageous than Rousseau: Rousseau confessed only his vices."

There is no room here for a volume of *jeux d'esprit*, spoken or written, and we must be merciful, too, in the matter of the stories told by Dumas; for he was a famous raconteur, and his autobiographical writings are enriched with capital anecdotes, neatly told. There are two, however, which we cannot bring ourselves to omit. One is of M. de Sesmaisons, "the fattest man in politics," who was so stout that he found it necessary when he travelled to reserve two places in the diligence for himself. On one occasion when he took this precaution, he discovered that his man had booked for him one seat in the coupé and the other inside!

The other story may be entitled the episode of Colonel Bro's macaw. Dumas called at that officer's house one day, went into the drawing-room to wait, and seeing a yellow red and blue macaw on its perch, he went up to it familiarly and commenced to scratch its head. The bird, it appeared, was in a vile temper that morning, and gave the unwelcome visitor a murderous peck. Dumas withdrew his finger, staunched the blood, and then, returning to the bird, wrung its neck, and quietly put the body out of sight under some of the furniture. Later on he left without anything having been noticed.

Some weeks afterwards Dumas dined with Colonel Bro, and the conversation turned on natural history. Reference was made to the habits of elephants, who kneel to say their prayers, and get out of sight to die secretly.

"As for that last trait," said the Colonel's wife, "it must be common to all animals." Then turning to Dumas she added, "You remember my beautiful blue yellow and red macaw?"

"Perfectly. Has some misfortune happened to it?"

"Alas! the poor thing is dead,—and would you believe it, Monsieur Dumas, we found it in a corner of the drawing-room, under the couch? That proves that this modesty before death is an instinct common to all animals in creation, and that our domestic parrots have it, just as strongly as the kings of the forest."

Dumas was duly impressed.

Take, with his gaiety and wit, Dumas's vanity. Here is Mr Lang's opinion of the worth of the reproach:—

"They call Dumas vain: he had reason to be vain, and no candid or generous reader will be shocked by his pleasant, frank, and artless enjoyment of himself and of his adventures. Oddly enough, they are small-minded and small-hearted people who are most shocked by what they call 'vanity' in the great. Dumas's delight in himself and his doings is only the flower of his vigorous existence, and in his 'Mémoires,' at least, it is as happy and encouraging as his laugh, or the laugh of Porthos; it is a kind of radiance, in which others, too, may bask and enjoy themselves. And yet it is resented by tiny scribblers, frozen in their own chill self-conceit."

There is an amusing story told of how this vanity was very neatly snubbed on one occasion. Dumas was giving evidence in a trial, at Rouen, and was asked his profession.

"I should say 'dramatic author,' if I were not in the city of Corneille," he answered.

"Oh, M'sieu," replied the judge, "there are degrees." . . .

We cannot resist quoting here how Dumas took his revenge on the Rouen folk, who it appears had also hissed his plays. "One day," he says, "a Neapolitan boasted to me of having hissed Rossini and Malibran, the 'Barbiere' and 'Desdemona.'

"'That must be true,' I answered, 'because Rossini and Malibran boast, on their part, of having been hissed by the Neapolitans. So I boast of being hissed by the Rouenese. The Rouen people,' he added, 'hiss me because they object to me. Why shouldn't they? They objected to Joan of Arc!'"

"Vanity," says Villemessant, "was a part of his talent; just as a balloon cannot rise, until it is filled with air." "The public," adds Du Camp, "are too exacting: they expect a man to have every talent in the world, and not to know it." Dumas's artless self-admiration was made the moral of a hundred malicious stories. It is said that his son remarked of him: "he is so vain that he would like to get up behind his own coach to make people think he owned a black footman." We have not traced this speech to its source, but we shall not believe that Dumas *fils* said it, without the strongest proof. There is, however, a story told by Mr W. H. Pollock, which is more probably authentic, being in better taste and more *spirituel*.

Dumas *père* is supposed to have written to his son, as to a stranger, proposing that they should collaborate. (He had more than once urged his son to do this, adding, "it would bring you in 40,000 or 50,000 francs a year,—you would only have to make objections, to contradict me in the subjects I proposed, and to give me the germs of ideas which I would develop without your help.") On this occasion Dumas *fils* replied that he disliked collaboration, but added, "I am the more sorry to refuse what you ask me because my sympathies are naturally enlisted by the great admiration which you have always expressed for my father's works."

"He believed in himself, it is true," writes Du Camp, "and it was quite legitimate for him to do so; but he believed in others, too." "People who complain of Dumas's vanity," adds Mr Lang, "may be requested to observe that he seems just as 'vain' of Hugo's successes, or of Scribe's, as of his own, and just as much delighted by them. Dumas had no jealousy," Mr Lang goes on, "no more than Scott. As he believed in no success without talent, so he disbelieved in genius which wins no success. '*Je ne crois pas au talent ignoré, au genie inconnu, moi.*' Genius he saluted wherever he met it, but was incredulous about invisible and inaudible genius." So little gall had Dumas in his disposition that he found ability everywhere—he praised heartily, gladly. His good-nature often led him to fancy that there was talent in people who possessed none.

"I can't make out what Mallefille lacks, in order to be a man of talent," he said one day.

"Perhaps he lacks the talent," some one suggested.

"By Jove! That's it! I never thought of that!" answered Dumas ingenuously.

With all his failings—and we will admit them in due time—Dumas had one splendid quality which might well outweigh a host of sins heavier than his. He was charity itself. His was indeed "a voice of comfort and an open hand of help." "He was like a cornucopia, shedding bounty perpetually from his outstretched hands," says Du Camp. "Half, if not more, of the money he earned he gave away." Another great writer has told us how Dumas would take his work and sit by the dying, would tend them and help them in their need. His heart was open to the suffering, his purse to the needy, his house to the homeless. "I was sick and ye visited me." We can fancy the Preacher of Galilee would have found something in Alexandre Dumas which the world never saw.

One day, when Dumas and du Chaffault were

talking together, a poor Italian was shown in, begging for help. The author was, as usual, at the end of his resources, but that did not check his charitable desire.

"My friend," he said, "I am no richer than you are; I have nothing, but I can never send away with empty hands a man who is in want. Take down one of those pistols from the mantelpiece; go and sell it, and leave me the other for the next poor devil that the good God may send to me for relief."

Theodore de Banville tells us in his "Souvenirs" how a poor starving devil, Montjoye by name, was ready to take his life in despair, when the thought of Dumas came to him like an inspiration from heaven. He found the great man deserted—all the servants had gone a-holidaying—but the host hurried into the kitchen, and prepared with his own hands a feast for the gods, for this stranger. It is a pleasant picture that the poet sets before us—the penniless beggar eating, and making witty remarks on the dishes as he attacked them, and Dumas beaming with delight and roaring with laughter, as he heaped the strange guest's plate with good things.

But the charity which gives money only is not complete in the great apostle's sense, and happily Dumas had his full share of that other and greater generosity. Of such was his surprise for Maquet, on the first night of the "Trois Mousquetaires." Maquet was the artisan and Dumas the artist of that collaboration, and the henchman had no thought of any public acknowledgment of his share of the work. But at the fall of the curtain Mélingue, the famous "D'Artagnan" came forward and named "Messieurs Alexandre Dumas and August Maquet." Maquet gave a cry of joy and pride, and fell sobbing on his master's neck.

The young and ambitious author always found a kind, genial, helpful friend in Dumas. One day a novice came to ask the great man a favour. Would he listen to a play in verse? Dumas, whose time was golden, nevertheless good-naturedly agreed. After the first act the great man remarked thoughtlessly:

"My boy, your verses are not very rich in poetry."[1]

"Not rich . . ." the young man exclaimed in dismay, letting the manuscript fall from his hands.

Dumas, regretting that he had given such pain to a beginner, picked up the play and handed it back to the youth, saying hurriedly:

"Don't be discouraged by such a little thing, my

---

[1] The word "riche" here implies a certain form of line-ending in French verse, but for the purposes of the story our use of it is as appropriate, and more comprehensible.

boy. Your lines are not *rich* in thought, it is true —but—but—they're fairly well off!"

Asseline, one of the staff of the ill-fated *Mousquetaire*, wrote in the *Indépendance Belge*, at the time that his old master was dying, a loving appreciation of him, in which he recalled a characteristic incident in their journalistic relations. Asseline was writing a *feuilleton* in the journal and was at a loss to know how to tell the story of a duel which was necessary to his plot. He took his cares to the famous editor, who, turning from his own work, cross-questioned the writer on his plot, characters, motives, and the rest, and then, having rapidly grasped the situation, sat down and wrote the chapter himself. Asseline received general congratulations on his masterly handling of the duel scene, but Dumas never made known the service which he had rendered his pupil.

There was a truly noble generosity, too, in his "confession," after he had written adverse critiques on plays by three of his *confrères*. He discovered, by self-analysis, that it was personal pique which had provoked his judgments on others, and not a lofty desire to defend his art. He cried shame on himself, published his self-condemnation to the world, and wrote no more criticisms. "What I had done," he says, "was perhaps good from the point of view of literature, but truly it was by no means good from the point of view of humanity, and the brotherhood of art."

His delicacy was equal to his kindness. One day he found an old friend who was in needy circumstances, and bore him off to dinner. As they parted the host said casually:

"Thou knowest, old comrade — I expect thee here again to-morrow."

The friend came again — and for ten or twelve years dined with Dumas. At last, overcome with remorse at eating the bread he did not earn, the guest declared that he must make some return for his dinners, or he would not come again. Dumas thought a moment.

"You can do me a great service," he said at length. "Go to the Pont Neuf every day at noon, and note the temperature of the Chevalier thermometer for me. That is very important, in connection with the receipts at the theatre. Will you oblige me?" The friend agreed delightedly, and the "situation was saved." Both men were happy once more.

On another occasion a man entered the "master's" room, begging. Dumas, without waiting to hear of his particular need, drew fifteen francs from a drawer. It appeared that the caller was collecting to raise funds to bury a *huissier* (or sheriff's officer.)

"To bury a *huissier*!" cried Dumas, who knew

those gentry only too well. "Here — here are another fifteen francs—go and bury another!"

The many stories which are told of Dumas's shifts to get money, and of his prodigality, are some of them amusing, but most of them untrustworthy. He himself was conscious of his failing, but was never able to cure himself of it. "When my hand closes on anything it can grip," he said laughing, "anything but money. Ah! money is so smooth, t slips through my fingers!"

One evening Dumas promised his theatrical company a *bal masqué*, followed by a supper.

"Ah!" cried a young and pert actress, "and who will pay?"

"*Parbleu*, I shall," answered Dumas, "shan't I be disguised?"

In later years, when the struggle to keep his revenue up to his expenditure became very keen, Dumas was almost as great at borrowing as at giving, and showed the same magnificent carelessness as to the sequel. Frequently he brought his wit to the service of his needs, as, for instance, when Porcher, who had advanced Dumas money on the prospects of his first play, and always been of service to the dramatist on similar occasions, begged the great man to "tutoyer" him. This form of the second-person-singular implies, with the French, familiarity in friendliness.

"Very good," answered Dumas, amused at Porcher's naïve request. "Wilt *thou* lend me fifty louis, Porcher?"

"Nothing," says Villemessant, "was more odious to him than avarice, which was entirely repugnant to his own nature." Leaving a soirée one evening Dumas found himself side by side in the cloak-room with an archi-millionaire who, in exchange for his *paletot* gave fifty centimes (fivepence) to the servant.

The writer, blushing with shame for the financier, drew out his purse and threw down a hundred-franc note.

"Pardon, sir, you have made a mistake, I think?" said the lackey, offering to return the note.

"No, no, friend," answered Dumas, casting a disdainful glance at the millionaire; "it is the other gentleman who has made the mistake."

But Dumas's extravagance, so far as his own pleasure and glorification were concerned, has been much exaggerated. We have seen, ourselves, that the palace of "Monte Cristo" was neither so big, so gaudy, nor so costly as has been represented. Again, Maxime du Camp refutes the charge that Dumas lived in luxury at Naples, declaring that the great man worked there in modest rooms, poorly furnished. "People," he adds, "spread false reports because slander is the first need of fools."

"Though for forty years," says Vandam, "Alexandre Dumas could not have earned less than £8,000 per annum; though he neither smoked, drank, nor gambled; though in spite of his mania for cooking, he himself was the most frugal eater—the beef from the soup of the previous day, grilled, was his favourite dish — it rained writs and summonses around him, while he himself was frequently without a penny."

No wonder, when the veriest stranger could farm himself upon the indulgent host, and then send the cabman, who took him to the station, back to the house to ask for the fare! Truly Dumas had a right to say, "If I have been a spendthrift *I* haven't made all the holes in my purse!"

This leads us to a delicate topic, with which Blaze de Bury, who knew Dumas intimately, deals in this fashion:—

"There are no parasites worse than rapacious women, and to these Dumas gave way as long as he lived. As one left another entered. The place was never empty, and the disgraced favourite, leaving one evening, would locate herself somewhere else the next day, carrying all sorts of things away with her, even to furniture.

"Take all," cried the master, looking on at the dismantling; "take all, but for heaven's sake leave me at least my genius!'"

In the matter of morals it is impossible to judge Dumas on general principles and by ordinary standards, and still more unfair to let British prejudice distort our judgment. His lax code of virtue in this respect must be considered simply in connection with his own nature and training. Except for a brief period, love of women never played the important and disastrous part in Dumas's life which it did in the case of so many of his contemporaries, like De Musset, for example. He was too sane-minded for that. But his ardent, semi-tropical temperament felt the overwhelming need of feminine society and the sensuous charms which fair women possess. His gallantry, good nature, and artless vanity rendered him a prey to the siren type of womanhood; although we have ample proof that he could appreciate the higher qualities of the other sex, as witness his honest, friendly admiration for Madame de Girardin and George Sand, and the chivalric way in which (as we see in "Une Aventure d'Amour"), he could treat a young and charming woman who trusted him completely and put herself under the protection of his honour.

We have spoken of the love of Dumas father for Dumas son. They were, indeed, the complement of each other—"not like in like, but like in difference."

"I know of no two characters more opposite than

Alexandre's and mine," said the father one day, "and yet they go together excellently. We certainly have some very good times when we are far away from each other, but I fancy we are never happier than when we are together."

They loved each other madly, and yet lived such different lives that sometimes they entirely lost sight of each other. At these periods, if the old Dumas saw a friend, he would stop his carriage and hold out his hand, asking for news of his son:

"What has become of Alexandre? Do you ever see him? For my part I never come across him, except to say 'good-day' when I meet him at funerals." On another occasion he added half-bitterly, half-jestingly, "Perhaps I shan't meet him again until my own!"

The passionate love between Dumas *père* and Dumas *fils* began with the birth of the one and did not end with the death of the other. Blaze de Bury tells a pretty anecdote, showing how deeply-rooted was this feeling, even in early childhood:—

"One day the young Alexandre fell from the top of the staircase. The accident seemed to be very serious: the child fainted, and the mother, thinking him dead, was quite overcome. She sent at once for Dumas, who was out on guard, and also for the doctor, who arrived first. The child, however, had regained consciousness, but he was very pale and faint, and when the father saw him in this state he fainted too!

"The doctor ordered leeches, but the child resisted strongly. The father implored and besought the boy to obey, vowing before God that it should not hurt him, to which the child replied, 'Oh, very well then, put them on yourself, and then I will let them put them on me afterwards.' Dumas consented, and put the leeches in the hollow of his left hand."

After the first natural pang of jealousy the elder playwright not only recognised, but acclaimed his son's dramatic powers.[1] At the "first night" of one of the successful plays of Dumas *fils* the proud father wept with joy and happiness. "He took my hand," writes Villemessant, "saying, 'He is my best work!'" Even wittier was Dumas's reply, on a similar occasion, to a friend who remarked that the play was so good, it was surprising the father had no share in it. "Oh, but I had," said the veteran dramatist, "the author is by me!"

The light-hearted gaiety of the father and the sardonic gravity of the son, offered a contrast too marked to be missed by the wits. "Alexandre is

---

[1] The latter has left a very charming account of his father's attitude towards "La Dame aux Camélias." He did not think it would dramatise, but catching the guilty youth with the MS. under his arm, he insisted on hearing it. The elder dramatist became interested, absorbed, moved, delighted, enraptured!

Dumas *fils*, but you—you are not Dumas *père*—you never will be!" said "the Lady of the Camélias" to the great man. "He is a big child of mine, born when I was quite young," said the son. Each seemed to provoke wit in the other. The elder was one day dining with his son, who had taken a house where the trees in the garden quite blocked up the light. "Open your windows," said old Dumas, "and let your garden have a little fresh air!"

By kindness of Madam Dumas *fils* we are enabled to add two "documents" in connection with this love between father and son. The first is Dumas *père's* formal, yet indignant, protest when the censor prohibited his son's most famous play :—

"I declare, on my honour, and on my literary experience, that 'La Dame aux Camélias' forbidden by that stupid institution called the Censorship, is an essentially moral play, and I have a right to an opinion on morality, seeing that I have written 700 volumes which might safely be included in a school library, or be read in a convent, by the young girls.—Paris, 4th October 1851.

"A. DUMAS.

The other is a little gem, which we do not dare to translate. It is written by the father to the son, on New Year's day :—

"Mon Cher Enfant,—Encore un an de plus que je t'aime, encore un an de moins à t'aimer.

"Voilà le côté triste.

"Mais en attendant, sans calculer ce qui nous en reste, aimons nous tant que nous pourrons.—1er Janvier.—*À toi,*

"A. Dumas."

We have been led away by seductive paths into a tardy recognition of one of the great facts about our author—his energy. Henley tells us that at times he wrote for sixteen or eighteen hours a day; and it is quite credible in the case of a physique so magnificently healthy, and a brain so greedy of work. Yet, until his final decline, the great writer never suffered from this abnormal devotion to the desk, except in one way.

"Dumas," says Blaze de Bury, "would never rest except when fatigued; consequently a curious phenomenon came upon him. Almost every year a fever seized him for two or three days; he was not simply ill, he was vanquished. Knowing this, he went to bed, and dozed there; from time to time he opened his eyes, and hastily taking up the glass of lemonade which the occasion required, he drank it, and then lay back with his face to the wall, and gave himself up to his fever. This was his violent manner of taking rest. The crisis lasted about three days, at the end of which Dumas arose and returned to work. The overtaxed organs had insisted upon a halt."

M. Edmond About gives an interesting account which describes Dumas's method of working. "I can still see on our hotel table," he says, "the first draft of the 'Compagnons de Jehu.' It was a thick pile of school-paper, cut in four, and covered with a neat little writing — an excellent rough sketch drawn up by a skilled assistant according to the master's original design. Dumas worked at it in his own manner—scattering wit broadcast through the pages as he wrote, each little slip of white (? pasted) on a great sheet of blue."

If it can be truly said of Dumas that "panting Time toiled after him in vain," it is just as true that he was ever toiling in the arrears of his own work—ever striving to keep pace with the demand for copy. "To be continued in our next"—it was the slave's warning cry at the classic feast. In his amusing preface to Grisier's "Arms and the Duel," Dumas confesses that there were certain extraordinary pledges which he could not fulfil unless forcibly detached from his regular work. This pressure on his time, coupled with a dislike of ridicule, made him, like Balzac, shun his days in uniform, on duty as a National guard, and accordingly the hours of "guard-room" imprisonment due from him mounted up enormously. Monpeou the composer, struggling vainly to get from the busy writer an opera-comique libretto which our good-natured author had undertaken to do, heard of the facts of the case. He learnt, moreover, that Dumas was dodging his military pursuers by sleeping in different houses, entering by side-doors, and departing by windows, "as if he wanted to be a fairy, and was rehearsing the part." Monpeou, for his own base ends, "gave information which led to the capture of the criminal." (It appeared that Dumas had aggravated his offence by an answer which he gave to a superior officer—one of his own tradesmen!—who, with more feeling than culture, declared that it was very "painible and terrible" for him to be obliged to arrest Dumas; to which that gentleman promptly replied, "Do you think it wouldn't be painful and terriful to me to go?") Monpeou begged that Dumas should have a private room to work in, and a piano, and when the prisoner arrived to undergo his punishment he found the traitorous musician busy composing the overture to the comic opera! The result was "Piquillo."

One last touch to complete the picture of "Dumas at work," not forgetting the invariable companion of his labours—the tea of which he drank such inordinate quantities. Mr Albert Vandam, in his "Englishman in Paris," describes a call which he made on his friend Dumas.

"'Is Monsieur at home?' I said to the servant.

"'He is in his study, Monsieur,' was the answer; 'Monsieur can go in.'

"At that moment I heard a loud burst of laughter from the inner apartment, so I said:

"'I would rather wait until Monsieur's visitors are gone.'

"'Monsieur has no visitors; he is working,' remarked the servant with a smile. 'Monsieur Dumas often laughs like that, at his work.'

"It was true enough; the novelist was alone, or rather in company with one of his characters, at whose sallies he was simply roaring."

That Dumas lived to work rather than worked to live, is obvious to all who read of his astonishing fertility, and devotion to his desk. M. de Bury quotes a passage from our author, in which he showed himself doubly indebted to his books—for the pleasure they brought in the writing and the memories they evoked, in the re-reading.

"'I am never alone as long as one of my books is near me,' he says, in a passage full of a deep and delightful emotion, which was not always usual with him. 'Every line recalls to me a day that has passed away, and this day is once more with me, filled from dawn to dusk with all the old atmosphere and all the same people who were there, in the days gone by. Alas! already the best part of my life is in my memories; I am like one of those trees, crowned with bushy foliage, which at noon is full of silent birds, that wake up towards the close of the day. Then, when evening has come, they will fill my old age with the beating of wings and with songs; with their joy, their loves, and their clamour they will enliven it until death, in its turn, lays its hand upon their hospitable home; and the tree, in falling, frightens away all these merry singers, of which each is simply an hour of my life.'"

It is this man whom most of his critics denounced as an idler! In his boyhood, the peasants, with more reason and less malice, said the same of him. He tells us as much, and overhears in imagination the neighbours shaking their heads over him, muttering:—

"See the idler; he prefers rambling along the high-roads to going to college. He will never do anything!"

"I don't know that I have done much," comments our author, "but I know that I have worked deuced hard since then!"

"Truly, this work has had no brilliant result; I should have done better, I believe, instead of piling up volume on volume, if I had bought a corner of land, and put pebble upon pebble, there. At any rate I should have had a house of my own, to-day."

"Bah! Have I not the house of the good God—

the fields, the air, the wide world and nature—which are denied to those who do not possess the power of seeing what I see?"

The most striking, most intuitive intellectual quality which Dumas possessed was what is known as the "dramatic instinct." He seems from the first to have seen life from the vivid, picturesque point of view. As a lad, ignorant of the stage, and collaborating with much more experienced men, his "cockney sportsman" was the successful feature of "La Chasse et l'Amour," the first piece performed in which he had any share.

His method of preparing his plays was interesting and characteristic.

"When I am engaged upon a work which occupies all my thoughts," he says, "I feel the need of narrating it aloud; in reciting thus I invent; and at the end of one or other of these narrations I find some fine morning that the play is completed. But it often happens that this method of working—that is to say, not beginning a piece until I have finished the plot—is a very slow one. In this way I kept 'Mademoiselle de Belle-Isle' in my head for nearly five years."

We may add that finally the piece was not read, but *described* to the committee of the Comédie Française, and at the end of Dumas's vivid recital, was accepted by acclamation! The fact was, it was already composed; it only required to be set on paper.

An anecdote told in connection with the dramatised version of the "Trois Mousquetaires" shows how thoroughly Dumas knew his public, and trusted his natural critics.

"Behind one of the scenes," says Dumas *fils*, "we had seen the helmet of a fireman, who listened to the play very attentively during the first six tableaux. In the middle of the seventh, however, the helmet disappeared."

"'Do you see that fireman's helmet?' asked my father.

"'No, it's not there now.'

"After the act the author went in search of the fireman (who did not know him) and said:

"'Why are you no longer listening to the piece?'

"'Because that act didn't interest me as much as the others.'

"This reply was enough for my father; he went straight to the office of Director Beraud; he took off his frockcoat, his tie, his waistcoat, his braces, opened the collar of his shirt, just as he did when he sat down to work at home, and asked for the copy of the seventh tableau. It was given to him, and he tore it up and threw it into the fire."

"'What on earth are you doing?' cried Beraud.

"'It didn't amuse the fireman: I have destroyed it. But I see exactly what it wants.'

"And he rewrote it, there and then."

The day before the production of his comedy "Halifax," at the dress-rehearsal, Dumas decided that the piece needed a prologue. He told the actors that if they would learn the parts straightway, he would write it. They were willing: the prologue was written, learnt, and acted in twenty-four hours. "Read it," says Blaze de Bury, "it is a gem!"

Dumas and Rossini were present at the first night of a play called "La Jeune Vieillesse." The piece was a shocking failure, and as it proceeded dolorously, to the tune of laughter and hisses, Dumas muttered "What a fool the man is! He has gone right past a splendid subject! I'll make a note of it." And from this germ grew "Le Comte Hermann," one of the most notable of its author's later plays.

Whenever he felt his dramatic energies flagging, he tells us, he opened Schiller or Shakespeare at random, to refresh and revive his powers by reading. But the slightest opportunity or impulse was sufficient to arouse the creative faculty and set it in action.

One day Dumas had been out shooting since six in the morning, and had killed twenty-nine birds.

"I'll just make it thirty," he said, "then I'll go

away and have a good sleep; I'm tired, I've done enough."

"He brought down his thirtieth partridge," says Blaze de Bury, "and we saw him making his way towards the farm. When we returned at five o'clock, he was sitting before the fire in the kitchen, gazing at the flames and twirling his thumbs.

"'Whatever are you doing there?' asked his son.

"'As you see, I am resting.'

"'Have you had any sleep?'

"'No, impossible! There is such an abominable uproar in this farm,—sheep, cows, labourers,—it's impossible to close one's eyes.'

"'Then all this time you've been twirling your thumbs?'

"'No, I have written a play in one act.'

"As a matter of fact he had just written 'Romulus,' which he amused himself by getting Regnier to read at the Comédie Française as being by 'a young, unknown writer.' It was accepted with unanimity." (The version which Dumas himself gives in "Bric-à-brac" of the origin of this play differs only in unimportant details from his friend's account.)

The father's analysis of the son's play "La Dame aux Camélias" shows his knowledge of stage-craft in a striking light. The elder Dumas added to his criticism his opinion that the courtesan on whose career the play and book were based, was immoral by heredity. Subsequent research proved the soundness of this deduction.

Dumas's talent was not confined to exertions on his own behalf. "How often," says Blaze de Bury, "has he served as the anonymous collaborator of his confrères![1] I have seen him thus deny himself any credit for a score of plays which have been signed with other names, but of which he had written two-thirds." In one case a friend brought Dumas a play which had been sent back from a theatre to be cut down, as they considered it too long. The great man read the piece, which was a short one, and told his friend that far from being too long, it was not long enough. He pointed out how the theme should be developed and extended, and made into a full-sized play. The author followed the advice he had received; and the piece thus remodelled was duly accepted and performed.

But "the dramatic instinct" is not without its disadvantages, as Dumas has amusingly shown.

"At a first night," he mourns, "I am the worst spectator in the world. If it is an imaginative piece that is being played, the characters have scarcely appeared before they are no longer the author's, but mine. In the first *entr'acte* I take them; I appropriate them. Instead of their unknown future of the next four acts, I introduce them into four of

[1] See the "Théâtre Inconnu d'A. Dumas, *père*," by Glinel.

my own composition; I enter into their characters, I utilise their originality. If the interval lasts only ten minutes, it is more than I require to build for them the house of cards in which I instal them, and my own particular paste-board house is scarcely ever the same as the author's. With historical pieces it is much worse. I bring my play, of course, built upon the title, and as it is written with all my natural defects—that is to say, with abundance of details, absolute rigidity of characters, and double, triple, quadruple intrigue — it is very seldom that my play resembles in the least the one which is being played. This is a real trouble to me, although to other people it is a source of amusement."

The great romancer's frank confession as to his lack of education as a youth has prompted his detractors to pronounce him ignorant. They pretend that the author of "Antony" wished to destroy the fame of Corneille and Racine; because Dumas's sentiments towards the two national poets was a discriminating admiration rather than blind worship. In reality he admired the highest in literature; and as a rule instinctively recognised it, and judiciously proclaimed it. We know him as yielding to no Frenchman, not even Hugo, in his veneration for Shakespeare; Andrew Lang, no mean authority, testifies to Dumas's sound appreciation of the greatness of Homer; and this passage in the "Mémoires" gives the lie to many jeers directed against the "great low-comedian" as his foes called him:

"Bad Latin scholar as I am, I have always adored Virgil; his compassion for the wandering exiles, his solemn pictures of death, his intuition of an unknown God, touched my heart supremely from the first; the melody of his verses ... had an especial charm for me, and I knew by heart whole passages of the 'Æneid.'" Unlike most scholars Dumas studied with enthusiasm, and he never forgot.

"Partly by diligence, partly by divination, Dumas had great knowledge," says M. de Bury. "Having received no early education, he set himself deliberately to repair the misfortune, filling in the gap by the thousand ideas which he gathered daily from conversation, from travel and from reading. History, travels, natural history, foreign literature —he read all, from the "Ramayana" to Shakespeare, Goëthe, Schiller, Thackeray, Dickens, Cooper, Scott, his admiration of literature ever increasing. Hugo delighted without influencing him, but Balzac had little attraction for Dumas, who didn't see human nature from that point of view."

As will readily be understood, the great realist and the great romanticist were at opposite poles of the literary sphere. On one occasion these extremes did meet, being invited by a well-meaning friend, but the result was not happy. Balzac had spoken contemptuously of his rival in popularity as "a nigger," and Dumas was not disposed to forget it. It was a Quaker's meeting, for neither guest spoke until they were both leaving. Then alzac said:

"When I am written out, I'll take to writing dramas."

And Dumas replied—

"You'd better begin at once, then."

And they parted. Yet Balzac saw that Dumas, like George Sand, had none of the low jealousy and littlenesses which obscured so many contemporary talents, and Dumas, who always wrote with appreciation of Balzac's talents, followed his coffin to the grave when the author of "Père Goriot" died in 1850.

A still greater *bête-noire* of Dumas's was Buloz, the editor of the *Revue des Deux Mondes*, for which periodical the "Isabel de Bavière" chroniques were written. The pair had quarrelled over the production of "Caligula" at the Comédie Française, for at that time Buloz was commissary of the national theatre. For some months afterward Dumas, who was witty even in his dislikes, "embroidered" his correspondence with varying but consistently uncomplimentary references to Buloz. For instance, he would address a letter

"To

"M——,

"Havre,

"Sixty kilomètres from that idiot of a Buloz." Or again, would begin a letter:—

"MY DEAR PORCHER,—You, who are in every respect superior to that idiot, Buloz." . . .

There was a third exception to Dumas's general "friendly relations with all the other powers." This was M. Jules Lecomte, and the circumstances of the case are worth recording, as being "significant of many things." Lecomte, when a young man, was recommended to Dumas by a mutual friend, and the author of course opened his house to the poor and friendless fugitive. In return for this kindness Lecomte ordered costly clothes, and left his host to pay the bill, sponged on the generous author in various ways, and finally disgusted him altogether by masquerading as Alfred de Musset, also at his benefactor's expense. Further, Lecomte, under a pseudonym, sent to Paris by way of Brussels articles containing references to Dumas and Ida Ferrier which were not in the best of taste.

When the great man was staying in Florence, Lecomte had the impudence to call once more on his old host. The authorities had required some particulars concerning Lecomte, and he had given them Dumas's name as a reference. The novelist duly furnished the officials with such facts about the gentleman in question that he was ordered to leave the city at once. Then the other, foreseeing a public disturbance, armed himself with a stout cane.

The precaution was a wise one. As the romancer was standing by the door of a carriage, chatting with a lady friend, in a public avenue one day, Lecomte, accompanied by a "backer," strode up, and without a word of warning struck at his old patron. Dumas parried the blow, and cut the rogue across the face with his cane. Then, turning to his assailant's "second," one Prince Korsakoff, he declared that he would not cross swords with a creature like Lecomte, but would willingly meet the Prince, if he chose to take up his companion's quarrel.

Korsakoff at once accepted, but before the duel came about he wrote to Dumas stating that he had heard certain truths about M. Lecomte, and now refused either to fight for him or to continue his acquaintance.

There are several morals to this incident, which have their bearing on Dumas's success—and failure—in life.

As a rule, however, the great writer was not a good hater, and bore little malice. Meeting one day a critic who had abused him, he stepped up to him, saying, "Hein! What a splendid article I have provided you with!" It is true that the persistent shout of "Collaborators! collaborators!" annoyed him. Once, after keeping a company of friends roaring at his witty sayings, Dumas added, "You find the jest a good one? Well, to-morrow one of my collaborators will swear it's his!"

Our author has expressed his opinion of collaboration in general, in his "Souvenirs dramatiques." The passage is written in his most vivacious style. But for Fiorentino, one of the many young men he befriended, and one of his best "'prentices," Dumas had a very real affection.

One day the master begged his secretary to take a letter to Fiorentino and wait for a reply. An hour after, the secretary returned with a letter from the ex-'prentice, then critic of the *Constitutionnel* and the *Moniteur*. Dumas opened it:

"Here is a man whom I have rescued from misery," he cried, "and whom I have taught his trade. Well!—would anyone believe it?—when at odd times I ask him to do me a service . . . he never refuses me!"

It is a proof of the many-sided nature of Dumas's genius that he was at once the rival of Balzac,

Scribe, and Hugo. Towards Scribe his attitude was one of admiration, mingled with a little good-natured tolerance—the smile of the gay grasshopper, as he watched the industrious ant toiling through a hot summer's day to get in his winter stock. The one had talent and amassed a fortune; the other had genius, made half a dozen fortunes, and died poor.

With the bulk of his fellow-writers Dumas was on excellent terms, and numbered amongst his friends Chateaubriand, Lamartine, Lafayette, George Sand, Rossini, Hugo, De Musset, Heine, Soulié, Béranger, Merimée, and Nodier. With Janin, it is true, he engaged in a wordy duel over "Les Demoiselles de St Cyr."[1] Mr Swinburne thinks that one of the poems in "Toute la Lyre" was addressed by Hugo to his two friends, suggesting reconciliation. We have seen that Dumas and Janin were on good terms again in 1849, and at the former's death the latter wrote a little "appreciation" of him, full of sincere affection and admiration.

We have mentioned Victor Hugo, and the friendship between these two men, so strangely unlike in character, played an important part in Dumas's

---

[1] The pair even met on the "field of honour." Janin would not fight with swords (so the story went) because he knew an infallible thrust; Dumas refused pistols because he could kill a fly at forty paces. So the foes embraced!

life, although the genius of each was quite unaffected by his admiration and affection for his *confrère*. It is true that the plays of one suggested ideas to the other, but the influence went no deeper. Dumas first met Hugo about the time of the production of "Henri Trois,"— in a show on the Boulevard du Temple, he tells us!—and Hugo invited his new acquaintance to attend the private reading of "Marion Delorme." The two young "Romantics" became instant friends, and Dumas never wearied of singing the praises of the poet, who on his part, although of a less demonstrative nature, seems to have remained a loyal friend throughout.

We have referred to Dumas's eulogy of "Marion Delorme," and Hugo's noble championship of his comrade, on the occasion when the Legion of Honour was conferred on him and then withdrawn. Unfortunately, a bitter attack on Dumas, written by Granier de Cassagnac, appeared in 1833, against Hugo's wishes, in a journal with which the poet was known to be connected. An attempt was made by ill-advised partisans to set the rival dramatists in opposition to each other. It may have been this which caused the coolness to exist between the two friends in 1837-8, but in the latter year Madame Dumas died, and her sorrowing son forgot the old enmity and invited Hugo to the funeral. This was the poet's reply:

"I could have wished a less mournful reason for clasping your hand once more. You will see me to-morrow, and with the first glance which we exchange, you will know that you did wrong ever to doubt me.

"You were right in counting on me. It is a return to a state of noble trust worthy of you, and of me."

It is a matter of history that after the *coup d'état* Hugo went into exile. The other soon followed his friend to Brussels, and we have already spoken of their intimacy during this period. On his return to Paris, Dumas proclaimed his admiration for Hugo in the very first number of his *Mousquetaire* — a bold thing to do, when one remembers that the author of "The History of a Crime" was anathema to the soul of "Napoleon the Little." The following year our author dedicated his play of "La Conscience" to Hugo as "a proof of a friendship which has survived exile, and which will, I hope, outlive even death." The compliment is acknowledged in the fifth book of the poet's "Contemplations," in which Hugo recalls their parting on the quay at Antwerp, and adds:

> "Tu rentras dans ton ceuvre, éclatante, innombrable,
> Multiple éblouissante, heureuse où le jour luit,
> Et moi dans l'unité sinistre de la nuit."

When Mademoiselle Augustine Brohan attacked

the exiled poet in the press, Dumas wrote to the Comédie Française to demand that the actress who had insulted his friend should not be allowed to play in his comedies in the future. Hugo in writing to thank his comrade for his loyalty, added, " I feel I must write to tell you that I love you more every day, not only because you are one of the wonders of the century, but because you are one of its consolations." The letter ended with an urgent invitation to visit the poet at Guernsey. Dumas duly journeyed to see the exile (in 1857), an act on which Charles Hugo comments admiringly. It was not only brave of him (he says), it was thoughtful. The bond between the two great men remained unbroken till the end, and Hugo wrote to the younger Dumas on the occasion of his father's death one of his characteristically noble and tender letters.

With all his defects of training and his semi-plebeian birth, Dumas was a man of taste. Pictures, music, bric-à-brac, ancient art in sculpture and design, all that was best in the artistic sense, appealed to him. His admiration for architecture was real and ardent, and when during his travels in La Vendée he visited the cathedral at Angers, and found an architect busy "restoring" the church—by scraping it!—his comment was severe in spite of its wit. "Alas, it takes twenty-five years to make a man: a Swiss mercenary in the royalist pay shoots him, and he dies. It takes six or eight centuries to 'colour' a cathedral: an architect with 'taste' comes on the scene, and scrapes it! Oh, why doesn't the Swiss shoot the architect, or the architect scrape the Swiss?"

If his enemies had not insisted on the contrary, one would hardly have thought it necessary to claim courage for a man who was in the streets of Paris during the days of July 1830, who chose to be "out" with Garibaldi, and who fought two or three duels and sent goodness knows how many challenges. As a fact, Dumas's courage was of the best quality.

"In manhood his earliest impulse," Mr Lang tells us, "was to rush at danger; if he had to wait he felt his courage oozing out at the tips of his fingers, like Bob Acres, but in the moment of peril he was himself again." His bravery greatly resembled that of Henri Quatre in "Les Quarante Cinq": it was a fear of *fear*, which overmastered any fear of the event that menaced him.

Once, when serving in the National guard, Dumas was summoned to help to arrest the Chamber of Deputies! He and another comrade met at the doors: they waited, but no one joined them. The "false alarm" appears to have been in the nature of a test, which the author passed successfully.

The great man's disdain of danger was partly due

to his superb health and strength. He was truly the son of the general who choked a horse with his knees; it was veritably the father of Porthos who tackled the leader of a crowd which threatened to mob him. "He turned round," says M. Du Chaffault, "seized on the biggest, carried him to the parapet of the bridge as if he'd been a bundle of straw, and cried, ' Beg my pardon, or I'll throw you into the water!'" His confidence rested also on his perfect familiarity with all kinds of weapons. He fenced admirably, and was an excellent shot, as became an ardent sportsman, for in all the pleasures of Dumas's life sport took a commanding place. As a boy we have seen him companion of keepers and poachers; as a man he loved the chase from the spearing of trout by midnight to the hunting of wolves. His travels contain the stories of his own exploits: his "Causeries" tell of the triumphs of others; everywhere in his books you may read of some form of *la chasse*; in one it is Charles IX. chasing the boar, in another Ferdinand of Naples breaking up a Council at the call of his *piqueurs*.

When wearied of desk-work, or intent on thinking out a new romance or play, Dumas would disappear from Paris for a few days. His old friends at Villers-Cotterets would be rejoiced to see their young friend (he was always "young" to them) walk in unexpectedly one fine day, looking gay and hearty, and ordering his dinner even as he shouted a greeting! Then would follow the jolliest of dinner-parties, everyone crowding round the table to exchange banter and chaff with the "King of Paris," who was happy and content to be hail-fellow-well-met with the poorest peasant in Villers-Cotterets.

It has been made a subject of reproach against Dumas—and which of his qualities has not been made use of in that way?—that he knew how to "cook his hare" after he had caught it. This prejudice is especially strong in England, where the word *gourmet* is confused with *gourmand*, and popularly translated to mean "glutton." Ordinarily, the writer lived simply, and if he knew how food could best be cooked, if he liked it cooked well instead of badly, and if he had the skill to cook it himself, there is surely no need to think any the worse of him. He was not (*pace* Stevenson) a "great eater" in the sense of eating much; he boasted of his appetite, it is true, but there is no reason to believe that it was out of proportion to his giant frame and the enormous amount of work he got through. So much of a "glutton," in short, was our Dumas, that when engrossed in his writing he refused to stop to take food; whatever his servant chose to prepare for him was placed at his elbow, and he ate mechanically as he wrote on and on!

ALEXANDRE DUMAS

To those who have so far followed the progress of this sketch of Dumas's life and character it will be a matter of no surprise to learn that he was a humanitarian. His father had earned the nickname of "Mr Humanity" from the fierce *sansculottes* of the Revolution, because he drew down the blinds of his room rather than witness the execution of some poor wretches whom the fanaticism of the time had doomed to the guillotine. And as the love of one's kind is only a grander form of charity, Dumas the charitable was never found wanting. Sometimes he used his influence to save a coiner from the gallows; sometimes he racked his wits to prevent a duel which was likely to end fatally; sometimes he would write autographs and aphorisms by the hundred, that some wretch in poverty might benefit by the sale. When "Notre Dame des Arts" was founded, Fitzgerald tells us, Dumas took the translation of a little German play, shaped it, disposed of it for £800, and presented the money to the charity. A poor monk journeying from Palestine, to obtain funds for the rebuilding of his monastery at Carmel, appealed to the writer, who laid the good man's petition before the public through the columns of a friendly journal. No less a sum than 300,000 francs was raised, and the monk went home joyfully, his quest accomplished.

Brunswick, who provided the base-idea on which

"Mademoiselle de Belle-Isle" was founded, sold his share—a third of the profits—for 300 francs, to a friend, who re-sold it to Dumas. When the play was written and produced, and proved a success, Brunswick hinted to the author that the sum was not adequate. The other replied:—

"I heartily thank you, my dear friend, for wishing to have your *share* in the good fortune that has just befallen me. I fancy I am more skilful in putting dialogue together than figures. I left out an 'ought' in the sum we agreed upon for 'your' piece. It is worth, my dear Brunswick, not 300, but 3,000 francs."

The description given by Dumas of the last days and the last moments of Marie Dorval is full of pathos, and most feelingly, unaffectedly told. The dying actress begged her old friend to see that she was not laid in a pauper's grave, and he promised. He had only 200 francs of his own; Hugo and M. Falloux between them supplied another 300; and the "vain *farçeur*" pawned a cherished decoration to make up the necessary balance. He struggled vainly to obtain pardon for Marie Capelle (Madame Lafarge), niece of his playmate Collard, whose crime was one of the tragic mysteries of the day. He had better fortune in the case of a hussar named Bruyant, a native of Villers-Cotterets, who was condemned to death for killing a superior officer, in an attempt to desert. By energetically attacking first his young patron the Duke de Chartres, and then M. Guizot, Dumas obtained a commutation of the sentence, for, as he had foreseen, the man proved to be mad, and was finally taken care of.

In his epilogue to "Comte Hermann" the author pleaded, with much earnestness and good sense, that executions should not be held semi-publicly, a way which summons false pride to the heart of the condemned and hardens him to die unrepentant. He asked that the sentence should be carried out in the prison cell itself, and should be accomplished, more swiftly and painlessly, by electricity. Since the words were written the French have advanced somewhat towards Dumas's ideal; the Americans have realised it to the full. As in private life our author was a friend of the poor, the sorrowing and the suffering, so in the world's history he invariably championed the cause of the fallen. "In his stories," says Ferry, "he never lost an opportunity of re-crowning the vanquished, of raising up fallen causes, and of asking the pity of posterity for those men who had sacrificed themselves for it."

Dumas passed through that evolution of the soul so frequent with thinkers,—dogmatism,—doubt—and a new faith, based on reason, and the divine intuition within man. As a boy he passed through a period of religious ecstacy; yet in his youth when he was in the depths of Byronic gloom, he prefaced his play of "Antony," as we have seen, with what was intended to be a very wicked invocation to the Spirit of Evil, in which he declared he would give up to it his life, and his soul too,— "if he believed in it!" Twenty-four years later, he wrote to Victor Hugo, "I believe in the immortality of the soul." In the verses which he composed on his mother's death, he shows a passionate piety. All these conflicting sentiments were uttered with perfect sincerity — they were really felt at the time they were expressed. But his true confession of faith, the conclusions of his maturer years, is given in the "Mémoires." Here, after protesting "a great respect for holy things, a great faith in Providence and a great love for God," he continues:

"Never in the course of a somewhat long life have I felt, in the most wretched hours of that life, one moment of doubt, one instant's despair. I will not dare to say that I am sure of the immortality of my soul; I will simply say, I hope for it."

At a certain dinner-party given by an opulent banker, the company discussed the existence of God, "over the walnuts and wine," and a certain general was very scornful on the subject, wondering how people could trouble to discuss such trifles.

"For my part," he added, "I can't conceive of the existence of this mysterious being whom they call 'the good God.'"

"General," replied Dumas, "I have two hunting-dogs, two monkeys and a parrot at home, who are of your opinion exactly."

Dumas *fils* has examined his father's religious sentiments and analysed them, in the introduction to the "Mousquetaires" before quoted. He finds that his father was too sane, too busy in good work, to dwell much on the hereafter; but believes that the kind, charitable soul need not be blamed very severely for living for this life, without considering its own precious self too closely—and most of us will agree with him.

Even in the last darkening hours of his mind Dumas was capable, at brief intervals, of something like his old wit. We quote his last *mot* from M. Ferry's "Dernières Années d'A. Dumas":

"When they took him away from Paris he had twenty francs on him. That louis was the total fortune of this man, who had earned millions.

"On arriving at Puys, Dumas placed the coin on his bedroom chimney-piece, and there it remained all through his illness.

"One day he was seated in his chair near the

window, chatting with his son, when his eye fell on the gold piece.

"A recollection of the past crossed his mind.

"'Fifty years ago, when I went to Paris,' he said, 'I had a louis. Why have people accused me of prodigality? I have always kept that louis. See—there it is!'"

"And he showed his son the coin, smiling feebly as he did so."

. . . .

We may add, by way of appendices, three character-sketches which will supplement the impression given by our own. They present by way of contrast, a view of Dumas's character, which is, as it were, focussed and compact.

The first is a phrenological description given by Dr Castle, a professor of that "pseudo-science," which purports to be a cold-blooded estimate of its subject's virtues and vices:

"Frank in the expression of all that he feels and thinks, he is loath by nature to take any roundabout way of attaining his end: his is the very opposite of the intriguing instinct.

"He is expansive, affectionate, and caressing in manner; and his affection is of that kind which extends itself in all directions, being in fact, the confession of his need for comradeship. This tendency to make friends of all whom he meets means practically an absence of exclusiveness in affection.

"He has a natural love for the weak, the suffering, and the young, and by a logical antithesis, a love, too, for the aged.

"He possesses confidence in himself, and yet needs the approbation of others; he has a desire to please, coupled with a respect for others.

"As one may see, such a character is subject to a great number of opposing impulses. These contradictory instincts will have an effect on our writer, a subtle inward effect, which is more apparent to Dumas himself than to any of his friends, however well they know him.

"He feels the need of love, of loving and being loved: this need is elemental in him, and is felt perhaps the more strongly by the sensuous than by the spiritual side of his nature.

"He is subject to irritable, rather than to irascible moments, and capable, on rare occasions, of violent and blind passion. Also he is liable to show himself vindictive, or, more often, stubborn, in controversy or quarrel. This obstinacy is prone to seem like vindictiveness, because our subject will probably be infuriated by resistance to his desires, although he feels no hatred towards the cause of his anger.

"There is a tendency towards covetousness, very

slightly indicated, but present. He is generally inclined to see the best side of everything, and view all things through *couleur de rose* spectacles. He is pious by instinct and religious by intelligence, more brave than courageous, and more resolute than brave."

The second is a portrait of Dumas in his thirties, by a *confrère* and a contemporary, M. Hippolyte Romand, who looks upon the author from a more human point of view:

" Passionate by temperament, subtle by instinct, and courageous by vanity, he has a good heart and bad judgment, and is a spendthrift by nature. He is a veritable 'Antony' for love, almost a 'Darlington' for ambition: he never will be a 'Sentinelli'[1] for vengeance. Superstitious[2] when he thinks, religious when he writes, sceptical when he speaks, light even in his most fiery passions, his blood is a lava, his thought a spark. His personality is as illogical as it is possible to conceive, and the most unmusical that we know; he is a liar in his capacity as poet; generous, because he

---

[1] The character in "Christine" who, impelled by private hate, kills Monaldeschi, by Queen Christine's order.

[2] Pifteau tells us that Dumas had a belief in the "evil eye," and a rooted distrust of monks as harbingers of evil. Vandam tells us that "although far from being superstitious," the romancer prophesied that the notorious Lola Montès would bring ill-luck to all who joined their destinies to hers, and the after career of that courtesan proved him to be right.

is an artist and a poet; too liberal in friendship, too despotic in love; vain as a woman, resolute as a man, and egoistical as a God. He is sincere to imprudence, kind without discernment, forgetful even to thoughtlessness, a wanderer body and soul, cosmopolitan by taste, patriotic in opinion, rich in illusions and caprices, poor in prudence and experience; light in spirit, cutting in speech, witty in season, a Don Juan by night, an Alcibiades by day, a veritable Proteus, escaping from everybody and from himself; as lovable for his defects as for his good qualities; more seductive for his vices than for his virtues—that is M. Dumas as we love him, as he is!"

We make no apology for adding, as the third "opinion," that of one whose partiality inspired a frank eulogy. It is Dumas *fils* who is speaking, a man of critical insight, who may at least be relied upon to praise the praiseworthy qualities of his father, and not to extol the bad ones. He speaks in apostrophe:

"In this century, which seems created, above all, to devour all things, you were in truth the one man it needed, for you in turn were born to produce perpetually. What precautions nature took, what provision she made in thee, for the formidable appetites, for which she was forced to prepare! It was beneath the American sun, and with African blood, that she moulded him of whom you were born, and who, soldier and general of the Republic, strangled a horse between his legs, broke a helmet with his teeth, and, alone, defended the bridge of Brixen against a vanguard of twenty men! Rome would have bestowed the honours of a triumph upon him and made him consul: France, calmer and more economical, shut the doors of the college upon his son. That son, growing to manhood in the wide forests—in the open air and under the blue heavens—urged on by want and by his genius, flung himself, one fine day, into the great city, and marched into literature by the breach he made, as his father marched into the camp of the enemy.

"Then commenced that cyclopean work which lasted for forty years. Tragedy, dramas, history, romance, comedy, travel, you cast all of them in the furnace and the mould of your brain, and you peopled the world of fiction with new creations. The newspaper, the book, the theatre, burst asunder, too narrow for your puissant shoulders; you fed France, Europe, America, with your works; you made the wealth of publishers, translators, plagiarists; printers and copyists toiled after you in vain. In the fever of production you did not always try to prove the metal you employed, and sometimes you tossed into the furnace whatever came to your hand. The fire made the selection: what was your own is bronze, what was not yours vanished in smoke. You have turned out some bad work thus; but on the other hand, how many amongst those who would have remained obscure have been lightened and warmed at the forge of your genius; and if the hour of restoration sounded, how immensely would you gain, simply by taking back what you have given, and what has been taken from you!

"Sometimes you placed your heavy hammer upon your great anvil, and rested on the threshold of the glittering grotto, your sleeves turned back, your chest open to the air. With smiling face, you wiped your forehead; you gazed at the calm stars, breathing the freshness of the night, or perhaps you rushed off upon the first path you met, hailing your freedom as a prisoner would; you crossed the ocean, you climbed the Caucasians, you scaled Etna—it was always something colossal! Then, your lungs filled anew, you returned to your cave. Seeing your big shadow outlined in black against the glowing hearth, the mob clapped their hands; for at heart they love fertility in work, elegance in strength, simplicity in genius, and you have fertility, simplicity, elegance—and generosity, which I had forgotten, but which has made you a millionaire for others and poor for yourself.

"Then one day there came a change—indifference, ingratitude, seized the crowd, whom till now you had swayed and dominated. They went elsewhere, wishing to see something fresh; you had given them too much. You even heard it whispered, 'I declare the son has far more talent.' You well might laugh at that, but you did not; you were merely proud of me, like some ordinary father, and perhaps you thought that they were right. You would have given me all your glory, just as you used to give me all your money when I was an idle boy. Let others of my time claim to be your equals: as they do not bear your name, that is their own affair; but I wish those who come after me to know, when they shall see our two names one above the other on the scroll of this century, that whatever people may say, I have never felt you other than my father, my friend, and my teacher; and that, thanks to you, I have never become conceited, always considering myself a mere pigmy by the side of you."

Reading this filial tribute, in which the regret for the father's lost popularity seems to be sincerely greater than the writer's own pleasure in his success, one may well agree with Hugo, when he wrote to the younger Dumas on the death of his father:—

"That soul was capable of all the miracles, even that of bequeathing itself, even of surviving itself. Your father lives in you."

PART II
HIS WRITINGS

His Writings

"Suppose," wrote Victor Hugo, "that in place of the romance of narrative, and the romance epistolary, a creative brain produced the romance dramatic, wherein the action should unfold itself in a series of faithful and varied pictures, just as the events of real life occur; which should know no other division than that which the changing scenes demanded—which should be, in short, a long drama, in which the description supplies the scenery and the costumes?"

Dumas was destined to realise this ideal much more extensively and closely than Hugo himself. He possessed, in the first place, the constructive, dramatic skill; he only needed the impetus. He found it in the love of history; but it was needful that he should first find the historians who would reconcile him to the task.

"What France is looking for, is the historical novel," said Lassagne to Dumas once, in the early days of the writer's career.

"But the history of France is so dull and tedious!" answered the ignorant young dramatist dogmatically.

"Indeed—how do you know that?"

"I've been told so."

"Poor boy! Read it yourself, first, and then you'll change your mind."

Dumas took his friend's advice, and read Thierry, and a high ambition possessed him.

"One day," he tells us, "Lamartine asked me to what I attributed the success of his 'Histoire des Girondins.'"

"'To the fact that you raised history to the height of the romance,' I replied."

"In Dumas," says Swinburne, "the novelist and the dramatist were thoroughly at one." We are told, and can well believe, that when the immense success of "Les Trois Mousquetaires" called for a dramatised version of the book, little more than scissors and paste, some skill in selection, and a change of form, were needed to turn the romance into a play. On the other hand, "Henri Trois et sa Cour" and "La Tour de Nesle" read like cape-and-sword romances in stage dress.

We know that in Dumas a desire to write fiction had always lurked behind the lust for theatrical fame. About the time that his first vaudeville was performed, the first book, a little collection of short stories, appeared. These, as we have said, were the "Nouvelles Contemporaines" of 1826, afterwards included in the "Souvenirs d'Antony" of

1835. As this was Dumas's first book, and is now a great rarity, we may give it a little attention.

"The first of these stories," he tells us, "was entitled 'Laurette,' the second 'Blanche de Beaulieu,' and the name of the third I have utterly forgotten. 'Blanche de Beaulieu' I afterwards utilised in writing 'La Rose Rouge,' and the third (the one of which I cannot remember the name), I subsequently reconstructed into 'Le Cocher de Cabriolet.'" We may add that the third story was named "Marie," and that the book was dedicated to the author's mother in "Homage—love—gratitude." Of the four (or six) copies sold, one is now in the possession of Robert Garnett, Esq., and the title-page is here reproduced with his permission.

Of the three (later the five) stories, "Blanche de Beaulieu" was the most striking. It is noteworthy that in this sombre but powerful little story General Dumas, the author's father, appears, though in its first form he was alluded to without being named. "Le Cocher de Cabriolet" (afterwards destined to form the basis of the author's drama of "Angèle"), is a pretty story, of a kind differing strongly from the terrible poignancy of its companion, "Un bal masqué," which is in the true "Antony" vein. This last, indeed, is the

NOUVELLES

CONTEMPORAINES,

PAR

Alex. DUMAS.

Fils d'un soldat, j'aime à choisir
mes héros dans les rangs de l'armée.

PARIS.

SANSON, LIBRAIRE

DE S. A. R. Monseigneur le duc de Montpensier,
Palais-Royal, galerie de bois, n° 250.

1826.

TITLE PAGE OF DUMAS'S FIRST BOOK.

sole excuse for connecting these stories with the famous play, as it is supposed to be told by that Byronic personage himself. The remaining story, "Cherubino et Celestini," appeared as one of the "Cent-et-un Nouvelles" in 1833, under the title of "Les Enfants de la Madone" ("The Foundlings"). The main incidents contained in this "nouvelle" were told to Sir Walter Scott as local history, when he visited Naples shortly before he died, and are given in his "Journal" as "The Death of Bizarro." Tennyson versified it from that source in "The Bandit's Wife." How cleverly the theme has been elaborated, and how its interest has been heightened, by the skill of the Frenchman, may be seen by those who will compare the outline in Scott's journal with "Cherubino et Celestini."

The novelist in Dumas lay dormant for nine years — his period of dramatic triumphs. Then, an acquaintance with Scott's novels, and an introduction to history picturesquely told, in the shape of Barante's "Histoire des Ducs de Bourgoyne" combined to excite his imagination, and gave direction to the ambitions called forth by Thierry. In his fine preface to "Isabel de Bavière" he faces the difficulties and exults over the glories of the career which he foresees for himself:

"One of the most magnificent privileges of the

historian, that lord over the Past," he wrote, "is the power to rebuild palaces and reanimate the dust of dead heroes. With the touch of his pen, at the sound of his voice, as at the call of a God, the scattered bones reunite; again the living flesh covers them; they are clothed once more in the gay robes of their other life, and from out that immense gulf of oblivion whither the three thousand centuries have flung their offspring, he has but to choose the favoured elect of his caprice, and call them by name, to see them instantly raise with their brows the walls of their tombs, part with their hands the folds of their shrouds, and answer him, as Lazarus answered Christ: 'Lord, here am I: what wilt Thou with me?'"

"True, one needs a firm step to descend into the abyss of history, a voice of power, to question the phantoms who dwell there, a hand that shall not tremble, to write the words that they shall speak, for often the dead hold terrible secrets which have been 'interrèd with their bones.'"

Dumas's early ideal of the historical romance, although it changed with the development of his genius, is also interesting. At the beginning of his career, he wrote:

"The great difficulty (it seems to us) is to avoid two errors—not to attenuate the past, as history has done; not to disfigure it, as the romance does. The only way to steer clear of both these mistakes will be, then, immediately one has chosen one's historical epoch, to study thoroughly the interests which moved the three classes of society — the people, the nobility and royalty—at that time; to choose from among the principal personages of those classes such as took an active part in the events to be comprised in the narrative; and to enquire minutely concerning their appearance, character and temperament, so that, whilst making them live, speak, and act in this triple unity, one may show the development in these historical types, of the passions which brought about those catastrophes which are recorded in the pages of the century by dates and facts and in which one can only interest one's public by showing them the actual living manner in which the same deeds were added to history."

Such was Dumas's view of the romance in the days of "Isabel de Bavière," and "La Comtesse de Salisbury." We have already explained how the former "chronique" came to be written. Dumas selected the most effective portions of Barante, and vivified them. He was destined in the future to make a brilliant success by the way in which he painted romance on a foundation of history; but on this occasion, as Mr Saintsbury pithily puts it, "the canvas shows through." There is a want of coherence in the book: it is absorbingly interesting, but it is neither romance nor history. "La Comtesse de Salisbury," published four years later, in 1839, is less readable. An admirable opening chapter is succeeded by long tracts of history, and only at brief intervals do the characters take life. This is the more to be regretted, as the episode of Edward III.'s guilty passion for his vassal's wife was a subject of which, in after-years, our more experienced author, emancipated from history, would probably have made much. The preface, which treats of the influence of Scott on the author and his fellow-romancers in France, is by far the most valuable part of the book.

Absorbed in travel and the drama, once again our romancer neglected the historical *métier*. "Pauline," a powerful little novel, some first indications of which appeared in his "Impressions de Voyage en Suisse," was published in 1838, and was much praised; and "Pascal Bruno," an episode of the days of Murat, was also suggested by the author's travels in Italy, and was coupled with "Pauline" in a volume entitled "La Salle d'Armes."

When Dumas produced his drama of "Caligula," he said to himself, "to study the corpse it is best to visit the tomb." He therefore went to Italy, and also "read up" the epoch, and the result was a romance as well as a drama. "Acté," which was published in 1839, is not translated into English, but in some respects it is a most notable book. "Scott could never have written the first two hundred pages," says Parigot truly; "Renan would not have been ashamed of them. Every step that Dumas takes his foot rests on a document—Nero's entry into the city over the *débris* of its walls, which had been levelled in his honour, the suppers, the games at the circus, the letters from Gaul which interrupt the spectacle—the whole story is taken from authentic sources, not forgetting Nero's flight, and his death at the house of Plancus. And with what grace, with what imaginative facility is this prodigious epoch conjured up, living and breathing, before our eyes! To these marvels of illusion, gathered together by the artist in Dumas with great effort and skill, he adds the vivid illusion of his own story."

It is a pity that such excellent work should in the end "drag itself to death in plagiarism and prolixity"; but the fact was that Dumas's mother died whilst the book was being written, and this probably accounts for the fact that the novel varies so markedly in merit. Either the writer, absorbed in his sorrow, left some other author to finish it, or he lost interest in the romance, and being as usual pressed for time, made use of Chateaubriand's "Martyrs" to supply the place of his vanished inspiration.

ALEXANDRE DUMAS

Sienkiewicz, who has studied Dumas's works to admirable purpose, probably found in "Acté" the basis for "Quo Vadis." The "Acté" of Mr Westbury, although it does not resemble Dumas's in plot, would seem to have been suggested by the older romance.

"Le Capitaine Paul," published in the previous year, relates to the celebrated privateersman Paul Jones, and professes to be a sequel to Fenimore Cooper's "Pilot." Although Alphonse Karr in "Les Guêpes" makes fun of the sea-terms employed in the story, the comparative non-success of the book is due rather to the fact that Dumas, in his admiration for the American novelist, was working with unfamiliar and uncongenial material. The plot seems to have been suggested to him. "Dauzats invenit, Dumas sculpsit," he wrote. He was more successful, two years later, with the "Aventures de John Davys," a book somewhat after the manner of Defoe. Thackeray in the *Revue Britannique* for 1847 accused Dumas of having stolen half of it from another book, which he did not specify. Cherbuliez, a contemporary critic, who was usually severe on our author, admitted that the book could be numbered amongst the best and most amusing of his early works.

Three other books published in 1840 deserve attention, although not one of them is accessible in

English. Of these perhaps the most noteworthy is "Maître Adam, le Calabrais," which is unknown to many of the admirers of the romancer, even to those who pursue him in the huge list of Calmann-Lévy. According to his witty epilogue, Dumas first heard the story from the lips of a peasant at Mugnano; but the intimate knowledge of Calabrian life, customs, and superstitions displayed suggests the assistance of Fiorentino, Dumas's Italian assistant. The result is an admirable story, told in most humorous fashion.

The "Maître d'Armes," the second book of this trio, Mr Saintsbury has pronounced "very poor stuff." Yet it was translated by a peer of the realm, and has been issued also for the use of schools. We fancy that on this occasion our author is to be taken more literally than usual in his explanation of the story's origin. Dumas supplied an introductory page to his friend Grisier's journal of a visit to St Petersburg, and possibly selected passages and rewrote them. "The public are warned that nothing of what follows is mine," writes Dumas, "not even the title." That is plain enough, and the internal evidence proves it. The story of the exiling of a Russian noble for complicity in the plot of 1825,[1] and of the devotion of the mistress who followed him to far Siberia, forms only a minor portion of

[1] The plot forms the subject of Jokai's romance, "The Green Book."

the book, and is not developed, as Dumas would have found himself forced to develop anything of his own. It may be added, that during his travels in Russia in 1858, our author was introduced to the hero and heroine of the adventure. The book had the honour of being forbidden in Russia.

The remaining work of this year was " Le Capitaine Pamphile," which narrates the adventures of a sort of nautical Crusoe in northern America. It should appeal particularly to children, for whom it was written, and if the entertaining digressions respecting the author's pets be forgiven or skipped, the rest of the book will be found capital reading. The note of humour in Dumas, which appears first in this book and in " Maître Adam," is not too frequently present in his later works.

Yet it is rather gaiety than any other quality which pervades the only attempt at story-telling made by Dumas during 1841 and 1842. It may be remembered that he was busy writing his three comedies for the Théâtre Français at this time, and also his " Impressions de Voyage " in the south of France and Mediterranean. At Marseilles, Dumas and his friend Méry enjoyed an experience which each utilised in his own way. Hayward, in his essay on our author, says, " One of the most amusing stories composed by Dumas is 'La Chasse au Chastre,' in which he depicts the trials and perils into which a worthy professor of music is hurried, by the reckless pursuit of a field-fare." Gautier in one of his books refers to " that *chastre*, whose adventures Dumas has told so vivaciously and wittily." The two authors heard the story from the lips of the unfortunate musician himself, and "de Mirecourt's" assertion that Dumas stole the tale from Méry is disproved by that writer in the preface to his own version.

"Le Chateau d'Eppstein" or "Albine" was the outcome of a social gathering at Florence in 1841, and was told to Dumas and the company by one of the guests. That is our author's explanation: his "commentators" declare "Albine" to be a story of the Rhineland (title and author not given). "Jacquot sans Oreilles"—not, one is disappointed to find, a pillorying of M. "de Mirecourt"—was similarly "supplied" to Dumas by an officer whose acquaintance he made during his Russian travels in 1858. The "Aventures de Lyderic" which appeared in 1842, is the story of Siegfried, made familiar to the public by Wagner.

We now enter upon the most important period of our author's career as a writer of romance. Up to this time he has possessed some very praiseworthy ideals, but has failed to devote much care—except, perhaps, in the case of "Acté"—to the realisation of them. We have seen him displaying wit and humour, skill in picturesque narrative, and his native sense of the dramatic, but all without any very definite aim. He had vowed, he tells us, to write the history of France in fiction, but, as we have seen, he had made little progress.

At this juncture the great man made the acquaintance of an unknown, unappreciated writer, named Auguste Maquet. The latter wrote a short story, in which he had great faith, and had the mortification of seeing it refused by an editor. Let Charles Reade (who supplies these details, in his " Eighth Commandment ") take up the story :

"As Maquet paced the boulevards, smarting, he met Dumas, who asked him if he had nothing ' by him.'

" 'I have only the " Bonhomme Buvat," ' said Maquet, sorrowfully.

" Dumas pricked up his ears. 'That is a good title,' he said. ' Come, tell me something about your " Bonhomme." '

" Maquet glowed, and poured out a part of his story.

" 'That will do : send me the manuscript,' said Dumas. ' I am off to Italy to-night.'

" Dumas took the 'Buvat' with him, worked on him, and in a few weeks it came out and charmed all Europe as the ' Chevalier d'Harmental.' "

"And then," adds Reade, " began that intellectual alliance to which the world owes the most brilliant romances of the century."

The episode of "The good-man Buvat" will be remembered by readers of this romance (known also as "The Conspirators"). It is a clever piece of character-drawing, but has only a slight connection with the main plot. The Cellemare conspiracy has provided the principal theme.

This is one of the best of Dumas's stories, and is not yet fully appreciated. Thackeray refers to it admiringly in his "Roundabout Papers"; and Mr. Saintsbury commends it as the most perfect of its author's novels in form—for unhappily Dumas was not always particular about unity and completeness. The contrast between the witty, voluptuous society of the Regency and the fresh, innocent life of Bathilde, is admirable in taste and effect. Captain Roquefinette is the first (off the stage) of the adventurers who occupy such a large place in Dumas's gallery of portraits. He dies finely, too, as do his comrades who come after him—Porthos, D'Artagnan, Maison-Rouge, La Mole, "Morgan," Bannière, and the rest.

"Une Fille du Régent," a sequel to the "Chevalier," was published two or three years later by the same collaborators. It contains one entertaining episode (treating of the Cellamare conspirators, and their life in the Bastille); but it is the plot of

"D'Harmenthal" again, with judicious variations. Worse still, there is a gloomy note of fatalism throughout the whole story. Nevertheless, "Une Fille du Régent" is well worth reading, if only for the study of Dubois, the Regent's minister, which shows Dumas's talent for intrigue at its best.

"Georges," which also dates from 1843, is a story of Mauritius, or the "Ile de France," and is probably the work of our author in combination with some "'prentice" who knew the colony. This may or may not have been Mallefille, to whom the credit of the whole work has charitably been given. But the hero, who suffers social ostracism for the black blood in his veins; the hero, who allows nothing to stand between himself and his desires— in short, "Dumas-Antony,"—betrays his origin unmistakably. With the struggle between the French and English for that tropical paradise the novelist has interwoven a revolt of the slaves, told with great dramatic force and truth, and a love story.

"Cécile," or "La Robe de Noce," is chiefly interesting as affording a first glimpse, in the author's writings, of the days of Revolution, afterwards to be turned to such full and effective account. So popular was this pathetic story that two pirated editions were issued in Belgium in the course of a few months. "Cécile" dates from "the great year," 1844, as does "Fernande," which has been claimed by M. Hippolyte Auger as at least half his own. It is impossible to test the truth of that author's assertions at this remote date, so that the degree of blame—if any—which can attach to Dumas cannot now be measured, but we may add that we believe the story is not the great writer's. "Amaury" was also published about this time, and Dumas gives an account of its origin in which he disavows the authorship; but it may or may not be genuine, for he always delighted in this form of mystification. It is probably true that M. Paul Meurice wrote the story with Dumas, for the style is not our author's. He has told us, however, that it was suggested by the case of his friend Felix Deviolaine, who was consumptive, and who, happily, recovered; but in the story Madeleine D'Avrigny is not cured, and so faithful and poignant was the description of the malady's progress that one M. Noailles, whose daughter was also suffering from the disease, appealed to the author to suspend the serial publication of "Amaury," if Madeleine was meant to die. The *feuilleton* was therefore suspended until after the poor girl's death, and the kind-hearted Dumas went so far as to improvise in manuscript a miraculous recovery and happy fate for the poor heroine, for the especial benefit of the doomed girl and her husband.

One of the best of Dumas's minor romances is that of "Sylvandire," at one time known in England as "Beau Tancrède." Its historical interest is slight, but it affords a glimpse of the court of Louis XIV. in his latter days, under the domination of Madame de Maintenon. Chronologically "Sylvandire" precedes the "Chevalier d'Harmenthal," and possesses many of the merits of that romance. It has little or nothing of the pretty sentiment of Bathilde's love story, but instead, is told with much ironic humour.

M. About, at the unveiling of the Dumas statue in Paris, told a story of M. Sarcey, who was in the same class at school with a little Spanish boy. The child was homesick; he could not eat, he could not sleep; he was almost in a decline.

"You want to see your mother?" said young Sarcey.

"No: she is dead."

"Your father, then?"

"No: he used to beat me."

"Your brothers and sisters?"

"I have none."

"Then why are you so eager to be back in Spain?"

"To finish a book I began in the holidays."

"And what was its name?"

"'Los Tres Mosqueteros!'"

"He was homesick for 'The Three Musketeers' (says Mr. Lang), "and they cured him easily."

That boy would almost seem to have been the young Castelar, the great Spanish orator, statesman, and author, for he has written of the famous story in manner quite as fervent:

"I can never forget the impression left upon my mind by the reading of that book. The characters are life-like, and stand out in such high relief, that I seemed to see them, to speak to them, to distinguish their features and manners, and even to compare them with real persons among my acquaintances. So absorbing was my interest in the story, that I watched for each new number with feverish impatience, to read the end of these adventures, as if they were intimately connected with some one beloved, with my former friends, with my nearest relations, with my own soul. . . . That exciting narrative; that flashing style; those characters, so boldly described; those scenes, so marvellously woven together; that ever-increasing interest in the story—all this worked upon my imagination, and by the magic of art the fictitious world was changed into the world of truth and poetry, and became as real as society or as nature."

Is there any man who has not read "The Three Musketeers"? It has become one of the world's books. As Méry, Dumas's fast friend, jestingly put it,

"If there exists a second Robinson Crusoe in any part of the world at this moment, be sure that the exile is whiling away his solitude reading 'Les Trois Mousquetaires,' under the shade of his parrot-feathered umbrella."

In his preface to the romance, Dumas has confessed the chief source of his inspiration—Courtils de Sandraz's "Mémoires de D'Artagnan," which in turn was probably more than half-fiction, although, of course, a soldier of that name lived, fought, sinned, and died in those times. "I think I like D'Artagnan in his own 'Mémoires' best," wrote Thackeray. Mr Lang does not agree with him, nor, if we may add our testimony, do we. To read the "Mémoires" and then the romance is to undergo a revelation. Mingled with this sordid story of closet-intrigue and kitchen-amours, Dumas, with his keen scent for the picturesque, found excellent material for a splendid story; and his admirable taste is shown not only in what has been utilised, but in what has been omitted. Only one questionable incident has been employed, and that because it has an important bearing on the plot of the romance and its sequel. "It has passed through a medium, as Dumas himself declared, of natural delicacy and good taste." These chapters about Kitty and Miladi, Sir Herbert Maxwell reminds us, in his article on "The Real D'Artagnan," did not escape their author's criticism.

"It is told that Dumas in after-life expressed

bitter regret that the said episode had not been omitted, with the rest of like nature; and there is evidence given by M. E. de Goncourt of how greatly Dumas differed in taste on these matters from less scrupulous French writers. M. de Goncourt tells us that he once heard Victor Hugo declare that, had he not been above filching from other authors, he must have yielded to the temptation to appropriate the story of 'Ketty,' '*et de lui donner une forme d'art.*' 'Think,' exclaimed Hugo, 'of the marvellously human *dénoûment*, far finer than any *dénoûment* of the utmost realism!'[1] It is not difficult to imagine to what luxuriance these materials might have blossomed, under the florid touch of Victor Hugo."

M. Parigot recommends students of Dumas to make the comparison between the romance and the "Mémoires," and judge for themselves how the man of imagination has glorified the material he worked on. "Dumas borrowed, but Dumas selected," he adds.

We may supplement this opinion with a short comparison of our own. Briefly, Dumas owes "D'Artagnan," first, the facts of the hero's life, so far as they concern history. All these are retained, and the famous character goes through the

[1] This incident is not to be found, as the reader will infer, in Dumas's romance.

very necessary process of renovation, elaboration, and elevation.

The names — and little else — of the three "brothers-in-war" are to be found in the "Mémoires." Athos, Porthos, and Aramis are but shadows, and the little that we do learn of them there is not exactly to their credit. They are actually brothers; whereas the romancer by making them brothers-in-heart gains enormously in effect.

Roughly speaking, Dumas has expanded, in the first six chapters of the "Mousquetaires," the opening chapters of "D'Artagnan." "The man of Meung," the hero's evil genius, was evidently suggested by an aristocrat named Rosnay, with whom the real D'Artagnan had an encounter early in his career, and who figures throughout as a coward, who endeavours to get D'Artagnan assassinated. In a later part of the "Mémoires" a hint is given that Louis XIII.'s Chancellor, Séguier, once attempted to take from the Queen a letter concealed upon her person. In "D'Artagnan" the letter was suspected to be from Spain, and political; in Dumas it was thought to be from Buckingham, Anne's secret lover. The most important extract from the "Mémoires" concerns "Miladi," and our author has borrowed freely from the young cadet's amour with the beautiful Englishwoman. The chapters describing the intrigue, D'Artagnan's rivalry with De Wardes, his subterfuges, and "affair" with the chambermaid, are mostly "fact"; but strange to say, Dumas entirely ignored the real beginning of this, D'Artagnan's greatest "passion."

The story is interesting. The musketeer had just returned from England (where he had fought with Charles at the battle of Newbury), when he was sent for by the exiled Queen, and questioned concerning his visit. The too-candid youth declared, in the course of the interview, that "he would as soon live with bears as with the English"; and this so deeply provoked one of the Queen's maids-of-honour, that she sent D'Artagnan, after the forward fashion of the time, an invitation to pay court to her. The soldier readily responded, and fell straightway in love. When, however, he at length avowed his passion, "Miladi" coolly informed him that she had acted thus in order to punish him for his abuse of her countrymen, and proceeded to mock him pitilessly. The story of his revenge is told by Dumas, to whose imagination, however, is due the incident of the *fleur-de-lis*, and all the tragic sequel.

These detailed comparisons may, perhaps, be more interestingly summed up in a few words. From the loose, casual jottings of a soldier, telling of his amours, his campaigns, and the politics of his day, Dumas extracted, by some wonderful mental process, a stirring and dramatic story, full of incident and character. Of the spiteful wanton "Miladi" he made a powerful and tragic figure; and the three names Athos, Porthos, and Aramis, in his hands, assumed individualities and became immortal. The whole plot concerning the Queen's studs, the sad story of Constance Bonacieux, the tragedy of Fenton and Buckingham—all these were either devised in the French novelist's fertile brain, or skilfully introduced by him into the framework provided for him by the "Mémoires." After the first six chapters (of which the dialogue, wit, and character-drawing were wholly his own), Dumas launched out for himself, and the plot begins.

Our author, too, makes use in this and subsequent romances, of Madame de la Fayette's "Histoire d'Henriette d'Angleterre," and also of the court chroniques of the time, omitting to avail himself of their most scandalous passages. He borrows from La Porte's memoirs the incident of Bonacieux's abduction; he finds the faint outline of his episode of the Bastion St Gervais, in an account of a scene at the siege of Casal in 1630. To Maquet probably belongs the credit of discovering these picturesque incidents; to Dumas the glory of giving them colour, shape, and life on his great canvas.

Of the other source of information—the "Mémoires

de M. le Comte de la Fère," nothing can be said here, for a very excellent reason. When Dumas had the audacity to ask at the Bibliothèque Royale for that book, the librarian retorted, "You know that it doesn't exist, because you yourself have said it does!" Indeed, the good man's sharpness was natural; since the publication of the "Mousquetaires" he had been appealed to perpetually for the book, by readers eager for "more"!

Mr Saintsbury complains that there is no central idea in " Les Trois Mousquetaires," and indeed there are at least two main plots. Professor Carpenter even analyses the story into

" A series of smaller tales (they are more like plays), each a hundred pages or so in length. In ' Les Trois Mousquetaires" the main problem is this, How can four adventurers, by their combined force, outwit *The Cardinal* and all his powers, temporal and spiritual? Viz. (1) How can a friendless and awkward but dashing young Gascon become in three days the talk of Paris and a sworn companion of the best three blades in the city? (2) The *Queen's* honour is at stake; how can this band of brothers fetch her jewels from England in time? (3) *D'Artagnan* is fascinated by *Milady*: how can his reckless passion be turned to hate and fear? (4) *Milady*, with good reason, is determined on *D'Artagnan's* death, *Richelieu* on *Buckingham's* assassination: how can both catastrophes be averted? (5) *Milady* is a prisoner in England: how can she escape and murder *Buckingham*? (6) How can the 'brothers' avenge their wrongs on *Milady*, and avoid the punishment of the *Cardinal*, whose agent she is?"

But it is obviously wrong to treat a book of adventure as if it were an ordinary novel. We do not expect a central plot in "Don Quixote," "Robinson Crusoe," or "Gil Blas."

Every lover of the "Mousquetaires" has his own particular hero, in one of the famous four. Thackeray, for instance, writes:

"Of your heroic heroes, I think our friend Monseigneur Athos, Count de la Fère, is my favourite. I have read about him from sunrise to sunset with the utmost contentment of mind. He has passed through how many volumes? Forty? Fifty? I wish, for my part, there were a hundred more, and would never tire of him rescuing prisoners, punishing ruffians, and running scoundrels through the midriff with his most graceful rapier. Ah! Athos, Porthos, and Aramis, you are a magnificent trio."

Stevenson had a weakness for Porthos. "If," he wrote to a friend, "by any sacrifice of my own literary baggage I could clear the 'Vicomte de Bragelonne' of Porthos, *Jekyll* might go, and the

Master, and the *Black Arrow*, you may be sure, and I should think my life not lost for mankind if half a dozen more of my volumes must be thrown in."

Dumas himself shared this feeling. The great, strong, vain hero was a child after his own heart. One afternoon his son, seeing him looking careworn, wretched, overwhelmed, asked him,

"What has happened to you? Are you ill?"

"No."

"Well, what is it then?"

"I am miserable."

"Why?"

"This morning, I killed Porthos—poor Porthos! Oh what trouble I have had, to make up my mind to do it! But there must be an end to all things. Yet when I saw him sink beneath the ruins, crying 'It is too heavy, too heavy for me!' I swear to you that I cried."

And he wiped away a tear with the sleeve of his dressing-gown.

We have glided insensibly into "Vingt Ans Après" and the "Vicomte de Bragelonne," for it is the D'Artagnan of this last of the series whom Stevenson has so eloquently proclaimed as his hero. In his essay "On a Romance of Dumas's" in "Memories and Portraits," he writes of him thus:

"It is in the character of D'Artagnan, that we

D'ARTAGNAN. FROM THE DUMAS MONUMENT.

must look for that spirit of morality, which is one of the chief merits of the book, makes one of the main joys of its perusal, and sets it high above more popular rivals. Athos, with the coming of years, has declined too much into the preacher, and the preacher of a sapless creed; but D'Artagnan has mellowed into a man so witty, rough, kind and upright, that he takes the heart by storm. There is nothing of the copybook about his virtues, nothing of the drawing-room in his fine, natural civility; he will sail near the wind; he is no district visitor—no Wesley or Robespierre; his conscience is void of all refinement whether for good or evil; but the whole man rings true like a good sovereign. I do not say there is no character as well-drawn in Shakespeare; I do say there is none that I love so wholly. There are many spiritual eyes that seem to spy upon our actions—eyes of the dead and the absent, whom we imagine to behold us in our most private hours, and whom we fear and scruple to offend; our witnesses and judges. And among these, even if you should think me childish, I must count my D'Artagnan—not the D'Artagnan of the memoirs, whom Thackeray pretended to prefer—a preference, I take the freedom of saying, in which he stands alone—not the D'Artagnan of flesh and blood, but him of the ink and paper; not Nature's but Dumas's."

One secret of the charm of the four musketeers is perhaps to be found in the fact that they stand for types of the great national characteristics. Says Parigot:

"D'Artagnan, the adroit Gascon, caressing his moustache; Porthos, the muscular and foolish; Athos, the somewhat romantic 'grand seigneur,' Aramis, who pinches his ear to make it red,—Aramis, the discreet Aramis, who hides his religion and his amours, able pupil of the good fathers—these four friends, and not four brothers as Courtils imagined, typify the four cardinal qualities of our country. . . . If Danton and Napoleon were the prototypes of French energy, Dumas, in 'Les Trois Mousquetaires' is its national historian. His romance is quite as dramatic as theirs, but more pleasant, and with a more continuous charm."

The origin of the two sequels has already been partly indicated. It is said that Dumas *fils*, frightened at the thought of the prodigious task which the rash author set himself, asked his father

"In spite of the help of Madame de La Fayette, who furnishes you with the name and first-love of Athos's son, how will you manage to keep up the interest through these innumerable volumes?"

"Oh, well," answered his father, "all that happened to Athos will happen over again to his son."

But (not for the first time) Dumas did himself an injustice. One has no feeling of repetition about "Bragelonne." If it is, as some critics assert, "full of improbabilities," it is yet very faithful to the chronicles of the court. "Those who rage about the far-fetched incidents," writes M. Parigot, "with which these romances of Dumas are simply crammed, make us smile. Have they never read the history written by Madame de La Fayette? And Guiche in the chimney? And the women spies? And the caskets of Malicorne? And the plots of de Wardes?"

The Trilogy of the Four is, after all, one great prose epic on friendship—the love of man for man. Professor Carpenter has seen this clearly, and expressed it well:

"So far as I am concerned there is no more poignant scene in literature than that in which, after twenty years of separation, the four who once were but a single will and a single force—hence, dauntless and invincible—found in the gloom of battle their swords clash on those of their peers, and realised that they were arrayed against each other. How paltry beside this seem lovers' quarrels! And yet there is nothing of the mock-heroic in Dumas's treatment of the famous friendship. These were men of clay, prone to vice and error, redeemed only by their sense of the sacredness of the strongest human tie, save that of family."

The same writer also notices with what unconscious skill the characters of the musketeers are developed:

"These men grow, not of the author's set purpose, in the ordinary fashion, according to a rule of logic, but as men grow in life, naturally. He (Dumas) could not have planned it; at the proper time he simply knew it. The *Athos*, the *Porthos*, the *Aramis*, and the *D'Artagnan* of 'Le Vicomte de Bragelonne" are not those of 'Les Trois Mousquetaires,' or even of 'Vingt Ans Après.' But the author does not inform us of it, except in a single case, and then he is evidently as surprised as we are. They grow, and if they are honest men they grow better, on stepping-stones of their own baser selves. . . . These novels show more than the growth of man. They represent the slow development of a race and nation. Like Gibbon or Michelet, Dumas had a genius for history. France under Charles IX. and Henry III., France under Louis XIV., France in the Revolution—he knew them, and felt them to the core. His chronology may be weak and his facts faulty, the young doctor of philosophy may find flaws in every chapter, but the great laws he follows, so far as I can see: the types are sound."

ALEXANDRE DUMAS

Let us limit ourselves to the quotation of two passages from Stevenson, endorsing this opinion. He is still writing of "my dear 'Vicomte,'" as he called him:

"What other novel has such epic variety and nobility of incident? Often, if you will, impossible; often of the order of an Arabian story; and yet all based in human nature? Not studied with the microscope, but seen largely, in plain daylight, with the natural eye? What novel has more good sense, and gaiety, and wit, and unflagging, admirable literary skill? And once more, to make an end of commendations, what novel is inspired with a more unstrained or a more wholesome morality? There is no quite good book without a good morality; but the world is wide, and so are morals. . . . And above all, in this last volume, I find a singular charm of spirit. It breathes a pleasant and a tonic sadness, always brave, never hysterical. Upon the crowded, noisy life of this long tale, evening gradually falls, and the lights are extinguished, and the heroes pass away one by one. One by one they go, and not a regret embitters their departure; the young succeed them in their places, Louis Quatorze is swelling larger and shining broader, another generation and another France dawn on the horizon; but for us and these old men whom we have loved so long, the inevitable end draws near and is welcome. To read this well is to anticipate experience. Ah, if only, when these hours of the long shadows fall for us in reality and not in figure, we may hope to face them with a mind as quiet."

One day, about two years before his death, Dumas's son found him with a book.

" What are you reading? " he asked.

" ' Les Trois Mousquetaires.' I always promised myself that I would read it when I was an old man, so that I might be able to judge of its merit."

"Well, what do you think of it?"

" It is good."

Some days later the same thing occurred again, only this time it was another of his own books—" Monte Cristo."

" What do you think of it? " asked the son once more.

" Pah! It isn't as good as the 'Mousquetaires!'"[1]

Nevertheless " Monte Cristo," published in the same year as the " Mousquetaires," rivalled, and still

---

[1] It is interesting to note that there was announced, in the "Mousquetaire" (1853), a romance, "Le Maréchal Ferrant," in 4 vols., "a sequel to the D'Artagnan Cycle." We know that in those days it was a frequent practice to announce books before they were written. What would not such an MS. be worth now, if it could be discovered? The so-called "Stories by Dumas"—"Monte Cristo and his Wife," and "The Son of Porthos"—are, of course, forgeries and find no place in Calmann-Lévy's authorised edition.

rivals the other in popularity. The two romances were in point of fact written with great rapidity. Charles Reade's comment on the fact is amusing:

"This phenomenon astounded costive writers, and set them uttering, by way of solution, old wives' fables that turned the wonder into an impossibility. The account the authors themselves (Dumas and Maquet) gave was the only credible one. These works were flung off by even collaboration of two most inventive and rapid writers. Some of the work was written in almost less time than a single hand could have transcribed it. I believe they still show at Trouville, in a fisherman's cottage, the chamber and table where the pair wrote the first four volumes of 'Monte Cristo' in sixteen days.'"

According to the amiable Quérard (inspired by the equally kindly "de Mirecourt") "Monte Cristo" was written, the first half by Fiorentino, the second by Maquet. "It was so simple to believe I was the author, that they never even thought of it," says Dumas banteringly. He has given us his own account of the genesis of the book, in his "Causeries." We know already how the story got its "local habitation and its name"; and the evolution of the plot is no less interesting.

Towards 1843 Dumas had agreed with a firm of publishers to supply them with eight volumes of

"Impressions de Voyage" through Paris, the idea being a perambulatory tour of the city from barrier to barrier, anecdotic, historic, archæological and above all, picturesque. But Sue had just written his "Mysteries of Paris," and the publishers, anxious to imitate the success of that book, modified their idea and demanded a story in which Paris should be the background merely. Dumas bethought him of an anecdote, twenty pages long, from the "Police devoilée" of Peuchet, entitled, "La Diamant et La Vengeance," of which he had made a mental note. The story itself he declares was *tout simplement idiot*, but it contained the germ of an idea.

The first outline of the book was no more than this—that a very rich nobleman, living in Rome, and called the Count of Monte Cristo, should render a great service to a young French traveller, and should beg him, when that gentleman desires to repay the kindness, to act as the Count's guide when he, in his turn, should visit Paris. Vengeance had inspired this thought, and when Monte Cristo "did" the French capital he was to discover enemies who were hidden there—his enemies, who had condemned him in his youth to ten years of captivity. His fortune was to furnish the Count with the means of revenge.

At this point Dumas acquainted Maquet (who, as we know, was his literary partner at the time) with the plot, and the assistant at once pointed out that "the master" was passing by the most interesting part of the story—the prologue, in which should be told not only how those enemies betrayed the Count in his youth, but also the story of his years in prison. From that moment the story developed: Dumas seized the idea, took for his text three cities—Marseilles, Rome, Paris—and the romance was made.

"Monte Cristo" owed part of its enormous success to its verisimilitude. The details were most convincing, and had, indeed, been studied on the spot.

"There is one thing I cannot do," Dumas tells us, in his preface to the "Compagnons de Jehu," " I cannot write a book or a drama about localities I have never seen. To write 'Christine' I went to Fontainebleau; to write 'Henri III.' I went to Blois; to write 'Les Trois Mousquetaires' I went to Bethune and Boulogne; to write 'Monte Cristo' I returned to the Catalans and the Chateau d'If. This gives such a character of truth to what I write that the personages I plant in certain places seem to grow there, and some people have been led to think they have actually existed; in fact, there are persons who say they have known them. I do not wish to injure worthy family-men who live by the little industry, but if you go to Marseilles they will show you Morel's house on the Cours, Mercedès' house at the Catalans, and the dungeons of Dantès and Faria at the Chateau D'If. When brought out 'Monte Cristo' at the Théâtre Historique I wrote to Marseilles for a drawing of the Chateau D'If, which they sent me. I wanted it for the scene-painter. The artist to whom I had written not only sent me the sketch, but he did more than I had ventured to ask of him; he wrote underneath it: 'View of the Chateau D'If, on the side from which Dantès was flung.' I have heard since that a worthy fellow, a guide attached to the Chateau D'If, sells pens of fish-bones made by the Abbé Faria himself."

One anecdote among many, will illustrate the fascination which this book possesses for its readers. *The Academy* not so long ago quoted an amusing passage from a speech made by Lord Salisbury at a literary gathering. The Prime Minister humorously told how once at Sandringham, he was surprised by his host, at half-past four one morning, reading his favourite book "Monte Cristo." The prince wished to know the name of the book which had dragged the Premier from his bed at such an hour. Three weeks after he confessed to his guest that the same romance had lured him from his bed that morning half-an-hour earlier still!

"'Monte Cristo,'" says Mr Lang, "has the best

beginning—and loses itself in the sands." There is a good deal of truth in this: some of us believe that Dumas's reputation suffers rather than gains by being so prominently associated with a romance, parts of which are undeniably dull. Mr Saintsbury declares the second part to be too "Balzac-like." But even admitting this, admitting also that the omnipresent count is not altogether the perfect gentleman his creator seems to have thought him; and that his appearances and disappearances are ultra-theatrical at times; yet, there is a grandeur of conception about "Monte Cristo" which more than redeems it from these drawbacks. It is Dumas's "Misérables," and the lesson it teaches—"Vengeance is mine, saith the Lord"—is taught so effectively, so honestly, and on so great a scale, that the book has a moral value which should preserve it from oblivion for generations to come.

"Ascanio" is variously said to date from this year or the previous one. It was suggested by Benvenuto Cellini's autobiography, wherein one or two of the most improbable incidents of the story are to be found, notably the employment of the head of the sculptor's gigantic statue as a hiding-place. The reader is introduced to François I., the monarch of Pavia, and the intrigues of his court, which as usual with Dumas are cleverly manipulated to attract and absorb the reader. It should be added that our author in his "Causeries" tells of a flattering and unexpected sequel to this book. It so inspired a poor potter of Bourg-en-bresse with an ambition to emulate its hero, that he studied and worked until from artisan he developed into an artist. Meurice is said to have been the collaborator in this instance.

"Gabriel Lambert" is the last chief product of this extraordinary year. Dumas professes that this story is true, and that he has met and spoken with the chief personages. "Gabriel Lambert" recalls "Richard Darlington," with a difference, for this novel is less a story of unscrupulous ambition, than a study of cowardice, made with a touch of that poignant realism which has since become so popular.

The "forties" proved the most brilliant and most productive period of Dumas the novelist. In 1845, the year following his great double triumph, the author produced (in addition to "Une Fille de Régent" and "Vingt Ans Après," already mentioned) "La Reine Margot," "La Guerre des Femmes" (or "Nanon"), and "Les Frères Corses."

First of the Valois romances as was "La Reine Margot," we must not forget that the success of "Henri Trois et sa Cour" many years before, had given the author a love for this historical period. The fatal passion of St Mégrin is repeated in the

ALEXANDRE DUMAS

ill-fated devotion of La Mole. The great personages of history here are drawn boldly, and with seeming carelessness, but how human they are—how full of character and life! The Charles IX. of history, as Parigot testifies, is not "betrayed" by the Charles of romance; the portrait of Catherine de Medici, if somewhat overdrawn, is full of that Italian guile with which the records credit her, and the frank, ingenuous, supple-minded Béarnais, Henri of Navarre, is one of the triumphs of Dumas's vivifying genius. The intrigue of the romance is full of absorbing interest: Will Henri of Navarre become King of France? Will Catherine be able to prevent him from reaching the throne? And with this, other threads are interwoven: the Huguenot-Catholic plots, the brotherly love of La Mole and Coconnas, these in turn being interspersed with those terrible episodes, the massacre of St Bartholomew, and the reading of the poisoned book:[1]

Yet, throughout "La Reine Margot" our "haphazard" author (the words belongs to his critics) has exercised a double restraint: he neither harrows the reader unbearably nor does he take advantage of the scandalous facts which informal history affords, relating to the court of the Valois. Mr Lang, in

---

[1] We would advise our readers to compare the romance with "The House of the Wolf" or "Count Hannibal" by Weyman, and the "Chronique du Régne de Charles IX." by Merimée.

his "Letters to Dead Authors" notes this judicious quality in our author. "In these romances," he says, apostrophising Dumas, "how easy it would have been for you to burn incense to that great goddess, Lubricity, whom our critic says your people worship. You had Brantôme, you had Tallemant, you had Retif, and a dozen others, to furnish materials for scenes of voluptuousness and of blood that would have outdone even present *naturalistes*. From these alcoves of 'Les Dames Galantes,' from the torture chambers (M. Zola would not have spared us one starting sinew of brave La Mole on the rack) you turned, as Scott would have turned, without a thought of their profitable literary uses. You had other metal to work on: you gave us that superstitious and tragical true love of La Mole's, that devotion—how tender and how pure!—of Bussy for the Dame de Montsoreau. You gave us the valour of D'Artagnan, the strength of Porthos, the melancholy nobility of Athos: Honour, Chivalry, and Friendship."

"La Guerre des Femmes," a story of the Fronde, and therefore contemporary with "Vingt Ans Après," is easily recognised as another of the romances in which Maquet had his share. Probably it owes its position in the second class to its sad, its fatalistic atmosphere. But "La Guerre des Femmes" has many merits: it develops rapidly, neatly, to its end, and Cavagnac and Canolles, like La Mole and Coconnas, are worthy of a place not far below those famous friends-to-the-death, the Musketeers.

Dumas's admiration for the historical plays of Shakespeare was chiefly owing to the skill with which the dramatist fused history into fiction and fiction into history, so that only the most expert eye could tell where the one ended and the other began. The little novel, "Les Frères Corses," possesses this virtue. It is obviously, as its author asserts, the result of his travels in Corsica; but it is equally certain that the supernatural element is beyond the credible and actual. Although the story forms a strikingly dramatic episode it hardly possesses the merits to which its popularity in England would seem to entitle it. Dumas himself, though much given to staging his novels, never made a play of the "Frères Corses,"[1] but two or three different versions were played simultaneously in London, and the craze gave rise to various burlesques on the theme.

In the following year, 1846, Dumas's publishers issued a remarkable advertisement respecting our author, which Mr Fitzgerald asserts (without advancing proof) to be written by the novelist himself. It offers the public Dumas's works "in a new shape"

[1] See Appendix C.

and at a uniformly low price. It proclaims the author as still young and in "wonderfully good health"; and declares that his unceasing flow of invention and *esprit* will in all probability add forty volumes a year to his already large library.

There seemed, indeed, every prospect that this extraordinary pledge would be fulfilled. The next few years brought their quota of lengthy and more or less famous romances, and " Le Chevalier de Maison Rouge" dates from 1846.

This epilogue to the series of novels dealing with the French Revolution was in reality the first to appear. The *raison d'être* of the book, which is full of revolutionary spirit, is easily explained in this instance, for France was beginning to feel the throes of that political upheaval, which was destined two years later to result in the Second Republic.

M. Blaze de Bury tells an anecdote respecting this story, which explains the rapidity with which our author worked:

" Dumas asserted that the actual writing of a book or a play was nothing to him—the conception, form, arrangement, and development of the theme, comprised all the difficulties. These once settled, the hand could go forward 'by itself.' One day some one avowed the very opposite. The romancist, who was preparing 'Maison Rouge' at this time, wagered with his opponent that he would write the first book in seventy-two hours, inclusive of time for sleep and meals. A bet of a hundred louis was made and recorded: to complete the volume [1] seventy-five great sheets were to contain forty-five lines of fifty letters each. In sixty-six hours Dumas filled them in his beautiful handwriting, without an erasure, thus gaining six hours on the specified time."

The incidents of the story, strange as they seem, were amply justified by history. Once again Dumas was "speaking by the book." M. Parigot suggests that "unbelievers" should compare the romance with M. Lenôtre's erudite work on the original hero; "Vrai Chevalier de Maison Rouge—A. D. J. Gonze de Rougeville, 1761-1814." "If I am not mistaken," he adds, "you will admire the discretion of our author, no less than his modesty." M. de Bury, in an appreciation of this romance, especially praises its creator for respecting and doing justice to the characters of Marie Antoinette and Madame Elizabeth, and adds that in spite of his republican sentiments, which he never loses an opportunity of expressing, Dumas gives those personages exactly their true sympathetic and historical value.

Even more famous than the "Chevalier de

[1] In the original editions of Dumas's works, there were at least twice as many volumes as in the present one-franc series—hence occasional discrepancies on this point.

Maison Rouge" is the second Valois romance, which appeared the same year—"La Dame de Monsoreau," commonly known in England as "Chicot the Jester." Dumas had already made acquaintance with Bussy D'Amboise, the *mignon* of the Duc d'Alençon in the old chroniclers, introduced him into "Henri Trois," and utilised the story of his assassination, as given in Anquetil, for the *dénoûment* of his tragedy. But in history the lady was on the side of the husband; our story-weaver turned her affections in the other direction, and the romance became at once sympathetic and moving. (A writer has taken the trouble to compile a book on the "historical inaccuracies" of this romance. Dumas knew quite well when it was wise to reconvey the spirit of the age, and ignore the form.) Critics have agreed that there are few finer historical portraits in fiction than that of Henri III., the effeminate, superstitious king, devoted to luxury and the most trivial pleasures. The sardonic Chicot, the Rabelaisian monk Gorenflot, the chivalrous and devoted Bussy, are three splendid additions to Dumas's picture-gallery. For the truth or untruth of detail in these stories it is probably only fair to praise or blame Maquet. We learn that a descendant of St Luc (one of the minor characters of the book) took umbrage at the description of that courtier, and brought an action, to prove that his ancestor was not one of Henri's *mignons*. The trial showed the collaborators to be right, even in this trifling respect!

The closing scene of the book—the death of Bussy—draws this warm tribute from Mr Lang:

"I know four good fights of one against a multitude. These are the Death of Gretir the Strong, the Death of Gunnar of Lithend, the Death of Hereward the Wake, and the Death of Bussy D'Amboise."

"Le Bâtard de Mauléon," or "The Half-Brothers," was written, as we know by a passage in the "Histoire de mes Bêtes," in the château of Monte Cristo, by Dumas and Maquet; and the dog Mouton, a new recruit for the menagerie of the "palace," was woven into the story by his master. The scene on this occasion is laid in Spain, in the days of Du Guesclin and the Black Prince; and those interested in comparing the methods of romancists should read Dr Doyle's "White Company," which is of the same period, and into which many of the same characters are introduced. Froissart's chronicles formed the base for Dumas's story, and even Agénor de Mauléon himself is to be found in the pages of the old chronicler. In spite of some "purple passages," however—Mr Saintsbury instances Du Guesclin's negotiations with the Free Companies, and the battle of Najara—this story of the days of Don Pedro the Cruel has not the best qualities of its author, for which, perhaps, we may blame the uncongenial time and place. Quérard states that the end is wholly Maquet's.

There remains for 1846 "Les Deux Diane," which, if a certain letter from Dumas be not a forgery, was entirely the work of M. Paul Meurice. It is probable, however, that the plot is "the master's." The style is certainly not Dumas's, being entirely sentimental, and the romance is said to have been suggested by "Une Fille Naturelle," by one Félix Davin.

Our readers will remember that in the autumn of this year Dumas departed hurriedly for Madrid, accompanied, it is true, by Maquet, but bent upon pleasure-seeking and the pursuit of material for further "Impressions de Voyage." "Joseph Balsamo" ("The Memoirs of a Physician"), which was appearing serially, suddenly suspended publication, leaving young Gilbert, the hero, lying senseless in the road whilst his thoughtless creator "did" Spain and Algeria. The unfortunate youth remained in this inconvenient position until Dumas restored him to life on his return. This suspension of consciousness suggests the magnetic trances of which our author so frequently makes use in this story. He has told us (in "Bric-à-Brac") that he experimented in mesmerism at the time that he was preparing to write "Balsamo," and that he succeeded in "putting to sleep" one of his servants, who then became *clairvoyant*. However much truth there may be in this, there is no doubt that "magnetic influence," or telepathy, is very ingeniously employed to give the charlatan Balsamo (or Cagliostro) his supposed supernatural powers.

For the rest the romance, if somewhat formless, is full of a number of varied intrigues and interests. We meet the king's mistress, Madame Dubarry, and learn how, in spite of all opposition, she managed to get presented at Court. We enjoy once more the witty society of Dumas's favourite libertine, the Duc de Richelieu, whom we met, in earlier years, in "Mademoiselle de Bellisle," and view Louis Quinze himself *en famille*. The first faint rumblings of the coming thunder of the Revolution are heard; Marat appears on the scene; Rousseau is disappearing from it. Then there is the weird story of Balsamo's love for Lorenza, and that of Gilbert for Andrée de Tavernay—all are interwoven in this gigantic romance, which is itself only a beginning. Either because Dumas wearied of his interminable subject, or left it to Maquet to finish—possibly the lawsuit with the seven journals distracted the author's attention—the closing chapters are dull; but, on the whole, "Balsamo" contains some of his best work.

In 1847 came "Les Quarante-Cinq," the sequel to "La Dame de Monsoreau." It tells chiefly of that lady's revenge upon the treacherous D'Alençon (now D'Anjou), who has caused the death of her beloved Bussy. The part of the book in which Chicot goes on an embassy to Henri Quatre is excellent, but the last volume is unsatisfactory. This year, be it remembered, was a stormy one in public affairs, and disastrous to Dumas personally. He dictated the last chapters to his son, being probably ill in bed.

Notwithstanding this blemish, the "Quarante-Cinq" was a favourite with one of our author's firmest admirers—George Sand. M. Victor Borie has told us that he chanced to visit the famous novelist just before her death, and found the romance lying on her table. He expressed his wonder that she was reading it for the first time.

"For the first time," she exclaimed, "why, this is the fifth or sixth time I have read 'Les Quarante-Cinq,' and the others. When I am ill, anxious, melancholy, tired, discouraged, nothing helps me against moral or physical troubles like a book of Dumas's."

During the next two years—troublous ones for our novelist—the rate of production slackened. With the very notable exception of "Bragelonne," and some historical studies, the chief work of importance in 1849 was "Le Collier de la Reine" ("The Queen's Necklace"), a continuation of the history-in-romance of the Louis XVI. period. So much has been written by Carlyle, by Funck-Brentano and others, about this famous episode in the career of Marie Antoinette, that there is no need to describe it here. Dumas (still with the valuable assistance of Maquet) tells the story of that extraordinary scandal in his own fashion, carrying forward, as he does so, the other "motifs" mentioned already. The comparative non-success of this book is probably due to the fact that history left so little to the imagination. "Les Mille-et-un Fantômes," said by some to have been written with Paul Bocage, by others with "Bibliophile Jacob," appeared this year. It is in great part a gruesome debate as to whether a severed head can speak, or retains knowledge of itself after parting from the body, and dwells on other similar matters,—being, in short, a book calculated to "make your flesh creep."

Of a very different nature was "La Tulipe Noire," which appeared in 1850. This book—"as modest as a story by Miss Edgeworth," Thackeray declared enthusiastically—has recently been issued as Dumas's contribution to the series of translations known as a "Century of French Romance." The subject—or at least the historical part of it—is said to have been suggested to Dumas by the King of Holland. (The novelist visited Amsterdam in 1849 to be present at the wedding of the Prince of Orange, who had recently ascended the throne, and with whom he had a corresponding acquaintance.) The tale, as Flotow used to relate it, is as follows.

When the author of "Monte Cristo" was first presented to the king at Amsterdam, the royal host said:

"M. Dumas, you have written many brilliant stories dealing with distinguished Frenchmen; have you not found any Dutchmen worthy of your consideration?"

"Your Majesty, I have not had time to make the necessary researches."

"Oh! you need not trouble about that," replied the king, whose own life and courtship had tinges of romance, "I will tell you a story." And so the king related the incidents of 1672 and 1673, of the murder of the De Witts, and the imprisonment of Cornelius Van Baerle—all upon wicked and shamefully wrong charges. At the end of the description, Dumas exclaimed,

ALEXANDRE DUMAS

"What a fine subject for a novel!"

"Write it," said the king, and Dumas promptly answered

" I will."

The dramatised version of the story produced at the Haymarket, and the consequent popularity of the book itself will have made the plot generally familiar. This is another case in which English managers, who have so generally disdained Dumas's dramatic work, have adapted for the stage a book which even the skilled instinct of its author failed to find suitable for dramatic use.

"Les Mariages de Père Olifus," rather loosely described as "a sequel to the 'Mille-et-un Fantômes,'" is said to have been written with Paul Bocage, and was one of the results of the trip to Amsterdam mentioned above. It is an extraordinary work, and decidedly deserves much more attention than it has received at the hands of critics. From a letter with which Mr W. M. Rossetti has kindly favoured us, it appears that the story was specially liked by Dante Gabriel Rossetti, a great admirer of our author.

" If a question were raised as to particular novels (by Dumas) specially admired by my brother," he writes, "I could mention 'Monte Cristo,' 'Trois Mousquetaires,' 'Bragelonne,' 'Père Olifus,' 'Ingénue,' 'Les Quarante-Cinq,' I think also 'La

Tulipe Noire.' He was also vastly amused with Dumas's 'Mémoires.'"

The tale, which purports to have been confided to Dumas by Olifus himself, is too strange not to have had some such origin. As we read it, it is told with as much reticence as the exigencies of the story and the promptings of humour allow; but the adventures of the seaman with his "sea-wife" too closely resemble the style of the narratives of "The Arabian Nights" or "Boccaccio," to recommend themselves to a prudish translator.

For his next story Dumas went to German history, and chose the time when the patriotic secret society of the "Tugendbund" was conspiring to assassinate Napoleon and to throw off the French yoke. Probably with the help of a 'prentice who "knew his Germany," Dumas wrote "Le Trou de l'Enfer," a powerful, poignant story, of how a young Antony living, *à la* Schiller's "Robber," a life sufficient unto himself, strove successfully to possess a young goatherdess, and the wife of his best friend, for whom he had conceived a self-willed passion. "Dieu dispose," which Mr Swinburne considers to possess great merit, was written in Brussels in 1852. It tells of the retribution which gradually overtakes the seducer, and the reader follows the sure though tortuous course of Nemesis with the interest which Dumas himself rarely fails to arouse and reward. The Revolution of 1830, and the secret "freemasonry" agitations connected therewith, are touched upon; but the dramatic effect of the story is borrowed from the author's own play of "Comte Hermann," produced three years before. We have indicated the sources of the story's strength; its weakness lies in a husband's non-recognition of his wife, after years of separation.

"La Femme au Collier de Velours," which also dates from 1851, contains by way of introduction an interesting account of Dumas's literary patron, Charles Nodier, and the society at the Arsenal. The tale itself, which purports to have been told to the narrator by the dying Nodier, and of which Hoffmann, the author of "Contes Fantastiques," is the hero, is as weird as any story by the German Poe. Incidentally it introduces the guillotining of Madame Dubarry the mistress of Louis XV., and presents a realistic picture of life in Paris in '93.

This story is associated by Calmann-Lévy with another essay into the supernatural—"Le Testament de M. Chauvelin." That noble, who was historically one of Louis XV.'s roués, makes a will for the protection of his wife and children, which he neglects to sign. He dies suddenly, but is seen to return to his chateau, and the will is found, duly completed. Powerful as the story is, its chief value lies in the introduction, which gives us a glimpse of the writer's youth, and in the full and vivid description of the last days of Louis Quinze.

One of the books of Dumas which is destined to become more appreciated in the future than it has been in the past, is "Olympe de Clèves," which dates from 1852. It was written before he retired to Brussels, and Maquet is credited with a share in the work. We, for our part, believe that the extent of that writer's connection with this story begins—if it begins at all—and ends with the discovery of Lemazurier's biographies of the French actors, from which the career of Bannière is taken, and with the preparation of the historical material repecting the debauching of the young king, Louis Quinze. The charm of the story lies for once in the characters of the lovable hero and heroine, and the unhistorical parts of the book, describing the life of a strolling company of French actors, in the early eighteenth century. We should like to echo the sentiments of Mr W. E. Henley, who proclaims "Olympe de Clèves" a masterpiece.

Probably most readers of "Ange Pitou" (also known as "Taking the Bastille"), published in 1853, will have noticed that the story ends abruptly—that, in fact, it cannot be said to end at all. An anecdote told by M. Parigot offers an explanation of this. One day, it appears, Maquet, reader and explorer of the obscure, burst in upon Dumas with an idea for a new romance, to be founded on a real historical character, Ange Pitou, ballad-monger, Royalist, and the rest. (M. Maurice Engerrand has recently given us a brochure on this historical personage similar to the one written by M. Lenôtre on Rougeville, or "Maison Rouge.") The master bade his assistant prepare the usual material, that is to say, make researches, and reconstitute the man in his moral and historical atmosphere. On the strength of this project the romancer entered into a contract with publishers to write and supply the story. Luckily or unluckily, Dumas and Maquet quarrelled; the book had to be written by a certain date; the romancer, pressed for time, ignored research, and created his hero from his own imagination, locating him at Villers-Cotterets, giving him his own personal boyhood, and sending him to Paris to take part in the capture of the Bastille. Then, when the novel had reached the requisite length, he abandoned the work.

Dumas's own explanation, given in an introduction to "La Comtesse de Charny," is that just at that time the Chamber imposed a tax on every copy of those journals which contained a *feuilleton*; and that De Girardin, editor of the paper in which "Ange Pitou" appeared, wrote to Dumas bidding him cut the story short. Presumably the *timbre* was taken off soon after. Those readers who care to compare the early chapters of "Ange Pitou" with the first volumes of the "Mémoires" will find that the hero and his author possess many interesting points of resemblance and dissimilarity.

Here, so far as we can trace, ended the connection between Dumas and his best collaborator. It has been said that without Maquet our author was helpless. It is true that he was at his best with that admirable 'prentice; but it is none the less true that both before and after him, Dumas wrote books which none but he could have produced, whilst Maquet never achieved anything like the same degree of merit or success under his own name.

During his exile in Brussels (1851-3) Dumas, as he tells us in the preface to "Père Gigogne," was far from idle. He instances "Conscience l'Innocent" (or "L'Enfant"), "La Comtesse de Charny," "Le Pasteur d'Ashbourn," "Isaac Laquedem," "Catherine Blum," and a portion of his "Mémoires" as the result of two years' work, and adds "it will one day be a source of trouble for my biographers to discover the 'anonymous collaborators' who have written those books!"

It was about this time that the novelist turned from the romance of cap-and-sword, and devoted himself chiefly to semi-pastoral stories, to tales of contemporary, and often humble, life. In the opening passages of "Conscience" he dwells on this.

"As one gets on in life," he writes, "and, losing sight of the cradle, draws nigh to the tomb, it seems as if the invisible ties which bind one to one's birthplace grow stronger and more irresistible. . . . A man's life is divided into two distinct parts: the first thirty-five years are for hope; the second thirty-five, for memory. . . . That is why, instead of always breaking fresh ground in literary work, consulting solely the caprices of my fancy, the resources of my imagination, ever seeking new characters and conceiving new, unheard-of situations, I return at times, at least in thought, to that beaten track, my childhood, retracing those days to their earliest hours, looking back along the path I have trodden, back until I see my little feet as they kept pace with my dearly loved mother's—which have traversed life side by side with mine from the day when my eyes first opened, to the day when hers closed for ever."

We have seen how Dumas made use, in "Ange Pitou," of his recollections of childhood. The preparation of the "Mémoires" probably further stimulated him to utilise his recollections of life at Villers-Cotterets, as a "milieu" for these semi-pastoral stories. Therefore, when he read a little story by Hendrik Conscience, the Flemish novelist, called "Le Conscrit," in which a young peasant is "drawn" for the war, is blinded in action, is brought home by his sweetheart, and is finally restored to sight, Dumas saw in this novelette (as he tells us in "Bric-à-brac") the outline of a story after his own heart. He wrote to Conscience, asking permission to use this story as a basis, and this the flattered author readily granted. In order to acknowledge his indebtedness publicly Dumas gave the name of Conscience to the hero of his own story, which is a considerable elaboration on the original. Our author changed the locale to Villers-Cotterets, introduced his boyish recollections of Napoleon's flying visits to that village, indulged in a little contemporary history, made the love of the peasant for the land a powerful factor in the story, created Bastien, one of the leading characters, and gave to the new "Conscrit" many times the length and strength of the original.

"Catherine Blum," published in 1854, had a similar origin. It is said to have been suggested by Iffland's "Gardes Forestiers," but its charm lies in the description of the people and atmosphere of Villers-Cotterets, and in the simple art with which it is told. There is a pleasant portrait of Abbé Grégoire, one of the boy Alexandre's preceptors. Mr Swinburne tells us that amongst Dumas's minor works he admires chiefly this pair of pastoral pictures, "Conscience" and "Catherine Blum," and we believe that if they were known to the English-reading public his judgment would be generally confirmed.

When he wrote "Conscience" Dumas was waiting for a copy of Michelet's "French Revolution," in order to begin upon "La Comtesse de Charny" (1853-5). Professor G. C. Carpenter, a thoughtful critic of Dumas's genius and writings, gives an appreciation of this romance, touching also upon the secret sources of our author's success:

"He read memoirs avidly, for one thing; he had a marvellous heritage of race, that made other times akin to him; submerged in his under-consciousness, out of reach of will or reason, were wondrous stores of association; his own life was rich and varied; his sympathy was extraordinary. On all these sources he drew, in that madly rapid writing of his. And the result is that in his pages, as in an allegory, are all the elements essential to the nation's life. Among a score of others, three are not to be forgotten: the violated *Comtesse de Charny*, who was the wrecked aristocracy; the brutal peasant boy *Gilbert*, who represented the uprising of men long down-trodden; and their child, who was the new France."

"La Comtesse de Charny," which links "Ange Pitou" with the "Chevalier de Maison Rouge" and thus completes the Revolution cycle, is full of picturesque history, although it is perhaps too long; and the fictitious interest, apart from the character of the countess herself, who develops into one of Dumas's most life-like heroines, is not very engrossing. We regret to find that in some English translations the "epilogue" to "La Comtesse de Charny," in which Ange Pitou and Catherine are satisfactorily brought together, is omitted.

In this cycle of revolutionary romance, which begins with the "Mémoires du Médecin," and ends with "Le Chevalier de Maison Rouge," there are several unsatisfactory gaps. The reader will find a consecutive and vivid panorama of the events of 1792, 1793, and 1794, from the battles of Valmy and Jemappes to the fall of Robespierre, in "Le Docteur Mysterieux" and "La Fille du Marquis." These volumes bear evident traces of Dumas's hand, touching as they do upon the restoration of reason to the imbecile, the use of "magnetic power," and the sense of life after death, in the case of a guillotined head (see "Le Mille-et-une Fantômes"). There is an interesting thread of fiction, and a translation of scenes from "Romeo and Juliet" may attract the curious. Chincholle tells us that when he visited the author in 1869, he was completing the dictation of these volumes, which were not published in book-form until after his death.

"Ever since 1832," Dumas tells us in one of his frequent bursts of confidence, "I have had in my mind the outline of a 'Juif errant,' to which I shall devote myself at the first leisure moment I get, and which will be one of my best books. Indeed, I have only one fear—that I may die without having written it."

In this case, "*l'auteur propose, le censeur dispose.*" Parigot is facetious, but misleading, when he writes: "Dumas, in commencing 'Isaac Laquedem,' thought to write the romance of the world's history. He soon stopped, as there did not seem sufficient material."

The story was interdicted by the censor of the Second Empire, probably as profane. It promised, says Henley, to fulfil its author's pledge, and be one of his best romances. M. de Bury devotes considerable space to it in his study of Dumas. It was, in truth, a gigantic task to undertake: "Isaac Laquedem" was telling us the story of the early days of the world and of the Bible with all sincerity and reverence, and in Dumas's most vivid and enthralling manner. The trial of Jesus; His encounter with the Jew and the terrible curse He laid upon him—all was as powerful as it was audacious. But the idea of the Passion told *en feuilleton* was too much for the authorities, and all that we possess of "Isaac Laquedem" is a fragment—a few scattered columns of one of the most daring literary edifices ever mortal man designed to erect. The MS.—all in Dumas's own handwriting—was presented by his son to the town of Villers-Cotterets.

The last of the "romances of exile," the "Pasteur d'Ashbourn," is said to have been drawn from an English source. On the other hand, Parran, who made considerable researches into the dates and origins of Dumas's works, believed both in its genuineness and its merit. "It reveals a new side to his talent," he declares. To this we are regretfully unable to subscribe. Apart from the story of "la Dame Grise" which it contains, and which may have been suggested by Marie Dorval's passionate and unconquerable grief for her dead child, the novel would seem to have originally been a German attempt to copy Goldsmith or Richardson. Probably something in this story attracted Dumas and caused him to translate and transform it. The novel is obviously incomplete as it stands, but we can find no trace of a sequel, which perhaps its lack of success did not encourage the author to supply. "La Boule de Neige" (or "Moullah-Nour") is also a translation or adaptation of a story by Marlinsky, but the humour with which it is told makes it our author's own, if not by right of ownership, then by right of "conquest."

The year 1854 saw Dumas back in Paris and installed in the editorial chair of the *Mousquetaire*. "Saltéador (or "The Brigand"), which appeared in the great man's journal, was announced in the master's introductory note as by another hand; but, according to a member of the family, it is certainly the work of our author—probably in collaboration. "La Princesse de Monaco" was simply *recueilli* by Dumas; "Une Vie d'Artiste" consists of the story of the early struggles of Mélingue, the witty actor and original stage D'Artagnan, most interestingly retold by his friend and patron.

In this year began "Les Mohicans de Paris," still another new departure for the inexhaustible romancer. Frequently with Dumas a new assistant meant a new field of enterprise; on this occasion the 'prentice was, we believe, Paul Bocage, and the story was at once the pioneer of the detective-story, and a reminiscence of the second part of "Monte Cristo," and "The Mysteries of Paris." Our author himself appeared in it, "athlete and poet," in the opening chapters, which take place in a night restaurant. The leading character, the detective, was a forerunner of Sherlock Holmes; but in this particular type of story Dumas was not at his best, and the same remark applies to the better constructed but too lengthy sequel, "Salvator," which commenced to appear the following year.

"Ingenue,"[1] also of this year's date, is of much

[1] It is stated that Maquet had a share in this work, but unless it was commenced before the rupture between the two men we doubt this. Certainly they would scarcely come together for the purpose of writing this small romance.

better quality, and we are surprised that the English translations of it have been allowed to go out of print. We find ourselves once more in the midst of the Revolution, the leading character of the story being Marat, to whom a love romance of his youth brings a strange sequel. The heroine is the daughter of Rétif de la Bretonne, a literary character of the time; but his descendants resented the freedom with which their ancestors were treated, and warned the public not to accept the story as true. Dumas's sincere apology, and declaration that he was unaware of the existence of any survivors of the family were accepted.

A sequel to "Les Deux Diane" also belongs to 1855—"Le Page du Duc de Savoie," and is obviously from the same pens—Meurice, instructed by his master.

We now come to another of our author's very best romances—"Les Compagnons de Jehu." This story, which appeared in 1857, was suggested (as we learn from the preface) by a page in Nodier's "Souvenirs de la Révolution." Dumas, in accordance with his practice, visited Bourg-en-Bresse to study the locality, and gives an instructive and amusing account of his visit, in the introduction to the book. At the time when he set off on the track of the young Royalist highwaymen he was preparing to write a serial to be called "René d'Argonne," and was studying Varennes for that purpose, along with Paul Bocage, so that the "neat draft" of the "Compagnons" which About saw on Dumas's table was probably by that young 'prentice. In our judgment this story of the days of the Directoire is one of the most dramatic and skilfully constructed of all Dumas's romances, and excels most of its more famous rivals in unity and form. Dumas *fils* took an interest in the story, and is said to have suggested to his father the characters of Roland de Montrevel, the young Republican, and Sir John Tanlay, the English aristocrat.

Once more, Villers-Cotterets! In "Le Meneur de Loups," which dates from this year, the narrator is Mocquet, the friend of the boy Alexandre, keeper to General Dumas, and hero of a wonderful trip to the moon. Dumas recalls how in his childhood Mocquet told him the tale of Thibaut, the man who became a wolf; and the weird adventures of the *loup-garou* are told engrossingly enough, not to say enthrallingly. But their chronicler-in-after-years modestly disclaims the credit. He speaks of the story as his, it is true, adding very sensibly, "when one has sat on an egg for thirty-two years one finishes by thinking one has laid it one's-self!"

"Le Capitaine Richard," known to the last generation of English readers as "The Twin Captains," is a good story spoilt by history. For once Dumas did not give sufficient attention to the fusing process, and story and history could almost be disentangled without damage to either. The plot, as we learn in the epilogue, was given to Dumas by Schlegel, the great critic, whom the former met when he was "doing the Rhine" in 1838. The period of the story is that of the "Trou de l'Enfer"; Napoleon is in Germany; and the account of the attempted assassination of the Emperor by Staps, and of the Moscow campaign, are both of the author's best. The tale finishes with such a dramatic situation that one is tempted to regret the evident haste with which "Le Capitaine Richard" was written, a haste which compressed matter for a full-sized drama into the last few pages of a novel.

We pass by "L'Horoscope," a fragment of the history of the short-lived François II., husband of Mary Queen of Scots, a piece of work of which the little we possess makes us ask vainly for more; "Black," a pretty story, based on the idea of the transmigration of souls into the bodies of animals; and "Ammalat Beg" (or "Sultanetta"), rewritten by Dumas from a translation of a story in Russian by Marlinsky.[1] This was published in 1859, being, of course, the result of Dumas's visit to the Caucasus

---

[1] An English version of this story, one of the best known in Russian literature, appeared in *Blackwood's*, 1843.

just previously. We may also briefly dismiss "Le Chasseur de Sauvagine," a charming story, the whole credit of which Dumas frankly gives entirely to his friend and collaborator, the Comte de Cherville. In spite of this avowal the authorship has been claimed by experts for Dumas, and in any case the story is well worth reading. It follows the fortunes of a Normandy wildfowl-hunter, and tells of his love, his sin, and his repentance. The story contains qualities not generally acknowledged to be possessed by our author, being in marked contrast with his better-known style. "Le Fils du Forçat" (or "Monsieur Coumbes"), published the following year, has also been ascribed to Dumas, and suggests the same collaborator as the previous work. Although the scene is laid in Marseilles, the tale resembles the "Chasseur" in manner. It is really a study of a "little" nature—that of Monsieur Coumbes, to wit, and is simply yet powerfully told. A splendid edition of "Le Fils du Forçat" was published in France not long ago.

"Les Louves de Machecoul," a product of 1859, deserves fuller notice. This tale gives the reader a graphic account of the rising in La Vendée in 1832, caused by the Duchesse de Berri—a description all the more trustworthy because, as we know, the author had not only foreseen the occurrence, but had visited the Royalist West a year or two before the outbreak. Mr Saintsbury remarks that the episode of Ewan of Brigglands in "Rob Roy" is "calmly translated verbatim" into this romance. This is somewhat of an exaggeration; the incident is undoubtedly "conveyed," it is true, but is retold in more graphic style. The character of Jean Oullier alone should give this book life: he is a fine study of the Breton peasant—cunning, dogged, devoted, pious—one of the best portraits from the hands of the master.

"La Maison de Glace," known to us in the sixties as "The Russian Gipsy," published in 1859, was another outcome of the visit to Russia two years before. It is a romance of the court of the Empress Anna, in the early half of the eighteenth century, full of intrigue and passion. We incline to believe, with Maurel, that the story is a translation.

Another excursion into unfamiliar regions was "L'Ile de Feu," known to a past generation in England as "Doctor Basilius." This was probably written with an assistant who knew Java well, for it is a weird story of that island, the interest afforded by the people and customs of that semi-barbarous spot being heightened by a suggestion of the supernatural. "Truly one of the gems of the collection," writes a deep student of Dumas, "the concluding volume being perhaps among his finest work."

"Le Père la Ruine," which dates from this period, resembles "Le Chasseur de Sauvagine," "Le Fils du Forçat," and "Parisiens et Provinciaux," so much as to suggest Dumas in collaboration with de Cherville once more. It is a pretty but sad story, in which, as in "Conscience," the love of the French peasant for the soil is powerfully shown.

A translation of Trelawney's "Adventures of a Younger Son," made under Dumas's orders, and known as "Un Cadet de Famille," and one of Gordon-Cumming's "Adventures of a Lion Hunter," known as "La Vie au Desert," were also issued in 1860, when Dumas set out on that tour which ended in the camp of Garibaldi. For some time the romancer was busy following the fortunes of the "red-shirts," editing a paper at Naples, writing the "Mémoires de Garibaldi," his own diary as amateur war correspondent, and the rest; and it was not until 1863 that he published another romance of any importance—"Madame de Chamblay." According to the circumstantial account given in the introduction, the manuscript of this story was sent to Dumas by a friend, whom he had met at Compiègne in 1836, when on a visit to the young Duc D'Orleans. The novel tells of a young wife, an unworthy husband, a lover, a potion *à la* Juliet, by which the lady escapes from bondage, and promises a happy life for lover and mistress in a distant land. In spite of this testimony, however, Mr Saintsbury believes Octave Feuillet to be the author of "Madame de Chamblay." Be that as it may, we have seen that Dumas does not claim the authorship for himself.

"Une Nuit à Florence," published in 1861, is a story based on the life-history of the Medicis—a favourite topic with Dumas. The night in question is the 2nd or 3rd January 1537,[1] and concerns the adventure of the Duke Alexander de Medici, who is finally killed by his cousin Lorenzino, the "Brutus" of his day. It would be interesting to compare this story with de Musset's play, "Lorenzaccio," which it closely resembles.

About this time (1862) appeared "Une Aventure d'Amour," which is more an autobiographical sketch and a record of the author's visit to Austria in 1856, than fiction. Incidentally it shows Dumas as the chivalrous friend of a beautiful woman in a risky and equivocal position. "Herminie" or "Une Amazone," which is bound with the same volume, is of earlier date—about 1845. It is a short story of a *bal masqué* intrigue, a sort of belated "Souvenir d'Antony," and is considered a model short story in its way.

In the following year—1864—came Dumas's last

[1] This is the date given by Dumas. Authorities disagree as to the day, and even as to the year.

ALEXANDRE DUMAS

long romance (if we except "Le Docteur Mysterieux," and its sequel), "La San Felice."

"La San Felice" is a word-panorama of the strange series of events which occurred in Naples in 1798 and 1799, when the Bourbon Ferdinand was overthrown by the French, in the former year, and was restored to the throne by Cardinal Ruffo in the next. We know, by passages in "Le Corricolo," that the events of this time had already aroused Dumas's interest. Pifteau, who was the author's secretary at the time the romance was written (and who vouches for its authenticity), tells us that Dumas whilst at Naples wrote a history of Ferdinand's overthrow and return known as the "Histoire des Bourbons," or "I Borboni Napoli," for the paper which he was then editing, and found the series of events far too exciting and extraordinary to neglect. Accordingly "La San Felice" was written. The characters are historical throughout, and the hapless Luisa San Felice, Ferdinand, "King of the Lazzarone," Nelson, Lady Hamilton, Fra Diavolo, Admiral Caracciolo[1] and a score more, appear "in their habits as they lived." This story shows strikingly the change which has come over

[1] Incidentally, the story of Nelson's hanging of Caracciolo is introduced, and treated from the French and humanitarian point of view. The "case for Nelson" is presented in Mr Sladen's book "The Admiral," which contains exhaustive quotations from original documents.

the author during the past twenty years. The "pace," is now comparatively slow; one is no longer swept off one's feet, as with the "Mousquetaires." The author unfolds his tale deliberately, but with much of his old charm, stepping carefully from document to document, and weaving half a score of threads together with a patience and dignity of style akin to Scott. "La San Felice" was followed by "Emma Lyonna," in which is told the story of Lady Hamilton's career, being a picturesque version, it is said, of that fascinating woman's "Memoirs." A supplementary sequel, "Les Souvenirs d'une Favorite," appeared in 1865. Lady Hamilton played a prominent part in the events described in "La San Felice," and Dumas was evidently led on by his interest in that picturesque personality to make her the central figure in succeeding volumes.

Readers who are inclined to disparage Dumas's later work, particularly the products of the "sixties," are advised to try "Parisiens et Provinciaux," issued this year, written with the Comte de Cherville. The scene shifts from Paris to the neighbourhood of the author's beloved Villers-Cotterets, and is in fact a humorous comparison of the city cockney (typified in the delightful person of M. Peluche) and the "rustic" Madeleine. The story might have taken the title of the author's first little play "La

Chasse et l'Amour," for the humours of the chase and a slight but pretty love-story are the chief attractions of this book, which is one of the best of that class of novels written by Dumas and yet so neglected by his admirers,—the slight, humorous story of modern humble life.

It is not generally known that in the closing years of his life Dumas tried his hand once more at a "romance of cape-and-sword." The reader will search the comprehensive list of MM. Calmann-Lévy in vain for any record of it. In the early part of 1866—so Ferry asserts—the editor of *Les Nouvelles* appealed to Dumas for an historical romance in his famous style, and Dumas agreed to think the matter over. He found an excellent subject in the career of "Le Comte de Moret," that illegitimate son of Henri Quatre who disappeared so mysteriously during the battle of Castelnaudary, and whose body was never found. He had already treated this subject in that charming story, "La Colombe." The first number of the *feuilleton*, Ferry tells us, promised an engrossing story; but unhappily other preoccupations, other work, took Dumas's attention from the romance, which flagged. He lost the thread of the narrative, which became merely a *chronique*, full of long extracts from the memoirs of Pontis, Delaporte, and from other historical documents of the seventeenth century. It suddenly ceased to appear, and was never heard of more. But although the romance is not now accessible, a wretched American translation published at the time, and happily preserved, shows that the story has been underrated by M. Ferry. Some of it, indeed, is excellent, notably the chapter in which Corneille is introduced to the *précieuses ridicules* of the day; and Richelieu's intrigues, and the incident of the "day of dupes," are Dumas as we know him best. The period of "Le Comte de Moret" just precedes that of the "Mousquetaires."

Two of the last volumes of fiction from the pen of the fast-ageing writer were of the revolutionary period.[1] "Les Blancs et les Bleus" (1867) like the "Compagnons," was suggested by Nodier's "Souvenirs de la Révolution," and Dumas in acknowledgment introduces his old friend into the story. It is interesting chiefly for the dramatic episode of Euloge Schneider the "red," who bargained for the hand of a Royalist maiden, as the price of her father's life. "Les Blancs et les Bleus," the scene of which is laid in Strasbourg in December 1793, was dedicated, with a gleam of the author's old wit, to the memory of Nodier, his

---

[1] "La Terreur Prussienne," although technically a novel, derives its chief interest and value from its historical matter, and is therefore dealt with in that capacity.

illustrious friend and "collaborator." "I have said 'collaborator,'" he adds, "because people would give themselves a lot of trouble in finding another one, and their time would be wasted." The veteran still held his grip of his facts, and of his reader; but the sequel, "Le Huitième Croisade," which now forms the latter part of "Les Blancs et les Bleus," is chiefly a spirited *chronique* of the siege of Acre. And on that last effort, made in 1869, the year before Dumas's death, the curtain falls.

* * * * *

At occasional intervals Dumas issued books of tales for children, one of which ("Le Capitaine Pamphile") we have already mentioned. Of the others, "La Bouillie de la Comtesse Berthe" is the most notable: it is a pretty story, in which the "Castle of Otranto" seems turned into a haunt for dwarfs and a delight for little readers. "Le Père Gigogne" opens with a story ("La Lièvre de mon grandpère") told to Dumas by de Cherville and recounted by him; but the rest of the two volumes contains fairy-tales, chiefly translations from Hans Christian Andersen and the German.

In reply to an enquiry from us Mr Lang writes to say that although he has not these stories by him, he thinks it unlikely that any are original. In spite of this weighty opinion we are reluctant to part with two or three tales, notably "La Jeunesse de Pierrot." This verdict also disposes of the tales in "L'Homme aux Contes": "L'Histoire d'un casse-noisette," is, we know, an adaptation of Hoffmann's story of the same name.

Next to the plays, with which we have not dealt for reasons already given, and to the romances, come the travels—if not in importance, at least in originality. These volumes abound in gaiety, in brief sketches of dialogue, of history, of archæology, of personal adventure—in short, they make a *mélange*, a savoury stew, with Dumas for cook! Parigot suggests that they should be called "Impressions produites par Dumas en Voyage," and declares "he is charming thus"; though with a touch of satire he adds, "one scarcely exaggerates when one says that the beauty of a country was to Dumas in proportion to the native admiration for his books." Of the first trip, "En Suisse" (1833), we have already given some account; then followed those on "La Midi de la France" and "Les Bords du Rhin" (1841), the former containing "La Chasse au Chastre" and other excellent reading; the latter, probably written with the help of Gerard de Nerval, telling, amongst other matter, of Waterloo and Marceau, of Rubens, and the devil-tempted architect of Cologne cathedral. Italy and the Mediterranean yielded the finest crop of "impressions," and there appeared in rapid succession "Une Année à Florence" (in 1841), and "Le Capitaine Arèna,"[1] followed by "Le Corricolo" and "Le Speronare" in the next two years. "It must be said," admits Fitzgerald, "that the 'Corricolo,' an account of Naples, and the 'Speronare,' an account of Florence —both written by Dumas's friend Fiorentin under his direction—are as spirited and amusing books of travels as can be found." "La Villa Palmieri" is another volume of souvenirs of Florence.

In 1846, as will be remembered, Dumas set out for Madrid, to be present at the royal wedding, and the following year his description of Spain was issued, in "Paris à Cadix." "Spain had had little influence on his genius, it is true," says Parigot, "but what impressions he has left us! The very custom-house officers respected the baggage of the illustrious Frenchman; the author of 'Monte Cristo' was received with open arms; the French schoolmasters left their work to escort him hither and thither, and the great hidalgos paid him homage of courtesy." As a consequence, "Paris à Cadix" is full of *verve* and gaiety, bull-fights, dances, and the rest. "Le Véloce," issued two years later, is a description of Dumas's adventures in that state-vessel along the coast of North Africa. Of the

[1] "Le Capitaine Arèna" tells of a tour round Sicily in a vessel commanded by that seaman. A "speronare" is a light coasting-vessel used by the Italians; a "corricolo," a carriage used by the Neapolitans—a sort of "tilbury."

travels "En Russie" (1865) and "Le Caucase" (1859) we have already spoken, and there only remains "Quinze jours à Sinai," written in 1839, a book remarkable for the fact that although Dumas was never in Palestine (he wrote the volume from the drawings of Dauzats and Baron Taylor's notes), it was declared by a Caliph to be the most faithful description of the Holy Land that he had ever read! Its author, we can believe, was delighted to find he had revealed the East to the Orientals.

We must not omit "Un Pays Inconnu," 1865 (an account of a visit to the land of the Aztecs in South America, and written from the notes of a certain Mr Middleton-Payne of New York), if only because of the incidental assertion, unmistakably made, that Dumas had *visited the United States*. It seems incredible that a man who travelled in the public eye, as it were, and whose journeys abroad were invariably turned to delightful account, could have gone to America unnoticed, and returned to leave his visit unrecorded. We know that Dumas *wished* to cross the Atlantic, but was restrained by a natural fear that his negro descent might lay him open to humiliating rebuffs. Probably, either Dumas "bluffed" his readers more hardily than usual, or else the introduction and notes were written by a 'prentice who had had the desired experience.

Not yet have we exhausted the catalogue of this

universal writer! Here are historical studies by the teens of volumes—a presentment of old facts from a refreshingly new point of view. "Gaule et France," a concise sketch of French history, began the series, being written, it is said, to divert Dumas's mind from the cholera epidemic. Its author is accused of having borrowed passages from Thierry and others; and this is quite possible. On the other hand, the form, design, and aim of the work were Dumas's own, and the closing passages which so faithfully prophesy the Second Republic of fifteen years later—with a president, elected by the people for five years, and so forth—is quoted by Blaze de Bury in full, as proof of the romancer's political foresight. Then came "Napoléon" (1839); "Les Stuarts" (1840)—in which Dumas largely availed himself of Scott's "Abbot"; "Jehanne la Pucelle," (1842), which is half a romance; "Louis XIV. et son Siècle" (1844), his most important history; "Les Médicis" (1845); "La Régence" and "Louis XV. et sa Cour" (1849); "Louis XVI. et la Révolution" (1850); "'93" (1851); and a "Histoire de Louis-Philippe" (1852). A series of portraits in undress, "Grands Hommes en Robe-de-Chambre," was sketched, but only "César" (1857), "Henri IV." (1866), and "Louis XIII. et Richelieu' (1866) appeared. "Perhaps," added Dumas. "if these studies meet with success, we shall try to go backward as far as Alexander, and forward as far as Napoleon." Evidently the series did not appeal to Dumas's public.

Of one of these books its author tells an amusing anecdote. He was chatting with a somewhat supercilious *savant,* and incidentally mentioned that he had written a history of Cæsar.

" You have written a history of Cæsar?" repeated the incredulous listener with a smile.

" Yes."

" You ? "

" Why not ? "

" Pardon! But it has not been spoken of amongst scholars . . ."

" Oh, the scholars never speak of me."

" But a history of Cæsar should have caused some sensation ? . . ."

" Mine caused none; people read it, that's all. It is the unreadable histories which make sensations; they are like the dinners which one doesn't digest; the dinners which one *does* digest, one has forgotten by next day."

Of these excursions into history "La Route de Varennes" (1860) and "La Terreur Prussienne" (1867) are two of the most valuable. The former was an attempt to write the story of Louis XVI.'s flight from Paris, of which historical accounts seemed confusing and contradictory. Dumas followed the course of the royal fugitive step by step, and Maxime Du Camp, who had himself studied the epoch carefully, testified to Dumas's accuracy and skill in the revision of the work of trusted historians. The "Terreur," in spite of its fiction-form, is practically a study of the Prusso-Austrian war, made on the spot, and full of shrewd observation and disquieting forebodings, soon to be justified. We should add here " Les Garibaldiens," Dumas's diary as amateur and volunteer war correspondent in 1860—a crisp, intelligent, restrained account of the Sicilian campaign.

Certainly not the least attractive of Dumas's writings are those in which he writes frankly of himself, his friends, his pets, and all that concerns his life and work. Of these, the first in order and importance is " Mes Mémoires," commenced in the forties, but written "in exile" in 1852-54, when leisure allowed the adventurous author to look back upon his early life. Dr Garnett speaks of them as "those wondrous 'Mémoires' which, as it is inconceivable that anyone but himself should have written them, alone suffice to establish his genius." The ten volumes cover the period of childhood, the early struggles and triumphs, the Revolution of 1830, and end abruptly at the time of the Swiss tour, 1832-33. But the "Mémoires" contain much more than Dumas's own history; he chronicles the political

[*Translation.*]

MY FATHER

My father, who has already been mentioned twice in the foregoing chapter, firstly, *à propos* of my certificate of birth, and again, in connection with his own marriage-contract, was General Thomas-Alexandre Dumas Davy de la Pailleterie.

He was, as we have shown in the documents cited by us son of the Marquis Antoine-Alexandre Davy de la Pailleterie, Colonel and Commissary-General of Artillery, who owned by inheritance the estate of La Pailleterie, raised to a Marquisate by Louis XIV. in 1707.

The arms of the family were: "*d'azur à trois aigles d'or, aux vols éployés pour deux, et un avec un anneau d'argent placé en cœur, embrassés par les griffes dextres et senestres des angles du chef, et reposant sur la tête de l'aigle de pointe.*"

My father, when enlisting as a simple soldier, or rather, when renouncing both title and coat-of-arms, adopted instead the simple device "Deus dedit; Deus dabit"—a device which would have sounded ambitious, if God himself had not countersigned it.

I do not know what secret discontent or speculative plan determined my grandfather to quit France, about 1760, sell his estate and go off to take up his abode in San Domingo.

As a result of this resolution he bought an immense stretch of land situated on the western side of the island near Cape Rose and known as La Guinodée, or the Trou de Jérémie.

It was there that my father was born, of Louise-Cessette Dumas and the Marquis de la Pailleterie, on March 25th, 1762. The Marquis was then fifty-two years of age, having been born in 1710.

My father first saw the light in the most beautiful spot in that magnificent island, queen of the gulf in which it is situated, and of which the air is so pure that no venomous reptile can exist there.

events of the time, and sketches the characters of his famous contemporaries. It is evident that even the stout-hearted Alexandre himself shirked the task of bringing such a record up to date. Needless to add, these volumes are full of entertainment. The "Causeries" (1860) contain the sketches of travel in England, chatty fragments of autobiography, and two *jeux d'esprit*. The two volumes of "Bric-à-brac," issued the following year, are similar in nature—" Propos d'art, de cuisine"—et de Dumas. "Les Morts vont vite" contains appreciations of the author's friends, de Musset, Chateaubriand, Béranger, and recollections of Marie Dorval, and others. The "Histoire de mes Bêtes" (1868) shows us Dumas as he was in the forties, *en famille* at Monte Cristo, amongst his dogs, monkeys, servants, and hangers-on. The "Souvenirs dramatiques" (1868) are written with an unusual degree of dignity for Dumas, and with a genial masterhood of stage-craft. The studies in criticism, the appreciation of Shakespeare, and the views expressed on the art of the playwright, and the management of the theatre, are all excellent in matter and manner.

Two volumes of "Mémoires" with which Dumas's name has been associated are not easy to classify. One is the "Mémoires d'Horace," published in 1860. It was supposed to be taken from an MS.

in the library of the Vatican, and is, Glinel tells us, "une grande fantaisie sur Rome ancienne." It is not now accessible. The "Mémoires de Talma," on the other hand, were written by Dumas from memoranda left by the great tragedian, and have been recognised by Fournel, J. Cherbuliez, and others, to be practically a biography of the actor, written by his young admirer, in after years.

One other work also stands in a class by itself. This is "Crimes Célèbres," which appeared in 1839-40. The series was founded on the "Causes Célèbres" of Gayot de Pithaval; the excellent material afforded by that industrious person was divested of formality and tediousness, and rewritten with all the animation and dramatic effect for which the novelist was noted. The records were compared by Dumas with the best authorities on the subject, and the romances of real life written with scrupulous attention to accuracy. Arnould, Fournier, Fiorentino, and Mallefille were responsible for some chapters, which consisted of the following: "Les Borgia," "La Comtesse de St Géran," "Jeanne de Naples," "Nisida," "La Marquise de Brinvilliers," "Les Cenci," "La Marquise de Ganges," "Karl Ludwig Sand" (the murderer of Kotzebue), "Vaninka" and "Urbain Grandier." (This last was dramatised by the author.) The whole scheme of the book is of course Dumas's, and some of the chapters appeared in his different " Impressions de Voyage."

Dumas the poet is perhaps best represented by "Charles VII. et ses grands Vassaux," and by "Christine"; but M. Glinel has collected a considerable number of fugitive poems, most of which appeared in the "Psyche."[1] They prove what, indeed, Dumas's tragedy-dramas show, that he had *le mouvement, la couleur et l'image*, and expressed passion with a rare vigour and warmth. "Although lacking a sure knowledge of syntax," says Parigot, "and deficient in mastery of form, he sparkled with gaiety and youth, even in verse. The man who wrote the lion chase, the dream of the desert, and the fifth act of 'Charles VII.'; the 'spirituel' couplets in 'L'Alchimiste,' and, above all, the prologue to 'Caligula' is not a poet to be despised." What, indeed, did this marvellous man attempt, that he did not in some degree achieve? Of the thirty or forty poems thus preserved, the elegy on the death of General Foy, the dithyrambe "Canaris," in praise of that heroic Greek, and the verses to Hugo and Sainte-Beuve, deserve mention. In selecting one of Dumas's poems for quotation, we have chosen what we believe to be one of the best and most typical.

[1] Dumas translated a number of poems from German and Russian writers, but these are not now accessible.

It is "La Sylphe," one of the fairy race which we meet in the "Rape of the Lock":

> Je suis un sylphe, une ombre, un rien, un rêve,
> Hôte de l'air, esprit mystérieux,
> Léger parfum, que le zéphir enlève,
> Anneau vivant, qui joint l'homme et les dieux
>
> De mon corps pur les rayons diaphanes
> Flottent mêlés à la vapeur du soir ;
> Mais je me cache aux regards des profanes,
> Et l'âme seule en songe peut me voir.
>
> Rasant du lac la nappe étincelante
> D'un vol léger j'effleure les roseaux ;
> Et, balancé sur mon aile brillante,
> J'aime à me voir dans le cristal des eaux.
>
> Dans vos jardins quelque fois je voltige ;
> Et, m'enivrant de suaves odeurs,
> Sans que mon pied fasse incliner leur tige,
> Je me suspends au calice des fleurs.
>
> Dans vos foyers j'entre avec confiance,
> Et, récréant son œil clos à demi,
> J'aime à verser des songes d'innocence
> Sur le front pur d'un enfant endormi.
>
> Lorsque sur vous la nuit jette son voile
> Je glisse aux cieux comme un long filet d'or,
> Et les mortals disent "C'est une étoile
> Qui d'un ami vous présage la mort."

We are far from pretending that the foregoing is a complete review of its subject. The task is an almost endless one, and there are limits to time and space and the patience of readers. We submit, however, that this analytical description is in advance of public knowledge in England and

America at least, and that it has served a two-fold purpose. It has, we hope, told the reader something new about the books he knows, and has given him an idea, however slight, of the nature and authenticity of other works by our author of which he has probably never heard. We trust we shall have led him to marvel, as we have marvelled, at the fact that so much which is good, and which is undoubtedly "genuine Dumas," should remain untranslated and almost forgotten. A good dozen of the minor romances have been translated into English and allowed to go out of print. Yet we have shown, we think, that there is plenty of excellent fish in this wide, wide sea which has not as yet been landed on our shores in the net of the translator.

One other point cannot have escaped attention. Our most serious admissions respecting Dumas's integrity have been made in the course of this examination of the authenticity of the various books attributed to him. In the case of collaboration, we declare that Dumas was ever the greater brain, the "predominant partner," and deserves the most credit. But in cases where his name is attached, obviously or confessedly to books untouched by his pen, his responsibility is grave. Yet even here it is well to discriminate between the man who issued the book with a frank disavowal of authorship, and the publishers of his day who sent it forth as "the master's."[1] Like Goldsmith, Dumas became a bondman to his publishers, and yielded weakly to them. His reputation has suffered accordingly, as was only right; but we believe that when the wheat of his own growing is sifted from the chaff, as one day it will be, and when the truth has prevailed over slander, Dumas, as a man and as a writer, will stand higher than he has ever done.

[1] We need hardly say that this in no way reflects on the *present* publishers of Dumas, MM. Calmann-Lévy.

PART III

HIS GENIUS

A DEFENCE—A COUNTERCLAIM

His Genius: A Defence.

DUMAS was once asked for a subscription towards a monument to a man whom everyone had reviled in the beginning of his career.

"You had better be content," he replied, "with the stones that people threw at him during his lifetime. No monument you can raise will be so eloquent of their imbecility, and his genius." There was a savour of bitterness in this speech which was only too natural.

"There never was a popular writer," declared Hayward thirty years ago, "who had better reason than Alexandre Dumas to protest against the contemporary judgment of his countrymen, or to appeal, like Bacon, to the foreign nations and the next ages." Charles Reade, writing in the French novelist's lifetime, implies the existence of the same attitude towards our author's genius in this forcible comment: "Poor Dumas! He has not only produced immortal stories and immortal plays, each by the dozen, but also a son who has shown himself master of the story and the drama. But what avails that treble fertility? If five generations of Dumas, novelist and dramatist, were now on earth together, instead of two, our puppy-dogs, drunk with moonshine, would manage to look at them all and not see any of them!"

It was the fashion to treat our author as the chief of a school of second-rate writers of popular stories, which were "turned out" hastily, and which therefore possessed no claim to criticism. "Dumas," adds Dr Garnett, "exceptionally passed for long as an example of this inferior grade of authorship. At one time it would have been thought absurd to parallel him with deep thinkers like Balzac, or exquisite artists like George Sand. 'Monte Cristo' and the 'Three Musketeers' were ranged along with 'The Mysteries of Paris' and 'The Wandering Jew,' and the circumstances of their reproduction in England showed that they were expected to appeal to readers of the same class. Yet as time passed, and mere clever melodrama gave place to other clever melodrama but Dumas retained his power and popularity, it became clear that his work really belonged to the domain of literature. In adjusting the relations between Dumas and his critics, it must be remembered that he did not, like some of the literary heroes of his age, take the world by storm with his earliest writings. . . . But Dumas had acquired a good sound reputation as a second-rate romancer before writing 'Monte Cristo,' and criticism was naturally slow to accept him as a genius."

We come down to 1880, and find Mr W. H. Pollock asserting in the "Nineteenth Century" that "Dumas has perhaps been more persistently underrated, in England at least, than any modern writer of his calibre;" and five years later Blaze de Bury, in his study of our subject, refers to public opinion in France, when he writes:—"Dumas is popular; he is not *known*. His method of life and his occasional worthless books greatly damaged his literary position. He is usually looked upon simply as an 'amuser,' and yet, like others, and more than many others, he had his moments of lofty thought and philosophy." "Even to be 'amusing,'" as Parigot drily remarks, "is not, when one looks round the world of literature, so commonplace and contemptible a merit, after all."

Nevertheless, in one province of literary opinion there has been a striking change during the past twenty or thirty years. The English literary critics and essayists of the romantic school, as we shall see, have more and more loudly proclaimed their admiration of Dumas. Still the public at large remains ignorant and unconverted. Its attitude towards the romance-writer is thirty years behind the times, and dates from the days when "Chambers's Encyclopædia" treated our author in this summary fashion:

"It may be said that the appearance in literature

of a writer like Dumas is a portentous phenomenon, and the avidity with which his invariably immoral and generally licentious fictions are devoured is the most severe condemnation of modern, and especially of French society, that could well be pronounced."

That is pretty well, and one is rather relieved, for Dumas's sake, to find that the biographer has previously declared that the novelist did not write his own books at all. We read further of "the savage voluptuousness" of his books (the "savage voluptuousness" of the "Tulipe Noire" is good), of his "astounding quackery," and of his "sweating system" of production. Need we add that the "brief biography" refers us to "De Mirecourt"?

Happily the "Encyclopædia" has retrieved itself, and its latest edition contains a sketch of Dumas's life, from the pen of Mr W. E. Henley, which, in the old-fashioned language of our fathers, "does equal honour to that writer's head and heart." We learn from R. L. Stevenson's "Letters" that his collaborator in "Beau Austin" was contemplating a book on Dumas some years ago. There is, indeed, a passage in "Memories and Portraits" which was written *at* Henley—"something about Dumas still waiting his biographer." It is truly a pity that the author of "Views and Reviews" never wrote this book, and did not obviate the necessity for the present work by giving the public an estimation of the great Frenchman which would say what should be said, with all the literary power and critical authority which that writer can command.

Unfortunately the other ordinary books of reference still repeat the old story of prejudice and spite. We have already mentioned that there is only one book in English dealing with Dumas's life and writings, a work which the critics have heartily condemned. We need only add, by way of summing up their views, that it ought fitly to be entitled " Dumas According to his Enemies: by One of Them." In France no adequate biography exists: on the one hand there are the "studies" of MM. B. de Bury and Parigot; on the other we have the bibliographical and biographical notes of Dumas's fellow-provincial, Glinel; but as yet the book which shall combine the two points of view is wanting.

The lover of Dumas could afford to laugh at the old-fashioned utterances of a cyclopædia in the sixties; he could forget a third-rate biography already forgotten by the public. But these are not the only obstacles in the way of a reconsideration of Dumas's literary merits. It is only a few years since a "Quarterly Reviewer" dismissed the claims of our author as a novelist in a few contemptuous words. True, nobody reads the *Quarterly Review*, but even straws show how the wind is blowing in certain quarters. In a recent work[1] M. G. Pellissier complacently remarks that Dumas "sacrificed his literary conscience to the vulgar taste of the public, and the necessities of the purse prevailed more and more over his work. . . . he was only the most popular of amusers." We are not surprised that this book was "crowned by the Académie." G. Brandès has repeated the same statement, which Parigot, who certainly possesses some knowledge of the subject, flatly denies:

"G. Brandès has declared that Dumas wrote firstly *en romantique*, and then *en industriel*—a doubly false estimate. 'Industriel' Dumas never ceased to be; 'romantic' he was also, if by the word we imply revolutionary; but dramatic he remained always, *con amore*, and by right of conquest."

M. Lanson, in his voluminous and comprehensive history of French literature, acknowledges Dumas to be a skilled stage craftsman, but no more; he ignores Dumas the novelist altogether!

These criticisms could only exercise a very distant influence on the ordinary English reader, and we need not concern ourselves with them further. But unhappily they seem to have furnished the sole sources of reference for Professor Dowden in his book on French literature. This

[1] "La Mouvement Littéraire au XIXe Siècle."

famous scholar confesses in his preface that "an adequate history of a great literature can be written only by collaboration. In this small volume I too have had my collaborators ... who have written each a part of my book." The list of authorities which the professor quotes includes the three critics we have mentioned, and contains no record of any direct study of Dumas himself. Hence we are not surprised to find that he "admits" our author's history to be untrue, his characters superficial, his action incredible. Dumas's work "ceased to be literature and became mere 'commerce' ... his money was 'recklessly squandered.' ... Half genius, half charlatan, his genius decayed and his charlatanry grew to enormous proportions."[1] Half-knowledge, at second hand, gives currency to those half-truths concerning which Tennyson held strong opinions. It is to be regretted that a great scholar meaning to deal fairly and even kindly with a personality should be misled into a flagrant under-estimate which is certain to be accepted by the public at large, who have a natural confidence in the professor's ability and

[1] We regret to find that Dr Garnett (in the introduction to the latest edition of the "Black Tulip"), repeats this charge in almost the same words. The epithet "charlatan," as applied to a writer, can surely only be taken to imply that he wrote without conscience and lowered his standard of literary production to catch the public taste. This implied charge we believe an impartial reading of Dumas's works at any period will disprove.

honesty of purpose. It is a relief to turn to Professor Saintsbury's " Short History of French Literature" and find our author dealt with more justly and sympathetically by one who has a fuller and more direct knowledge of his subject.

The attitude of the orthodox French critic towards Dumas is even more severe and contemptuous, and this is easily explained. A man of such irregular origin, who led such an irregular life, who produced his works in such an irregular way, was bound to shock the critics of the nation which takes pride in that triumph of literary convention and snobbery, the Académie Française. If Dumas had been content to live a quiet, " respectable" life, to stick to one class of writing, and conform to tradition in that branch of literature; if in addition he had refrained from disrespectful witticisms respecting the Institut, and maintained a non-aggressive attitude towards the world, a *fauteuil* might have been his. He would have gained the praise of the conventional and won, if not Immortality, at least an Academic fame. But he remained—Dumas—himself, and an eccentric individuality; and so we find Sainte-Beuve writing of him : " All that he has written is fairly bright, engrossing and amusing, *à moitié*, but spoilt by incompleteness, negligence and vulgarity." Still, elsewhere the same writer condescends to say:

"Quant à M. Dumas, tout le monde sait sa verve prodigieuse, son entrain facile, son bonheur de mise-en-scène, son dialogue spirituel, et toujours en mouvement, ce récit léger qui court sans cesse et qui sait enlever l'obstacle et l'espace sans jamais faiblir. Il couvre d'immense toiles sans fatiguer jamais ni son pinceau ni son lecteur."

Similarly, Desiré Nisard sneered at Dumas, in his attack on what he called the "easy" literature. It is characteristic of the French critic, this inability to see that for certain kinds of composition rapidity of thought and writing are essential to success. In short, the austere devotion to "form" and "style" which his countrymen profess and demand in others have always prevented Dumas, who cared little for either quality, from achieving honour in his own country — except, of course, from the ignorant public, who read him and enjoyed him.

The weight of official authority being cast against us, it is obvious that our own attempt to estimate the extent and value of Dumas's genius must firstly take more or less the form of a defence, in which we must pass in review the charges brought against our client, and produce evidence in support.

It is not at all our desire to deny all the accusations brought against Dumas; we hope, however, that we shall be allowed to extenuate some things, and be pardoned for setting down naught in malice.

We have admitted the many faults to be found in Dumas as a man and a writer; we have recorded, and shall continue to record, hard things said of him by expert and impartial critics. We do this not only for honesty's sake, but because we believe that the shoulders of his talent are broad enough to bear the burden. Mr Henley is by no means a mealy-mouthed witness, and this is how he faces the point:

"He is one of the heroes of modern art. Envy and scandal have done their worst now. The libeller has said his say; the detectives who make a speciality of literary forgeries have proved their cases one and all; the judges of matter have spoken, and so have the critics of style; the distinguished author of 'Nana' has taken us into his confidence on the subject; we have heard from the lamented Granier (de Cassagnac) and others as much as was to be heard on the question of plagiarism in general and the plagiarisms of Dumas in particular; and Mr Percy Fitzgerald has done what he is pleased to designate the 'nightman's work' of analysing 'Antony' and 'Kean,' and of collecting everything that spite has said about their author's life, their author's habits, their author's manners and customs and character: of whose vanity, mendacity, immorality, and a score of improper qualities besides, enough has been written to furnish a good-sized library. And the result of it all is that Dumas is recognised for a force in modern art and for one of the greatest inventors and amusers the century has produced."

Before proceeding to the counts in our defence it may be as well to "put into court" Dumas's own opinion of his place in and value to literature. From the "vain *farçeur*" something pompous and ridiculously big will be anticipated.

"Lamartine," he writes, "is a dreamer; Hugo is a thinker; as for myself, I am a populariser. I take possession of both: I give substance to the dream of one, I throw light upon the thought of the other, and I serve up to the public this excellent dish, which, from the hand of the first would have lacked nourishment, being too light, and from the second, would have caused indigestion, being too heavy; but which when seasoned and introduced by me, will agree with almost any stomach, the weakest as well as the strongest."

This passage, of course, refers to Dumas's position in the ranks of the Romantics, but it may fairly be taken as representing his general opinion of his own worth. The reader will be able to judge for himself as we proceed, whether our author is correct in this self-estimation, or whether he falls below it or rises above it.

The first attack which was made upon Dumas,

and the first therefore which we have to meet, is that his plays were "horrible," and immoral. The chief plays to be pilloried were "Henri Trois," "Antony," "Don Juan de Marana," "Caligula," and "La Tour de Nesle." Each of these received its due share of ridicule from the wits of the rival school, the classicists. The first, in which the intrigues of the Valois court were exposed, was the subject of an epigram which made fun of the "handkerchief" incident, (which no doubt was borrowed from "Othello"):

> "Messieurs et mesdames, cette pièce est morale ;
> Elle prouve aujourd'hui, sans faire de scandale,
> Que chez un amant, lorsqu'on va le soir
> On peut oublier tout . . . excepté son mouchoir !"[1]

Similarly, "Antony," the society drama which set the fashion in "foundling" or illegitimate heroes, and heroines fair and frail, inspired the couplet—

> À croire ces MM. on ne voit dans nos rues
> Que les enfants trouvés, et les femmes perdues."[2]

The author's classic tragedy-drama gave rise to the slangy word "caligulate," meaning to bore;

[1] "Ladies and gentlemen, this play is moral: it proves that now-a-days, when meeting one's lover by night one may without scandal forget one's self, . . . but not one's handkerchief!" (Alluding to the fact that the Duchesse de Guise's handkerchief, left in Ruggieri's rooms—where she has met St Megrin, her lover,—is found by the Duc, and, by arousing his jealousy, leads on to the tragedy.)

[2] "If we can believe these gentlemen (Dumas and others of the Romantics) one meets everywhere only women who are "lost" and children who are "found."

and Dumas was represented as being haunted, à la Richard III., by the ghosts of the authors from whose "Don Juans" he had borrowed.

"Henri Trois" is now by general consent beyond the reach of this injurious criticism. Of "Antony" Dumas himself in his "Mémoires" has submitted his own defence to the judgment of posterity. He certainly makes two palpable hits, firstly, in pointing out that the sinners Antony and Adèle do not prosper by their sin, for they live in stress and anguish and die violent and miserable deaths; and secondly, that in "exploiting" adultery as a subject for the stage he treats it in a far more worthy fashion than did Molière, and we may add, than the Restoration and eighteenth century dramatists. With them cuckoldry was a suitable theme for comedy; as the fashionable and amusing pastime of *le monde où l'on s'ennuie*. In fact, Dumas faithfully follows Shakespeare in "Othello," and "Much Ado about Nothing."

It should never be forgotten, especially by Englishmen, that many of the "horrors" with which Dumas's early plays are filled, are due to an ardent but indiscriminate admiration for Shakespeare. Schiller no doubt is also to blame, but we are obviously concerned with the Elizabethan playwright. Do those who condemn the murder of Monaldeschi, the unholy love of Queen Marguerite in "La Tour de Nesle," and the profanity of "Don Juan" forget not only the "horrors" of the old classic tragedies, which Dumas duly studied, but also the passages in "Titus Andronicus," in "Macbeth," in "Richard III.," and other plays, which no stage-manager would dare to present to the public to-day? For in more than one respect the Romantic movement in France, in the early part of last century, corresponds with the Elizabethan era in our literature. We have neither the desire nor the ability to present an elaborate comparison here: it is sufficient to note that political and social conditions favoured a reaction towards passion and action in poetry, drama, and romance, and this has been well shown by Dumas himself in his preface to "Comte Hermann," in which our author explains and defends the outcomes of his first dramatic period. He had taken part, as Castelar truly says, "in that war of giants, the struggle for the poetry of nature against the poetry of the Académie, breaking the chains of all literary codes, and loudly proclaiming liberty; ardent and daring even to folly, like a hero in the war of his age against past ages."

Why, we may fairly ask, should critics take eager note of the excesses of the young dramatist and ignore his second and last periods, when experience had taught a nature instinctively sane the folly of that Byronic mood, in which it had copied perhaps not the best qualities of Shakespeare? Dumas's three famous comedies are all "on the side of the angels"; and "Conscience," "Le Marbrier," and "Comte Hermann" are almost sermons in their didactic presentment of moral truths.

We may leave this point in our case, then, quoting in support the words of Brander Matthews, the American critic:

"The horrible is not necessarily immoral . . . morality is an affair, not of subject but of treatment, and Dumas's . . . is not insidious or vicious."

No sooner had the orthodox French classicists found Dumas's plays startlingly successful than they set themselves to discover the sources of his plots, and to their great delight, ascertained that he had "stolen" right and left, from English, German and other writers. In reply to this cry of "Thief! thief!" the author, in boldly characteristic fashion, stated his theory of defence in respect of plagiarism:

"It is men who invent, and not the individual. Each in his turn and in his time lays hands on something accomplished by his fore-runners, makes use of it in a new way, and then dies, after having added some small share to the sum of human knowledge. This he bequeaths to his successors, —a new star in the Milky Way. As for the creative completion of a thing, I believe that to be impossible."

After having quoted Shakespeare and Molière in support of his practice, Dumas adds:

"The man of genius does not steal, he conquers; he makes the province which he annexes a part of his own empire, peoples it with his own subjects, and imposes his own laws upon it. He extends his golden sceptre over it, and no one dares to say, as they look upon his fair kingdom, 'That piece of ground was not part of his patrimony.'"

One delightful sample of the knowledge and spirit with which Dumas was attacked by his detractors is recorded in the "Mémoires." "Isabel de Bavière" was, as we know, published serially in the first numbers of *Revue des deux Mondes*, which was at that time little known and read by few. Bourgeois and Lockroy joined some of the most striking scenes of the *chronique* together and made them into a play called "Perrinet Leclerc," which was very successful. At that time Dumas had collaborated with Bourgeois in a drama "Le Fils Emigré," which our author confesses to have been an "execrable" play. One of the leading critics of the day reviled Dumas as if he were the sole author of the latter drama, but praised the other to the skies; and not content with this, the journalist emphasised his own fatuity by calling attention to the rare literary and historical merits of the story of "Perrinet Leclerc," and comparing it, greatly to its advantage, with "Le Fils Emigré," for which Dumas was only partly responsible! But the best was yet to come; for when Dumas re-issued "Isabel de Bavière" in book-form the critics fell foul of him for stealing from MM. Bourgeois and Lockroy!

It is best to recognise that the charge of "plagiarism" has been brought against almost every dramatist of weight since plays first were written; and one of Dumas's defenders has made a full and instructive list of the "thefts" attributed to Shakespeare Molière, Sheridan, and even the classical writers themselves. It is in our view simply a question whether the "borrower" does or does not add to the value of the material he uses; whether he imprints the personality of his own talent upon it. Surely Dumas did that. "All his plagiarisms, and they were not a few," says Brander Matthews, "are the veriest trifles when compared with his indisputable and extraordinary powers . . . It irks one to see Dumas pilloried as a mere vulgar appropriator of the works of other men."

The cry "plagiarist!" was not raised so loudly or generally against Dumas's romances, and such charges as were brought we have already dealt with. It was now that the cry of "collaborators!"

was heard in the land; and this time the plays, with the exception of "La Tour de Nesle," of which we have spoken, were let off lightly, partly because Dumas's earliest plays were incontestibly his own, partly because he did not dispute the share of Maquet, Bourgeois and the rest, in the later productions. A new charge, therefore, was levelled at the romancer, whose second fame infuriated his enemies. He was represented as a rich, prosperous (!) spider who lured the starving flies into his web, and sucked their brains, "swelling wisibly" thus, whilst they dwelt in darkness, enduring an obscure, not to say empty, existence.

Dumas's reply to this terrible indictment was a challenge, which we need hardly say was never accepted. He informed these unknown but talented authors that he was supplying the *feuilleton* to one Paris journal only, and that therefore the rest of the press was open to them. This was their opportunity: now they could vindicate themselves, and win a reputation that was their own undisputedly. "Write a 'Monte Cristo' or a 'Trois Mousquetaires,'" he pleaded; "don't wait until I am dead—let me in turn have the pleasure of reading your books!" The answer was—silence.

Dumas was always the man of genius, whoever his co-worker may have been, and this is asserted by all critics of any standing. "That he was the moving spirit still, and the actual author of what is best and most peculiar in the works which go by his name," says Mr Saintsbury, "is sufficiently proved by the fact that none of his assistants, whose names are in many cases known, and who in not a few instances subsequently attained eminence on their own account, has equalled or even resembled his peculiar style." "Whereas Dumas could turn out books that live, whoever his assistants were," adds Mr Lang, "could any of his assistants write books that live without Dumas? One might as well call any barrister in good practice a thief and an impostor because he has juniors to devil for him, as make charges of this kind against Dumas." Theophile Gautier employs the same argument, in his "Histoire de l'Art Dramatique." "He has been reproached with having had collaborators," writes Castelar. "I declare that all these collaborators lost their brilliancy when they separated from Dumas; and I must add, that all of them united do not weigh in the literary balances of Europe half as much as Dumas weighed alone."

The implied accusation that Dumas injured and debauched his "assistants" has been ruthlessly spoilt by M. Edmond About. "The master," he declared, "took from them neither their money, for they are rich, nor their reputation, for they are celebrated, nor their merit, for they have it still, and in plenty. For the rest, they have never pitied themselves: on the contrary, the proudest of them have congratulated themselves on having been to such a good school, and it is with a true veneration that the greatest of them, M. Maquet, speaks of his old friend."

The great romancer frequently protested against the word "collaborators," and he was right, for it implies an equality in quantity and quality of the work done which was not justified. "Dumas's method," says Mr Lang, "apparently was first to talk the subject over with his *aide-de-camp*. This is an excellent practice, as ideas are knocked out, like sparks (an elderly illustration), by the contact of minds. Then the young man probably made researches, put a rough sketch on paper, and supplied Dumas, as it were, with his 'brief.' Then Dumas took the 'brief' and wrote the novel. He gave it life—he gave it the spark (*l'étincelle*), and the story lived and moved."

The testimony of one of the great man's best collaborators is valuable evidence on this point. Fiorentino, in his "Comédies et Comédiens," writes: "How many believed themselves his collaborators who were only his confidants!... In his books, but above all, in his plays, his collaborators had only the smallest share. He remodelled the scenarios, changed the characters, added or cut down entire acts, and wrote all in his own hand."

Thackeray, with a *camaraderie* and candour, both of which do him infinite credit, has stoutly defended this system in one of his "Roundabout Papers." The support it gives to our author is none the less valuable for having been written in a half-jesting manner. "They say," adds the English novelist, after a eulogy of Dumas, "that all the works bearing his name are not written by him. Well? Does not the chief cook have *aides* under him? Did not Rubens's pupils paint on his canvasses? Had not Lawrence assistants for his backgrounds? For myself, being also *du métier*, I confess I would often like to have a competent, respectable, and rapid clerk for the business part of my novels. . . . Sir Christopher is the architect of St Paul's. He has not laid the stones or carried up the mortar. There is a great deal of carpenter's and joiner's work in novels which surely a smart professional hand might supply."

We may venture to add to these "testimonials" from writers more or less expert or learned in fiction, our own strong belief that the ideal romance of fact or history in particular requires two workers at it— the one to prepare the material, and the other to make use of it. The case of Scott, of course, will be brought forward as evidence to the contrary; but surely those who recognise the existence of such a study as the Art of Narrative will admit that Scott the poetic novelist was often terribly hampered by Scott the antiquarian and archæologist. In searching out details, in verifying references, and the other work of preparation the imagination is naturally restrained, the fancy is deadened, the mental energies turn in the direction of the trivial, the precise, the formal. Charles Reade, a master of narrative, too frequently gives us a glimpse of Reade the compiler of cuttings-books. Dumas himself offers a still more glaring example; for when preparing "La San Felice" he made his own researches into the original documents, and, seeing the historical and picturesque importance of each, he wrote a story full of detail and long parentheses, which only his great skill saved from being dull and drawn-out. If the facts had been brought to him already ferreted out, he would have seen and seized on the salient points, and have written a romance half the length, but with ten times the brilliance and engrossing charm.

It frequently proclaimed, by people imperfectly acquainted with Dumas's novels, that they are immoral in nature and tendency. It must be confessed that this is true—if books dealing with pitch must of necessity be themselves defiled. He attempted to teach his fellow-Frenchmen the history of their nation, and the history of France, social and political, is full of improperly-behaved personages. We can quite understand the attitude of those people who wish to ignore great facts, such as the sensual as well as the ethereal side of love between the sexes, the passionate love which laughs at priests and lawyers, and other objectionable traits of human nature. We advise these readers to avoid Dumas, —and all the other great writers. "If," says Mr. W. H. Pollock, "his writing is not intended for boys and maidens, that is one quality which he has in common with such playwriters as for instance, Shakespeare, Racine, and Molière, and such novelists as Goëthe, Fielding, and Le Sage. His method was at any rate 'an honest method'; he did not palter, as the modern French school of playwriting does, with vice and virtue, keeping one foot in the domain of each, and casting a false glamour of splendour around corruption."

But hear the defendant in his own cause.

"I had, thank God, a natural sentiment of delicacy (as a boy), and thus, out of my six hundred volumes[1] there are not four which the most scrupulous mother may not give to her daughter." Dumas repeated this assertion in a letter to Napoleon III in 1864, twelve years later, adding, "I am as fatherly as Sir Walter Scott." We are afraid that

[1] See note, p. 225

Dumas gave mothers credit for too much breadth and independence of mind. When Stevenson, in defence of our romancer, wrote that " the world is wide and so are morals," he did not hope to win Mrs. Grundy's approval of the sentiment. Mr. Lang, dealing more directly with Dumas's reply, adds: " his enormous popularity, the widest in the world of letters, owes absolutely nothing to prurience or curiosity. The air which he breathes is a healthy air, is the open air, and that by his own choice, for he had every temptation to seek another kind of vogue, and every opportunity." Hayward, again, notices the difference between Dumas and so many other of the French writers with whom he is ignorantly and indiscriminately classed. " His best romances," says the author of " Biographical Essays," " rarely trangress propriety, and are entirely free from that hard, cold, sceptical, materialist, illusion-destroying tone which is so repelling in Balzac and many others of the most popular French novelists."

Professor Carpenter lifts the subject to a higher plane of thought.

" I find it impossible," he writes, " to admit that Dumas's ideals were low, unfit for common use. It is of honour that he tells most willingly—of man's honour and the constancy of men to men; of man's striving against the powders of the world by force and guile; of man's love of woman and the curb it puts on cowardice and sloth and selfishness; of man's strength and weakness; of a nation's slow progress onward and upward toward order and justice. Dumas was not an austere moralist, and his life was prodigal; but the reader will find on reflection that the ethical system revealed by his books is one which, the more we consider, the more we shall approve."

We may add that we made one or two experiments to test Dumas's books from this point of view. We have asked repeatedly at shops where French novels of the pornographic type have been displayed in large quantities, and have failed to obtain a copy of one of the master's novels. We have found that at free libraries (and at the committee meetings connected with such institutions Mrs. Grundy is always present in spirit) that Dumas's works are admitted fully and freely, where Fielding, Defoe, Zola, Boccaccio and others are forbidden. Lastly, we have followed Ruskin's advice and left our bookshelves open to the use of the Young Person, who has frequently chosen one of our author's stories, and returned it in due course with warm and ingenuous acknowledgment of the pleasure the book has given her.

We have already dealt to some extent with the charge that Dumas, in writing amusing stories of the past, has distorted or ignored history. In support of this indictment the critics have quoted the passages in "Vingt Ans Après" relating to our Civil War and the execution of Charles—together with the "General Monk" episode, in "Bragelonne," and the plot of the plays "Catherine Howard" and "Kean." As he has expressed it in a well-known sentence, Dumas deliberately violated history, when he had some set purpose to achieve which rendered it necessary. The word "fiction" implies something, even in historical romance, and the writer who has not the nerve to make a little history for his own purposes, and to take liberties with great personages, may contrive very accurate history, but we are afraid he will write a very dull romance. On the other hand, when Dumas set himself to reproduce a certain period in the past centuries, he was full of precise detail and historic fact. And he was supreme in what, after all, was the essential: he caught and revivified the atmosphere of those by-gone days with a fidelity, a power of conviction, a charm, and a subtle skill which no one before or since has excelled.

The warfare between the classicists and romantics in French literature was waged fiercely throughout Dumas's prime. Nisard, of whom we have spoken, fastened on Dumas the stigma of "easy composition." To this our author replied with his customary good-humoured banter, behind which lurked a good deal of sense and power :

"When one is a real romancer, you know, it is as easy to produce a romance as for an apple-tree to produce apples. This is how it is done.

"One gets one's paper, pen and ink; one sits down, as comfortably as possible, at a table not too high, not to low; one reflects for half an hour, one writes a little. After the title, comes Chapter I ; then one writes thirty-five lines to a page, fifty letters to a line—for two hundred pages, if it is to be a romance in two volumes—for four hundred pages if in four volumes—for eight hundred pages, if in eight volumes, and so on. And after ten or twenty or forty days, supposing that one writes twenty pages between morning and evening, which means seven hundred lines, or 38,500 letters daily, the romance is finished.

"That is the way I work, say most of the critics who are good enough to concern themselves about me; and these gentlemen only forget one thing.

"It is this : that before preparing the ink, the pens and the paper which must serve for the material in the development of a new romance, before drawing my arm-chair up to the table, before writing the title and those two very simple words 'Chapter I.,' I have sometimes thought for six months, a year, ten years, about the subject on which I am going to write. I owe to this way of working the clearness of my intrigue, the simplicity of my methods, the naturalness of my effects. As a rule I do not begin a book until it is finished."

A women of talent, Madame de Girardin, who knew and admired Dumas, put the case for her friend even more forcibly:

"This rapidity of composition, is like the swiftness of a railway train: both work on the same principles, from the same causes—an extreme facility obtained by difficulties overcome. You cover sixty leagues in three hours: it is nothing—you laugh at the swiftness of your travelling. But to what do you owe this marvel of transportation? To years of daunting toil, to money spent like water, all along your way, and to thousands of pairs of arms which have prepared the way for you, day after weary day. You flash past so swiftly that one can scarcely see you; but to gain that freedom of speed for you, how men have slaved, and grown old, bending over the pick and shovel! What plans have been made, and baulked; what cares, what struggles has it not cost, to whirl you from this spot to that, so smoothly and easefully, and without a care or a fear!"

Blaze de Bury further explains Dumas's facility

of working, doing justice to his friend's marvellous memory, and that power of intuition and divination which was almost second-sight.

"When other authors write," he says, "they are stopped every other minute—there is a detail to discover, or a reference to verify—a lapse of memory, or some other obstacle. Dumas was never stopped by anything. The practice of writing for the stage gave him great fluency in composition; add to these gifts sparkling wit, and inexhaustible gaiety, and you will understand how, with such resources, a man may achieve an incredible rapidity of production without sacrificing skill in construction or injuring the quality or solidity of his work."

The same writer adds shrewdly "the public were very ready to despise as 'shop-made goods' books written in such quantity, being unwilling to believe that there are certain favoured individualities like those blest places of the earth where the grain shoots into green and ripens in a few weeks. It is no sin to own these precious gifts: it is only wrong to abuse them."

It is difficult for most people to comprehend that a book quickly written can be well written; and the obvious course of trying the work on its merits does not seem to occur to them. As the old prejudices of fifty years ago are still held to-day, we shall do well to quote Maxime Du Camp's protest on behalf of his old friend, which has been excellently paraphrased and elaborated by Mr Lang.

"A writer so fertile, so rapid, so masterly in the ease with which he worked, could not escape the reproaches of barren envy. Because you overflowed with wit, you could not be 'serious'; because you created with a word, you were said to scamp your work; because you were never dull, never pedantic, incapable of greed, you were to be censured as desultory, inaccurate, and prodigal."

Having assured themselves that Dumas wrote rapidly and therefore badly, the critics proceeded quite confidently to dower that author with another literary vice.

In theology there is a sin so terrible as to be unmentionable; in literature there is a sin so awful as to be indefinable. Therefore, it was decided, in order to dispose once and for all of the French romancer's claims on the tender-hearted public, that he should be declared to have no "style." There is only one thing certain about this mysterious quality—that those who do not possess it cannot belong to the elect.

Far be it from us to dare to attempt to indicate the nature and habits of this mythical creation: we can only attempt to win a place for Dumas among the "stylists" (for we must "conform" to this creed in the literary religion) by putting forward the testimony of such as are "within the pale." If a sufficient number of these haloed great can be persuaded to gather round our sinner, perhaps it may never be noticed that he himself wears no such symbol of intellectual sanctity.

Our first witness (we grieve to betray his identity, but we must give chapter and verse), is R. L. Stevenson, whose manner of composition was the very opposite of Dumas's. He is allowed to possess "style," and truly he laboured hard and nobly to win it—the quality itself, not the acknowledgment of it.

"There is no style so untranslatable " (as Dumas's), he wrote; "light as a whipped trifle; strong as silk; wordy like a village tale; pat like a general's despatch; with every fault, yet never tedious, with no merit, yet inimitably right."

Next we have Mr Lang. In addition to his fame as scholar and critic, was he not the prize "stylist" of an "Academy" competition? That is as good as a degree at a University, it is an unofficial election to a *fauteuil* and Immortality (with a capital I). Then note with respect this evidence:

"When I read the maunderings, the stilted and staggering sentences, the hesitating phrases, the far-sought and dear-bought and worthless word-juggles; the sham scientific verbiage, the native pedantries of many modern so-called 'stylists,' I rejoice that Dumas was not one of these. He told a plain tale, in the language suited to a plain tale, with abundance of wit and gaiety. . . . but he did not gnaw the end of his pen in search of some word that nobody had ever used in this or that connection before. The right word came to him, the simple straightforward phrase. Epithet-hunting may be a pretty sport, and the bag of the epithet-hunter may contain some agreeable epigrams and rare specimens of style; but a plain tale of adventure, of love and war, needs none of this industry, and is even spoiled by inopportune diligence."

This misguided critic involves himself more deeply still. He praises Dumas's dialogue for its unsurpassed excellence, and dares to claim for some of Dumas's phrases that they are unconsciously Homeric!

"In your works we hear the Homeric Muse again, rejoicing in the clash of steel; and even, at times, your very phrases are unconsciously Homeric. Look at these men of murder, on the Eve of St Bartholomew, who flee in terror from the Queen's chamber, and 'find the door too narrow for their flight': the very words were anticipated in a line of the 'Odyssey' concerning the massacre of the Wooers. And the picture of Catherine de Medicis, prowling 'like a wolf among the bodies and the blood,' in a passage of the Louvre—the picture is taken unwittingly from the 'Iliad.'"

We are not, we confess, aware whether or no Balzac is admitted to be a "stylist," but at least two critics prefer Dumas's language to that of his great rival; for Brander Matthews favourably compares the running sentences of the romancer with the tortured "style" of the realist; and Nisard, in spite of his prejudices, acknowledges that Dumas "tells his story with more vivacity (than Balzac), in dialogue more witty and natural, and clothed in better words." Parigot admits that Dumas takes no heed of the literary merit of his writing, but claims that nevertheless he shows taste and care, and a choice of clear and sane language. Edmond About prophesied that Dumas would become a classic, "thanks to the limpidity of his style." Dumas a classic! Yet the history of literature tells us that more unlikely things have happened. We shall be laughed at when we point out that passages from the romancer's books are constantly being chosen and edited for use in schools and colleges, and yet the fact is not so puerile as its connection would seem to imply. Those who are responsible for such productions are men of culture, with a professional knowledge of French literature and with reputations to maintain. If they find in Dumas's books qualities which make them fit to be put before scholars as models of French composition, we may rest assured that there is some suspicion of "style" about our author's writing, after all.

We may return to the point touched upon by Mr Lang, that Dumas's style—we use the word in its uncanonical sense—was fitted to its author's purpose. "Of art, of careful choice, of laborious adaptation of words and phrases and paragraphs there is none," says Professor Saintsbury. "It is even capable of being argued whether, consistently with his peculiar plan and object, there could, or ought to be, any. A novel of incident, if it be good, must be read as rapidly the seventh time as it is the first." Quite so; the romancer's desire was to tell you a story in a way that would enthral you from beginning to end; if you stopped to admire the exquisiteness of a phrase, or to ponder over the possibilities which a thought suggested, you would lose the thread of the story, the charm that its narrator had woven about you would be broken, and his aim would be defeated.

Even when Dumas seems wordy there is, as another great story-teller saw clearly, an artistic reason for it. Stevenson, writing to one of his friends, touched on this point, and declared "if there is anywhere a thing said in two sentences that could have been as clearly and as engagingly and as forcibly said in one, then it's amateur work."

But he added: "Then you will bring me up with old Dumas. Nay, the object of a story is to be long, to fill up hours; the story-teller's art of writing is to water out by continual invention, historical and technical, and yet not seem to water; seem, on the other hand, to practise that same wit of conspicuous and declaratory condensation which is the proper art of writing."

One last word on this point. We have taken a solemn vow not to blaspheme by attempting to define the occult word, but if style can be said to imply distinction and individuality in a writer, and that in a praiseworthy sense, then we claim it for Dumas. Once the reader is acquainted with his style (in the French) he can hardly mistake it. And if it is justified in narrative by its artistic subservience to the story, it justifies itself in the lighter writings of its author. Unfortunately these are practically unknown to the general British reading public. "In the slightest and loosest work of his vainest mood or his idlest moment Dumas is at least unaffected and unpretentious," says Swinburne; and we may add that in the best of his "occasional writings" he exhibits qualities of wit, humour, and neatness of expression in a high degree.

The last count in this lengthy indictment is perhaps the most serious. It is asserted that

Dumas, at least in the latter part of his life, "wrote for money."

This is a loose phrase, and we must distinguish. Most authors write for money. "Intimate" biographies show that in private life all writers not born to affluence have valued the work of their brains in filthy lucre; that they have demanded—and quite rightly—the market price for their work. The questions which really touch the quick of the subject are: Did Dumas pander to the public for gain? Did he consciously lower and debase his abilities for money? Was money the prime object of his labours? We deny all these possible charges. Granted, that Dumas, like many another artist, turned out bad work at times; that he spoke of his books on occasion in commercial terms; that he was generally pressed for money, and obliged to turn to his desk to satisfy a dun, or fulfil a contract, and that in the last few years he resorted to shifts unbecoming in a man of genius. He never parted company with his literary conscience. A score of examples of this could be given: how he destroyed bad work; how he delayed or refused to commence work for which he had not found in his brain the plan of adequate treatment; and how he deplored the bad stuff which he had been coerced or persuaded into doing. He never wrote unworthily, or below his own level. The greed of money, for money's sake, for anything that money could give him, was foreign to the man's generous, *insouciant* nature. Before and after the writing of a story, the man of business was keenly alive in Dumas, as in all shrewd authors; once plunged into the story the man became the artist; he had no thought but for the story and the best way of telling it. If he had been miserly, if his work had not been the great enjoyment of his life, the whole story of Dumas's career would have left him open to base suspicion; but the more one learns of the man's nature and life-story, the more clearly one sees in him the artist, not the artisan.

COUNTERCLAIM.

In the hope that we have extenuated or disproved the charges against Dumas, and shown him guilty of literary faults rather than vices, we shall modify our metaphor and treat the case more lightly. Believing it only just to look upon the matter rather as a question for the civil courts of literature, we close our defence and proceed to put in a counter-claim of as modest a nature as our convictions respecting the true worth of our client's cause will allow.

It is noteworthy that whereas we in England look

upon Dumas simply as a writer of fiction, and are ignorant of his plays, the French regard him almost exclusively as a dramatist. "This," says Blaze de Bury shrewdly, "is because the imperturbable entomological public loves classification, and will only judge a man from one point of view."

Unable as we are to prove Dumas's merits as a playwright by instance and reminder, to readers unacquainted with his stage triumphs, we must again have recourse to "expert opinion," and show indirectly, and as concisely as possible, the high position which Dumas occupies in the ranks of the world's dramatists.

He possessed the "dramatic instinct" to the full. "He is not a dramatic author; he is the drama incarnate!" cried Fiorentino. Dumas has told us, with a pride which is justifiable, that all he needed was the bare apparatus of a stage, "two actors, and a passion." In this he is held to have been superior—as a craftsman—to his friend and rival, Victor Hugo. Whatever Heine was as a dramatic critic, he was a man of piercing insight where his prejudices did not obscure his view, and further, a keen student of the literature of his time; and this is what he says of the two authors, in his letters on the French stage:

"The best tragic poets in France are still Alexandre Dumas and Victor Hugo. I put the latter in the second place because his efficiency as regards the theatre is not so great or productive of result. . . . Dumas is not so great a poet as Hugo—far from it—but he has qualities which go much further, as regards the theatre. He has at command that prompt, straightforward expression of passion which the French call *verve*, and therein he is more French than Hugo; he sympathises with all vices and virtues, daily needs and restless fancies of his fellow-countrymen; he is by turns enthusiastic, comedian-like, noble, frivolous, swaggering, a real son of France, that Gascony of Europe. He speaks to heart with heart, and is understood and applauded.

"No one has such a talent for the dramatic as Dumas. The theatre is his true calling—he is a born stage poet, and all materials for the drama belong to him wherever he finds them, in nature or in Schiller, Shakespeare or Calderon. A very unjust criticism on art which appeared long ago under most deplorable circumstances in the *Journal des Debats* greatly injured our poor poet among the ignorant multitude. In it was shown that many scenes in his plays had the most striking resemblance to others in former dramas. But there is nothing so foolish as this reproach of plagiarism; the poet may grasp and grab boldly wherever he finds material for his works; he may even appropriate whole columns, carved capitals and all, so that the temple which they support be magnificent. Goëthe understood this very well, as did Shakespeare long before him."

Professor Brander Matthews in his consideration of our author as playwright cannot avoid the coupling of the two great names. "There is but one dramatist of Dumas's generation who will stand comparison with him," he says; "and even Victor Hugo, master as he is of many things, is less a master of the theatre than Dumas."

Dumas *fils* wrote of his father as one "who was and is the master of the modern stage, whose prodigious imagination touched the four cardinal points of our art,—tragedy, historic drama, the dramas of manners, and the comedy of anecdote,— whose only fault was to lack solemnity, and to have genius without pride, and fecundity without effort, as he had youth and health; and who (to conclude), Shakespeare being taken as the culminating point, by invention, power and variety, approached among us most closely to Shakespeare." And Professor Matthews adds, of the son's opinion: "Due allowance made, he is not so very far out."

"Dumas broke ground," writes Mr Henley, "with the ease, the assurance, the insight into essentials, and a technical accomplishment of a master, and he retained these qualities to the last. . . . He was the soundest influence in drama of the century." Sardou has similarly declared Dumas to have been "*le premier homme de théâtre du siècle passé.*" Castelar has this passage on Dumas as a revolutionary leader, a pioneer of stage liberty:

"A lover of the drama, he proved himself able to reanimate the theatre. To accomplish this purpose he chose pieces of lively interest, characters of a strongly marked individuality, descriptions of unbridled passions, which, though without the artificial rules of poetic conventionality, followed the inspirations of fancy in its native purity, and were powerful enough to awaken artistic attention."

Did Dumas in his ardour go too far? Goëthe uttered a warning note when, two years before his death, he addressed the young poet after the success of "Christine":

"Friend," he wrote, "don't go further than your masters, Delavigne and Béranger, Schiller and Scott. Beware of forcing your activity; production without respite ends in bankruptcy of one's talent. Whatever frees the fancy, without retaining it within the control of reason, is pernicious. Art must be at the command of the imagination, if it is to have an outcome in poetry. Nothing is more terrible than imagination deprived of taste."

Whether or no Goëthe's advice was necessary, and applicable, we leave to be discussed by others, and elsewhere; but we are inclined to suspect, by the choice of masters here prescribed for Dumas, that the sage neither comprehended the nature of our author's talent, nor foresaw its tendencies.

Certainly the drama of passion and intrigue, of which Dumas's own plays are the first great examples, developed extremes for which the originator cannot fairly be blamed. George Sand saw this, when, in dedicating her play on Molière to her friend and *confrère*, she pleaded for psychology as well as movement and action, as an element in the drama. She protested against the idea that her play, illustrating this theory, was in any way a challenge levelled against the school of which Dumas was the chief.

"I love your works too well," she continued, "I read them, I listen to them with too much emotion and appreciation to wish to cast the slightest slur on your triumphs. . . . You have lifted dramatic action to the highest power, without any desire to sacrifice psychological interest to it, but your imitators have abandoned this second essential, for one must be of strong calibre to keep both ideals equally to the fore."

In his expositions of the hidden motives of his plays, in his skilful analysis of his son's great play ("La Dame aux Camélias"), and in various chapters of his "Souvenirs Dramatiques," Dumas showed that he was something more than the teller of a stage story, something better than a clever manipulator of incident and intrigue, plot and passion. "A man?" cried Michelet, "no, an element, like an inextinguishable volcano or a great American river. . . . He remains the most powerful craftsman, the most *living* dramatist since Shakespeare."

Of Dumas's influence on the modern French drama, M. Parigot has written fully and learnedly in his " Drame d'Alexandre Dumas," showing the effect produced in varying ways and degrees by the playwright on the later nineteenth century,—on his son, on Augier, Sandeau, Daudet, Lemaître, Meilhac and Halévy, Sardou, and others. He "exercised a continuous and profound influence on the drama of the nineteenth century," adds the writer, and we need only supplement his verdict by calling attention to the case of the "latest discovery" in French dramatic literature, Edmond Rostand, whose success with "Cyrano de Bergerac" so closely recalls the triumphs of the author of " Les Trois Mousquetaires" and " Henri Trois."

On our English drama the plays of Dumas have had only a subtly indirect effect. As the founder of the " society drama " he has much to answer for; but for our sterile " West-End " fashion plays, and the modern French school which has been evolved from "Antony" and his successors, the old playwright cannot fairly be held responsible. He was the first to vivify the melodrama in its higher form, and the history-drama, at present so popular with us, owes its true birth to the author of "La Tour de Nesle." His three comedies have each been "adapted" and produced in London within recent years, but without much success; and we may predict, without going into the grounds for our belief, that his books may be dramatised from time to time, but that his plays themselves will never take root with us.

It is with a very judicious fear of our "entomological public" that we claim for Dumas a supreme place as a master of the art of narrative. True, Swinburne goes further, and acclaims him "the king of story-tellers;" and a poet-critic in many respects akin in taste to the author of "Atalanta in Calydon" held a similar opinion. Oliver Madox Brown once wrote to his father in great perturbation:

"(D. G.) Rossetti . . . has had several long discussions with me on the subject of novel-writing. . . . Thackeray he will hardly hear the name of; George Eliot is vulgarity personified; Balzac is melodramatic in plot, conceited, wishy-washy, and dull. Dumas is the one great and supreme man, the sole descendant of Shakespeare."

In reply to a letter from ourselves, Mr W. M.

Rossetti has kindly confirmed this record with his own testimony.

"It is perfectly true," he writes, "that my brother took the greatest delight in reading Dumas, and I think it may be said that, if he had been asked 'whom do you regard as the greatest novelist that ever existed—in those qualities which are most essential for novel-writing?' he would have replied 'Dumas.' Of course he would at the same time have been conscious that Walter Scott, as a precursor of Dumas, had to some extent served him as a pattern."[1]

Henley strikes the same note of praise. "Dumas is assuredly one of the greatest masters of the art of narrative in all literature," he says, and amplifies his assertion thus: "He was an artist at once original and exemplary, with an incomparable instinct of selection, a constructive faculty not equalled among the men of this century, an understanding of what is right and what is wrong in art, and a mastery of his materials which in their way are not to be paralleled in the work of Sir Walter himself."

The frequent references to Scott force us without

[1] Another passage in this letter is interesting, in connection with much that has been written above. "In my very early years—say 1846-7," adds Mr Rossetti, "my brother and I knew more of Dumas as a dramatist than novelist. 'Don Juan de Marana' was our favourite; next might come 'Antony' and 'Caligula.' 'Kean' we used to laugh over, for its amusing travestie of English manners and customs."

further delay to face a comparison as inevitable in the case of Dumas the novelist, as was that with Hugo in the case of Dumas the playwright. The two names—in the field of romance—are linked together inseparably by talents, time, and circumstance; but until recent years the ordinary English critic would not admit of any degree of equality between the two. It is no doubt an act of daring on our part to presume to discuss the relative merits of the two men, as if the Frenchman could seriously challenge the Scotsman's supremacy. Yet we venture to submit that, generally speaking, the two writers, as masters of the historical romance, stand on a level, and that Sir Walter, superior as he is in some respects, has been excelled by his pupil in the art of story-telling.

In claiming this point for our client we own that we should have none of that client's sympathy. Scott, as we have said, was Dumas's teacher, and the junior never wearied of expressing his praise, his gratitude, and reverence for the older writer. "Scott," he wrote in his "Mémoires," "had a great influence on me in the early days of my literary life." In another book he analysed the causes of his master's success, thus: "To the natural qualities of his predecessors Scott added knowledge specially acquired; to his study of the hearts of men, he added that of the science of popular history;

dowered with archæological zeal, a quick discerning eye, and the power to reanimate, his genius conjured into a new existence a past epoch, with all its manners, interests and emotions."

Dumas saw one of Scott's weak points, but dealt with it very pleasantly and tenderly.

"Scott," (he says in his "Histoire de mes Bêtes"), "had his own way of creating interest in his characters, which, though with a few exceptions always the same, and though at first a little disconcerting, succeeded none the less. This method was, to be wearisome, mortally wearisome, often for half a volume, sometimes for a whole volume. But during this volume he placed his characters, and gave such a minute description of their appearance, of their mental status, of the traits of their individuality; one knew so well how they walked, dressed, and spoke, that when at the beginning of the second volume one of these characters found himself in some danger, you exclaimed 'Ah, here's this poor limping chap in Lincoln green—how on earth is he going to get out of this?'"

And then our author goes on to set his own method of narrative by the side of Scott's, of course to the advantage of the latter, declaring that Sir Walter gives you the best dishes last and the worst ones first, so that one rises from the table delighted; but that he himself reverses the process, leaving the guests to go out on the house-tops and revile the stupid *chef's* bill of fare.

But it was another thing entirely, when Dumas thought of Scott as a possible pattern for himself, in the self-imposed task of writing the history of France in romance. In two important respects the genius of the younger man broke away from his teacher's style.

"The qualities of Walter Scott are not dramatic qualities," he declared. "Admirable in the portrayal of manners, costumes and characters, he was completely unable to paint passions. The only 'romance of passion' amongst his novels is 'Kenilworth.' . . . My analysis of Scott's books taught me to see the romance from another point of view to that familiar to us in those days. The same fidelity to manners, costumes, and characters, with a brighter, more natural dialogue, and with passions that were more life-like—these appeared to me to be what we needed."

In course of time Dumas applied these beliefs of his, enormously aided by the experience and discipline of fifteen years of play-writing. The result we know.

One of Sir Walter's most fervent admirers, Mr Lang, has underlined much that we have already implied, and though he probably ranks Scott higher than the Frenchman, both as a man and as a writer, he certainly seems to us to endorse all that we have claimed for our author. In "Essays in Little" he touches this point again and again:

"Speed, directness, lucidity, are the characteristics of Dumas's style, and they are exactly the characteristics which his novels required. Scott often failed, his most loyal admirers may admit, in these essentials; but it is rarely that Dumas fails, when he is himself and at his best." We venture to add that these are the qualities which the ideal story should possess. Further on we read: "It is admitted that Dumas's good tales are told with a vigour and life which rejoice the heart; that his narrative is never dull, never stands still, but moves with a freedom of adventure which perhaps has no parallel. . . . If Dumas has not, as he certainly has not, the noble philosophy and kindly knowledge of the heart which are Scott's, he is far more swift, more witty, more diverting. He is not prolix, his style is not involved, his dialogue is as rapid and keen as an assault-at-arms."

The qualities which have made Scott so great and so beloved are not part of his technical skill in narrative, and it is only with that particular quality that we are concerned here. Mr Saintsbury, in the "Short History of French Literature," although treating Dumas critically, as becomes one sitting on the judge's bench, does not hesitate to set the Frenchman, in his peculiar talent, above Scott and all others.

"His best work," the professor declares, "has remarkable and almost unique merits. The style is not more remarkable as such than that of the dramas; there is not often or always a well-defined plot, and the characters are drawn only in the broadest outline. But the peculiar admixture of incident and dialogue by which Dumas carries on the interest of his gigantic narrations without wearying the reader is a secret of his own, and has never been thoroughly mastered by anyone else."

An American critic, emancipated from any superstitious feeling concerning Scott, has put his opinion in blunt and unmistakable form. "What is it," asks Professor Carpenter, "that endears Dumas to us? The conventional answer would be, the exciting character of his plots. And his plots may well be called exciting. No other author—except Sienkiewicz, who learned the art from him—can match him there. He is better reading than Scott; for there are, as a rule, no elaborate essays, no dull dialogues, no stupid characters, satisfactory only to the antiquary. The characters act and talk; but they talk only to make the act more telling. The whole moves quietly, rapidly, but without unnecessary haste; every scene is to be enjoyed as it passes; and one is impressed throughout by the power that the author keeps in reserve for each of his climaxes."

In short, although Dumas found his inspiration in Scott, the style of the Frenchman's romances was essentially different. He wrote with a lighter, bolder touch. He got rid of all the impedimenta which baulked the Scotsman's speed. His books contain little or no background; he is not concerned with scenery; still-life has no attraction for him. Nor do his heroes indulge in the torments of mind which assail the old-fashioned English hero: they simply speak and act.

Nothing, however, can be so instructive as a test-comparison of novels by the two romancers—say "Waverley" and "Les Trois Mousquetaires." Take it as granted that it is a story's first duty to be readable, and that one's attention should be seized as quickly as possible; and with this common-sense fact in mind, dip first into the Scottish and then into the French romance.

"Waverley's" first nine chapters are devoted successively to an introduction, the hero's birth, his education, his day-dreams, his appointment to the army, and his departure from home, with a description of a Scottish "horse-quarter," a manor-house, and again, the manor-house. You have now reached page 40, and you have not yet begun the story. Turn then to the "Mousquetaires." You have a couple of pages of introduction, which go to paint the character of the hero; and on the third the story—the plot—begins, and with it the interest. Your sympathies are at once enlisted on the side of D'Artagnan by the Unknown's cruel behaviour toward him; your curiosity is aroused by the apparent mystery surrounding this same Unknown, by the theft of the letter, and by the vision of Miladi. The political intrigue has begun, also—and all in the first chapter.

Dumas saw clearly that dialogue was the life, the vitality of this style of story—the dramatic romance. It seems a truism now to say that the best insight into the characters of a book is gained by hearing them speak; but the old-fashioned novel relied upon description to convey these impressions to the reader's mind. Now we live in an era of "suggestion"; something is left to one's imagination, and the old "steel-plate-engraving" style is dying out in fiction as in art.

It would be foolish to carry the comparison any further. Scott possessed powers beyond the reach of Dumas, and each writer must be judged according to his aims and nature, and the materials at his command. Few can appreciate both writers, their styles are so opposite. To those who love the Scot Dumas is frivolous and *outré*; to those who are in sympathy with the French spirit, Scott is dull and sluggish. But there can surely be no reasonable doubt as to which is the master and pioneer of the story of adventure as we know it to-day.

The changes which have come over the historical novel within the last twenty or thirty years are striking indeed. The old school was perhaps founded by Scott, and certainly imitated by Lytton, G. P. R. James, Ainsworth, and a host of others. This style possessed several very marked features. Its pages abounded in description; it was not enough to be with our hero in his adventures; we were obliged to listen to the story of his birth, parentage and upbringing, with many other dreary details by way of introduction. We were regaled with lengthy accounts of scenery and buildings, costumes and customs. We found the heroine a very sensitive and sedate young lady, with supreme sensibility and a wonderful capacity for tears. We followed the course of the hero's thoughts, page after page, as he raved at fortune, or rhapsodised upon his love. As a consequence we cultivated a habit of "skipping," and no one to-day would blame us for so doing; for in truth there was a laborious heaviness about the old-fashioned, historical romance.

Scott succeeded in spite of his style—or lack of it—but his successors, one and all, died of theirs.

There is no need, we think, to labour the point as to the Frenchman's influence on present-day romance, if our readers will apply a simple test, and keep one or two dates in mind. Read firstly one of Scott's imitators—some romance of the thirties or forties, and note the rare and stilted dialogue, the padding, the lack of fire, of human interest—the tawdry dreariness of it. Then, after half an hour at the "Mousquetaires," let the reader take up some modern romance, say one of Mr Weyman's, "The Refugees," by Dr Doyle, or Anthony Hope's "Simon Dale." This subject, we are aware, deserves a whole essay, but for all practical purposes the object lesson we have suggested will be sufficient to carry conviction with it.

We are told that the influence of Dumas can be traced back as far as "Esmond," the scene of "the breaking of the sword" being suggested by more than one like incident in the Frenchman's romances. Of the many authors who have benefited by a study of the great *conteur*, one has acknowledged his indebtedness. This is Bret Harte, whom one would scarcely have expected to experience such an influence. He testifies to having received "the sacred spark" whilst reading Dumas—the burial of Dantès in the sack, in particular, having powerfully affected him. "The grandeur of effect, the simplicity of the means, the absence of all apparent effort, caused me an unspeakable joy." In after years he gratefully took the opportunity of proclaiming how much he owed to Dumas. The spirit of our author lives to this day, if Mr A. E. W. Mason's recently published story, "Clementina," be any criterion; and a more recent and more striking example is that of Maxime Gorki, who, though a sombre realist in temperament, was led on to read Gogol and Dumas when all other literature was distasteful to him. Forthwith the Russian was seized with an ambition to write. The fact that the optimistic romancer could awaken emulation in a nature so widely different is a strong proof of the vital power of his talents.

But the modern writer whom Dumas most strongly impressed was Robert Louis Stevenson. This Sidney Colvin acknowledges, in his preface to his friend's "Letters."

"The debate, before his place in literature is settled, must rather turn on other points, as whether the genial essayist and egoist or the romantic inventor and narrator was the stronger in him—whether the Montaigne and Pepys elements prevailed in his literary composition, or the Scott and Dumas elements—a question, indeed, which among those who care for him most has always been at issue." Although Stevenson could not fail to make use of his great knowledge of Dumas for his own ends, being a man of originality in talent, we seem to find traces of the great Frenchman here, there, and everywhere in his admirer's stories—subtle effects, twists of the plot, picturesque situations, chivalric touches, gusts of breezy freshness—all Stevenson, and yet instinctively familiar to the lover of Dumas.

To our master of narrative, those literary adornments of which nowadays we are so disproportionately proud were not entirely lacking. He possessed in supreme degree a third quality—wit. It was this which rendered his dialogue "brilliant" and "unapproachable"—dialogue "of which the quantity would be the most remarkable point, if its quality were not equally remarkable." Echoing Professor Saintsbury, Brander Matthews adds,—"dialogue such as none but Dumas could write. . . . He was witty without effort and without end." This gift, as we have seen, made the quadroon the king of Paris and the most delightful companion, the *causeur par excellence* in print; it made comedy-writing easy to him, and the telling of short stories a delight to reader and writer.

But the companion quality of wit, which is yet so rarely found in conjunction with it, was Dumas's also, although most critics ignore it, and one in particular denies it. "He had little humour, as we understand the word," Professor Matthews declares, "and what he had was on the surface." To say the least of it, humour is not a quality which should be hidden very deeply from observation. Hayward, whose essay shows a close knowledge of our author's writings, remarks "he had an exquisite perception of the humorous"; and we regret we have no means of showing our readers how truly discerning the essayist's words proved him to be. The distinction between the two forms of mirth is a subtle one and difficult to define, we are aware. Dumas's wit is at least quotable, and mostly to be found in dialogue: his humour is more airy and tangible, and frequently is at its best in the telling of a story.

Unluckily many of these tales are not known to the English reader, and a sly style is apt to evaporate in the process of translation. Nevertheless we are convinced that when Dumas's own genuine and complete writings are edited, and Englished by translators of literary taste, this quality in them will be recognised with delight as still another vein of riches in the mine of wealth left us by this versatile genius.

It remains to be seen whether Dumas's works will last. His plays, with one or two exceptions, are almost forgotten, even in France. His travels, which "discovered Europe" to the million, have been imitated so often that they have paid the penalty of their success and become common-place. The literary pendulum swings from romance to realism and back from realism to romance; at present Zola and his school prevail in France, and to a great extent throughout Europe and America. Dumas heartily disliked "naturalism." The Goncourts tell us that when he read "Madame de Bovary" he cried, "If *that* is good, all that we've written since 1830 is worthless!" But the "novel" to-day is, on the whole, better written than the "romance," and even in fiction of adventure psychology plays an increasingly important part.

But with the mass of readers these changes, these fashions of the moment, have little weight. In the higher strata of society Dickens and Dumas are as dead as last year's novels; amongst the people, untroubled by ultra-intellectual qualms, those despised authors flourish shamelessly. As the stress of daily life grows more acute, as the great primitive instincts of our natures become more and more obscured in the complex duties of civilised society, the more likely shall we be to turn with relief and gratitude to the welcome optimism, the refreshing simplicity, the engrossing charm of the two great writers, and the books which they devised for our delight.

It is acknowledged that Dumas is one of the amusers of the world, even by his detractors, who appear to think that to amuse is easy work, requiring neither skill nor effort, deserving neither recognition nor praise. (If the amuser *is* born, not made, the rarity of the species is perhaps accounted for.) Is this power so small a thing? "They say that Dumas has amused three or four generations," said Jules Claretie; "he has done better: he has consoled them. If he has shown us humanity more generous than it is, do not reproach him for that: he has painted it in his own image." "Old folk blessed him," wrote Jules Janin, "for he made easy the path to the grave; the women called upon him to aid them against their sadness, and the young men swore by the romances of their poet." "All our hospital patients recover or die with one of your father's books under their pillow," said a surgeon to Alexandre Dumas *fils*. "When we wish to make them forget the terror of an approaching operation, the tediousness of convalescence, or the dread of death, we prescribe one of your father's novels, and they are able to forget."

One great poet and great sufferer has left his appreciative gratitude on record:

"For six years," wrote Heine to his *confrère*, "I have been bed-ridden. During the worst part of the time, when I was suffering the greatest torment, my wife read your romances to me, and that was the only way in which I was enabled to forget my pains. Thus I have devoured them all, and sometimes during the reading I have exclaimed 'What an ingenious poet! What a grand fellow this Dumas is!' Certainly after Cervantes and Madame Schariaz, better known as the sultana Scheherazade, you are the most amusing storyteller I know. What fluency! what ease! and what a good chap you are! Truly, I can find but one fault in you: that is modesty. You are too modest. Good gracious! those who accuse you of boasting and swaggering have no notion of the greatness of your talent!

Nor are these "amusing" books ephemeral in their charm; there is, in despite of critics, something more than merely an hour's entertainment in Dumas's romances. Their particular qualities have been thus defined by Dr Garnett:

"Dumas stands out as the first among the truly eminent novelists of the world for exuberance of production. To class him thus is to assign him a high place. . . . Exuberance implies a vast fertility of invention; animated, impassioned style; and more particularly great facility in dialogue.

All these merits Dumas possesses in the highest degree; his invention moves within the limits of humanity, his characters are credible personages, neither monsters nor puppets."

"If his imagination was not of the highest quality," says Professor Bryce, "it was of almost unsurpassed fertility."

Mr Saintsbury, reflecting upon the charm which the romancer's books possess for him, is vaguely conscious of an abiding quality in what seems so slight, so fleeting in its nature:

"Dumas has the faculty, as no other novelist has, of presenting rapid and brilliant dioramas of the picturesque aspects of history, animating them with really human if not very intricately analysed passion, and connecting them with dialogue matchless of its kind. He cannot, as a rule, do much more than this, and to ask him for anything more is unreasonable, though in rare passages he rises to a much greater height. But he will absorb your attention and rest you from care and worry as hardly any other novelist will, and, unlike most novelists of his class, his pictures, at least the best of them, do not lose their virtue by rebeholding. I at least find 'The Three Musketeers' not less but more effectual for its purpose than I found it thirty, twenty, ten, even five years ago, and I think there must be something in work of such a virtue than mere scene-painting for a background and mere lay-figures for actors."

Professor Carpenter sees evidence of the "staying power" in these books, and does not hesitate to say so.

"I find one explanation of the deeper effect these volumes make on me," he writes, "in the fact that Dumas, recklessly as he apparently wrote, and in headlong haste, has somehow managed to build his characters out of genuinely human material. He seems to treat them like the veriest puppets; they wear their hearts on their sleeves; and yet neither the creations of Scott nor of Shakespeare are more truly alive. With women he was less successful; though *Marguerite*, the queen of folly, the gracious *Diane de Monsoreau*, and the proud *Comtesse de Charny*, are wonderful types of womanhood. But his men are men. *D'Artagnan, Athos, Porthos,* and *Aramis*; *Chicot, Henri IV., La Mole, Coconnas, Bussy d'Amboise*; *Balsamo, Philippe de Tavernay,* and *Gilbert*—not to mention others—these are as solidly and finely imagined as any characters in literature. How the author could have produced them we may never cease to wonder; but they do exist. He lived a foolish life; and he wrote in haste; but he wrote from his heart, and his heart was by nature *clairvoyant*."

And he adds in conclusion:

"Such are the considerations, in my judgment, which raise Dumas above the horde of vulgar romancers. His fame, like his genius, is not academic, and the critics may praise him with only half a heart, but his great public will be none the worse. One who reads him will pass the word to another; and each who knows him will be a better man."

Finally, Mr Lang sees, beyond the mere power of amusement possessed by Dumas, a philosophy and an ethical influence.

"In all he does, at his best, as in the 'Chevalier d'Harmenthal,' he has movement, kindness, courage, and gaiety. His philosophy of life is that old philosophy of the sagas and of Homer. Let us enjoy the movement of the fray, the faces of fair women, the taste of good wine; let us welcome life like a mistress, let us welcome death like a friend, and with a jest—if death comes with honour. . . That his works (his best works) should be even still more widely circulated than they are; that the young should read them, and learn frankness, kindness, generosity—should esteem the tender heart, and the gay, invincible wit; that the old should read them again, and find forgetfulness of trouble, and taste the anodyne of dreams, that is what we desire."

We have more than once dubbed Dumas "great,"

and possibly the reader has smiled to himself, or registered an inward protest at the time. And yet a threefold proof can be presented in support of the tremendous adjective.

To our thinking, the very reason advanced by many critics for refusing greatness to Dumas offers one of the strongest presumptions in favour of that claim. "There is perhaps hardly such another instance," says Dr Garnett, "of a man with so little moral or intellectual claim to rank among the *élite* of letters, taking so high a place upon the literary Olympus." (We have neither time nor space to do more than register a strong protest respecting the "immorality" of Dumas's claim to literary rank, and pass on.) "Inferior in intellectual power to his principal contemporaries, his instinct is often truer than their reason."

Roughly speaking, great writers may be divided into two classes—those whose work is based on reason and process of thought, and those whose utterances are prompted by instinct and inspiration. We refrain from suggesting instances of what we may call the "intellectual" writers and the "spiritual" writers; neither quality can claim to be higher in itself than the other, and some great men, like Shakespeare, possess both. The one type of mind tends to produce logicians, political economists, problem-novelists and playwrights, politicians, theologians, and so forth; the other gives birth to the poets, seers and prophets in all forms of art. To this latter class Dumas belonged. He lacked the power of poetic expression in its highest form, it is true; but there existed behind that barrier a nature akin in essentials to a poet's. Not only do his writings show this, but those who knew him or have studied him have testified to this fact again and again. He was "*clairvoyant*"; he divined in a flash what reason must laboriously discover; his intuitive instinct, guided by his intelligence, served him in place of experience, memory and logical thought. We have given numerous instances of his political foresight. Such qualities are of the highest, even if Dumas did not possess them to the uttermost; the soul is at least the equal of the brain.

This power, mysterious and inexplicable, too often produces the visionary, the fanatic. It had a very earthly abode in Dumas, and in one sense this was an enormous advantage. On a subject which appealed to him he could reason well and clearly, and grasp both principle and detail. Blaze de Bury tells us that the novelist once casually ventured to dispute with Geoffroy St Hilaire on a point of natural history relating to the whale's anatomy. Dumas imperturbably maintained his hypothesis; the great *savant* smiled with good-natured scorn. Will it be believed? When the standard authorities were consulted on the question, they confirmed the romancer's view!

It would seem that, according to Dr Garnett, Dumas was "great" in some respect, and by virtue of some high power. We presume that if Dumas is "high on Olympus" he has some right to be there: and if his is not the greatness of intellect, what form does his genius take? It must surely be a quality equal in calibre to that of brain-power, and there we are content to leave the matter.

Another of Dumas's claims to the rank of great" is pithily put by Hayward.

"A title to fame, like a chain of proofs, may be cumulative. It may rest on the multiplicity and universality of production and capacity. . . . Dumas will thus take rank as one of the three or four most popular and gifted writers that the France of the nineteenth century produced." Brander Matthews takes the same view. "Even more remarkable than the range of Dumas's work is its general level of merit. He had at least one element of greatness—an inexhaustible fecundity." He adds regretfully: "With his great powers one feels that he ought to have done something higher and nobler: that he had great powers, admits of no cavil." All who love Dumas and appreciate his work will echo this sentiment. Dr Garnett makes the same point when attributing to the Frenchman "a fecundity rivalled by very few novelists, and a standard of merit equalled by none who have approached Dumas's productiveness."

We find a third "reason for the faith that is in us" in the fact that so many great writers have proclaimed Dumas great, if not in so many words, still, unmistakably. It is not simply the ordinary reader who is astounded at the romancer's charm and resource, wit and skill; "the front row of the stalls"—the principal men and women writers of his day—applauded him just as heartily. We could wish nothing better than that the reader should compare the respective calibre, and worth, of our author's eulogists and detractors. For in addition to the great names we have already quoted there were others as "loyal" in their acclamation as Charles Reade himself. "I have an opinion of human things," wrote Lamartine, poet and historian; "I have none on miracles: you are superhuman. My opinion—of you—it is a note of exclamation! People have tried to discover perpetual motion—you have done better: you have created perpetual astonishment!"

"He was not France's, he was not Europe's, he was the world's!" cried Hugo; and he it was who wrote "*Ce qu'il seme, c'est l'idée*

Française." He has indeed taught French and the French to the whole world. Swinburne writes of Dumas's "excellent heart and brilliant genius"; Stevenson "would not give a chapter of old Dumas for the whole boiling of Zolas." Blaze de Bury, a sober critic, well acquainted with the literature of his nation and the great writers of his time, declared that "if there can be said to have been a French Shakespeare, it was Dumas. Hugo, who imagined that he was descended from the Elizabethan poet in a direct line, had far less claim to such parentage than Dumas." The most illuminating tribute to our author's genius was without doubt that of Michelet the historian. "Monsieur," he wrote, "*je vous aime et je vous admire, parce que vous êtes une des forces de la nature.*" This is strikingly true: there was something great, something primitive, elemental, about Dumas, which explains at once his strength and his weaknesses. "His virtues were colossal," says Dr Garnett, "and he had the defects of his qualities." The mixture of "white" and "black" blood produced a phenomenon of physical strength and energy in General Dumas; a combination of physical and mental energy and strength in Dumas *père*; and the "strain" survived to give us a remarkable instance of intellectual capacity in Dumas *fils*.

Briefly, our author was great because, being a natural force, with the great instincts of primitive man, without subtlety, or fear, or a doubt of self, he strove greatly and achieved great things, or failed as thoroughly. Ridicule never soured him nor baulked him of his end and aim; in heart and valour and confidence he was a giant. Such men are rare in these days, and "to encourage" any possible "others," we have laughed at this one for his failures; and measuring his stature with our eye, through the wrong end of the telescope, have decided that he was, if anything, rather below the middle height. In saying this we feel that we have added another inch or two to our own tall selves.

We have reserved for final quotation three very different estimates of our hero, which cannot, on the whole, be said to err on the side of eulogistic platitude. The first is from Castelar's essay on our author, and we present it with only one comment—that whereas the eloquent Spanish scholar obtained his knowledge of Dumas's genius direct from the writer's books, he received his impression of the Frenchman's life and conduct through the medium of "De Mirecourt" and others, as his article plainly indicates.

"Probably but few men have been born with so many and such brilliant qualities as Alexandre Dumas. His dramas are somewhat deficient in finish, but they are highly interesting. His novels contain nothing ideal, but much that is enchanting. Had he taken time for reflection, he would have produced some perfect work. With such great rapidity this was impossible. His creations are meteors when they might have been stars. Here we find a poet of a wonderful imagination, of an extraordinary power, fallen in the mire of the Parisian streets; punished for not having considered life as a reality, art as a religion, genius as a ministry, the world as a tribunal, and history, that conscience of humanity, as a judge."

In an oration full of feeling and eloquence, M. Edmond About pronounced a formal eulogy on Dumas at the unveiling of the statue in Place Malesherbes in Paris, in 1883.[1]

"This statue," said M. About, "is that of a great madman, who, into all his good humour and astonishing gaiety, put more true wisdom than there is to be found in the hearts of all of us here. . . . It is the likeness of a prodigal who, after having

---

[1] This monument owed its origin and completion to the loving admiration which the great romancer has so generally inspired. A. M. Villard, a traveller, had cheered so many of his hours of enforced idleness with the company of d'Artagnan and his innumerable comrades, that he set on foot a scheme to recognise publicly and perpetually the author's fame and worth. When the committee—a representative one, full of illustrious names—was still lacking the money for the sculptor's labour, Gustave Doré, the artist, offered to do the work, literally "for love."

THE DUMAS MONUMENT BY DORÉ, PLACE MALESHERBES, PARIS.

squandered millions in a thousand generous ways, left, without knowing it, a king's treasure behind him—it is the portrait of a 'man of pleasure,' whose life might well serve as a model for all men who work; of an egoist who devoted his life to his mother, his children, his friends, and his country."

As a summary of Dumas's character, an epitome of his greatness, and his failings—human and full of charity, we have not bettered this of Mr Henley's, in all our reading, and our own searchings of heart and brain :

" In life he was very much of a scapegrace and a madcap, and even more of a prodigal. His morals were loose, he was vain as only a man of colour can be, his literary conscience was (to say the least) imperfect, his veracity was that of the *romantiques* in general, he could—and did—commit astonishing offences in taste; but his humanity was boundless in degree and incorruptible in quality, he was generous to a fault, he is not known to have dealt a single foul blow . . . the fact is, that he was a prodigy of gaiety, kindliness, and charm, and a prodigy of temperament and power, and capacity of life and invention and achievement. He talked still better than he wrote; and he wrote without any affectations of style, and with an ease, a gusto, a sincerity of mind, a completeness of method that are irresistible. And the lesson of his greater books is one by which the world may well have profited. Love, honour, friendship, loyalty, valour, the old chivalric virtues — these were his darling themes; and he treated them with a combination of energy and insight, of good sense and good feeling, of manliness of mind and beauty of heart, that has ranked him with the greatest benefactors of the race."

Well may we add, with Villemessant, that "if during Dumas's long career there are some incidents which one ought to judge severely we should pass them by in silence, not only out of respect for the great name which he has left to French literature, but also out of sympathy with the excellent heart which did so little harm, and wrought such an enormous amount of good."

It has been our aim throughout, to leave the praise we fain would speak to come from the mouths of others, who would do the pleasant task more skilfully, and be listened to with the respect which their reputations can command. We are aware that as a result critics may dub us "compiler," or "book-maker." Had we "stolen the thunder" of our authorities, omitting acknowledgment and quotation-marks, we might have passed for being very clever, very conceited—or very dishonest. We preferred to speak by the mouths of others, the better to establish Dumas's reputation, and to let the captious say what they choose. "What matters it to the artist, so that the work be done?"

Yet we, too, have a word to say. The great men have spoken their glowing periods by the grave-side, and turned away. Before it is too late we, who have lingered behind, crave the right to come forward, take a last leave of our old friend, and

> "cast at his feet one flower that fades away."

Stevenson has said, half-stoically, half-bitterly, that an author must look to his pleasure in writing as the only reward for his work. If this be true, we have already received our best pay for our labours. Nothing that may happen to this book can give the author the pleasure which he has found in the preparation of it. With every day's research his wonder, respect and love grew and deepened. "What a man to love!" he thought; and then, "How this man was loved!"

That, we believe, was the secret of Dumas's success, of his lasting popularity, and of his greatness. He was, like Fielding and Goldsmith, a man who won affection without effort. "If any man could be loveable, in the true sense of the word,—that is, made to be loved,—he was that man," so wrote one who knew him well and intimately; and indeed all who knew him seem to speak of him with full hearts, almost with tears in their eyes, so fond and affectionate is their remembrance of the man. From the famous great ones who treated him as their equal, to the servants who strove to save him from his generosity, to the very dogs he rescued, Dumas earned love from all, by giving it, generously and without thought of return. A heart such as his will outlive many a cleverer brain.

"*Je suis tout en dehors,*" he once declared, in laughing self-disparagement. True, most of his vices, and some of his virtues, were on the surface, easy to be seen. But it would be truer to say of him that his was so transparent a nature that the sun of life shone through it, and that like a precious stone, its rays were reflected in myriad sparkling flashes of joy, gaiety, kindliness and generosity. The flaws were there; but there is no doubt this was a genuine diamond.

"*J'aime qui m'aime.*" It was his motto, that line from the Proverbs: "I love them that love me." Loving the world, cheering it in its wretchedness, brightening its hours of leisure, giving to it fully of his wealth of gaiety and wit, he failed at times to keep the respect of the more prosaic, and was delivered over to the mercy of the envious. But those who have loved the people, the people never forget. The dying Dumas feared he had written in vain, but he wrought better than he knew; and the rock of human nature on which he built will endure through ages of carking Time, and all the storms of change.

* * * * * *

TO MY FATHER

Oh, my father, thou the thinker, thou the poet—can it be
That naught will snap the chain of bondage round thy heart, and set thee free?
      Must thou ever give thy best
To the others who grow wealthy with the riches from thy store,
Leaving you not e'en as solace, when the long week's work is o'er,
      One brief seventh day of rest?

Bow thy head, then to thy labours! Not for thee the fields, the flow'rs,
Laughing song of birds, that echo in the leafy mountain bow'rs,
      Peaceful sleep of liberty,
Smiling valleys, in the glory of the setting summer sun,
And the sweet, faint breath of nature—Heaven's gift to ev'ry one—
      Free to all men, but to thee.

From thy study-window gleaming, one may watch and see, alway
When the twilight falls at even, when the dawn is dim and gray,
      Light of lamps that shine for thee.
Galley-slave of thine own talent, thou must toil, and toil in vain;
Thou canst not, with all thy weary years of labour and of pain,
      Buy a month of liberty!

Be it so, then—thou, the cornfield rich in flowing golden grain
Still must see the gladdened reapers in the season come again,
        Reap the harvest thou hast grown ;
Be thou still, the bright, the wondrous star, whose light all men may share,
Shining on, supreme, majestic in the studded heavens there,
        Distant—splendid—and unknown !

Work, then, for the coming ages, that shall hold thy days so dear ;
Strive, and testify, and suffer, like some ancient prophet-seer !
        Thou thy onward course shalt keep
Calm and peaceful, like the Rhine, that grand old river. To thy brink
Let all nations come, and, grateful, of thy flowing current drink,
        'Twill be still as clear and deep !

Work, then, freely ; work unceasing. I will watch beside the gate ;
What care I what others think me ? For I know that, 'spite their hate,
        Soon or late, fame will be mine.
But to-day my place is here ; for I the pious duty claim
Here to stand, to guard from wrong a father's glory and fair name,
        As it were a sacred shrine !

            (*From the French of Alexandre Dumas fils.*)

APPENDICES

APPENDIX A.

Comparative List showing the Events in French History covered by the Romances of Dumas

As we have said, it was Dumas's ambition to write the history of his country in romance. As even he quailed before the task of telling the story from the days of Cæsar, or of Charlemagne downward, he contented himself with biographies of those heroes, and began his task in the fourteenth century, when literature had so far developed as to afford the novelist some material for his background. It was Barante's work dealing with this era which fired the author to attempt "Isabel de Bavière," and he saw no reason for going backwards down history for his subjects. Henceforth, although there are gaps, there is scarcely a reign which he does not touch. We have thought it best to add the histories and historical plays to the romances, to show that Dumas fulfilled his intentions in one form or another. The task was practically completed with the Napoleonic romances, although one or two intermittent attempts to bring the record up to his own time were made by Dumas. The reign of Louis XI. was probably abandoned by the author because of "Quentin Durward," and the episode of the death of Charles the Bold, Louis's enemy, because of "Anne of Geierstein."

1328 The House of Valois—Philip VI. ascends—Edward III. of England claims the French crown—Anglo-French Wars.	"La Comtesse de Salisbury."
1350 John II.—Poitiers—Regency of Charles "The Dauphin."	

APPENDIX A

1364 Charles V.—Spanish Civil War—French interposition under du Guesclin.	"Le Bâtard de Mauléon."
1389 Charles VI.—His insanity—The feuds of the Burgundians and Armagnacs.	"Isabel de Bavière."
1415 Agincourt.	
1422 Charles VII. and Agnes Sorel, etc.	"Charles VII. chez ses grands Vassaux" (tragedy).
1429-31 Joan of Arc.	"Jehanne la Pucelle" (chronique).
1461 Louis XI.	
1477 Charles the Bold of Burgundy slain by the Swiss.	"Charles le Téméraire" (biography).
1483 Charles VIII.	
1498 Louis XII.	
15 Francis I.—"Field of the Cloth of Gold"—The Reformation (1517), etc.	
1540 Charles V. and Francis I.	"Ascanio."
1547-59 Henri II.—Calais taken from the English—War in the Low Countries.	"Les Deux Diane" and "Le Page du Duc de Savoie" (1555-57).
1559-60 François II. and Mary (Queen of Scots).	"L'Horoscope."
1560 Charles IX.	
1572 Massacre of St Bartholomew's Eve.	"La Reine Margot."
1574 Death of Charles.	
1574-89 Henri III.—Assassination of Duc D'Anjou—Death of St Mégrin, etc.—Huguenot-Catholic Wars.	"La Dame de Monsoreau" and "Les Quarante-Cinq"; "Henri Trois et Sa Cour" (drama).
1589-1610 Henri IV.—The wars of the Holy League—Edict of Nantes, etc.	"Henri IV." (biography).

APPENDIX A

1610-28 Louis XIII.—Richelieu—Capture of La Rochelle, etc.	"Le Comte de Moret," "La Colombe," "Les Trois Mousquetaires." (See also "Les Grands Hommes en Robe-de-Chambre.")
1643-60 Louis XIV.—Mazarin—The war of the Fronde—Colbert and Fouquet—The king's loves (De la Vallière and de Montespan)—The Man in the Iron Mask, etc.	"La Guerre des Femmes" (1650) and "Vingt ans Après" (the Fronde); "Le Vicomte de Bragelonne" (1660); "La Jeunesse de Louis XIV." (comedy); "Louis XIV. et son Siècle" (history).
1708 Old age of Louis—Marriage with Madame de Maintenon—Death of Louis XIV.	"Sylvandire."
1717 The Regency of the Duc D'Orleans.	"Chevalier d'Harmenthal" (Cellamare conspiracy) and "Une Fille du Régent." "La Régence" (history).
1727-29 The youth of Louis XV.	"Olympe de Clèves."
1756 The Seven Years' War—Canada won from France by the English (1760).	"Louis XV. et Sa Cour" (history).
1770-74 Last years of Louis XV.—Court intrigues, etc.	"Les Mémoires d'un Médecin."
1774 Death of Louis XV.	"Le Testament de M. Chauvelin."
1774 Louis XVI.—The affair of the queen's necklace (1784).	"Le Collier de la Reine."
1789 The Revolution.	"Ingénue," "Louis XVI. et la Révolution" (history).
1789 Taking of the Bastille.	"Ange Pitou" ("The Taking of the Bastille").

1791	The Royal Family's attempted flight from France, etc.	"La Comtesse de Charny," "La Route de Varennes" (history).
1793	Execution of Louis XVI. and Marie Antoinette—Reign of Terror — The Revolution, from Valmy and Jemappes to the fall of Robespierre.	"Le Chevalier de Maison-Rouge"; "Les Blancs et les Bleus" and "Blanche de Beaulieu"; "Le Docteur Mystérieux" and "La Fille du Marquis"; "Ninety-three" (history).
1798-9	French in Italy—Conquest and loss of Naples.	"La San Felice."
1799-1800	The Directoire — La Vendée—Rise of Napoleon—Royalist conspiracies.	"Les Compagnons de Jehu" and "Les Blancs et les Bleus."
1801	Napoleon in Egypt—Siege of Acre, etc.	"Les Blancs et les Bleus" (second series).
1805	Napoleon's Continental Campaigns.	"Le Trou de l'Enfer." and
1812	The Russian Expedition.	"Le Capitaine Richard."
1814	Louis XVIII.—The "Hundred Days"—Return of Napoleon from Elba.	"Black," "Monte Cristo."
1815	Waterloo.	"Napoléon" (history); "Napoléon" (drama).
1824	Death of Louis XVIII. and Accession of Charles X.	
1830	The Revolution of July—Charles X. flies to England, Louis Philippe, king.	"Dieu dispose."
1832	The Duchesse de Berri's "Second Vendée."	"Les Louves de Machecoul."

APPENDIX B.

The Chief Events in Dumas's Life, with their Dates.

Birth at Villers-Cotterets	July 24, 1802
Death of his Father, General Dumas	1806
Becomes a Clerk with M. Mennesson, the Notary	1816
Becomes a Clerk with M. Lefévre, Crépy	1822
Runaway trip to Paris	1822
Return to Paris—Clerkship in the Orléans Bureau	1823
Birth of Alexandre Dumas *fils*	1824
Production of "La Chasse et l'Amour"	September 22, 1825
Publication of "Nouvelles Contemporaines"	1826
Kean and the English Shakespeare Company in Paris	1827
Production of "Henri Trois," Théâtre Français	Feb. 10, 1829
Production of "Christine" at the Odéon	March 29, 1830
"The Revolution of July"; the Soisson Expedition	July 30 and 31, 1830
"The Revolution in La Vendée"; as Special Commissioner	August, 1830
Production of "Antony"	1831
Attacked by the Cholera	1832
Gaillardet and "La Tour de Nesle"	1832
Publication of "Isabel de Bavière"	1832
Swiss Travels	1832
Visit to England	1833
Travels in the South of France, Corsica, Calabria, Sicily	1834
Travels in Hyères, Etna, Naples, etc.	1835-6
Death of Dumas's Mother	1838
Travels in Belgium and on the Rhine	1838
Production of "Mademoiselle de Belle-Isle"	1839

APPENDIX B

Marriage with Mdlle. Ida Ferrier.	March 1840
Residence in Italy	1840-1-2
Production of "Une Mariage sous Louis XV."	1841
Voyage with Louis Napoleon	1842
Production of "Les Demoiselles de St Cyr"	1843
Finally rejected by the Académie	1843
Publication of "Les Trois Mousquetaires" and "Monte Cristo"	1844
Travels in Spain and along the N. coast of Africa	1846-7
Opening of Dumas's Theatre, the "Historique"	February 1847
Opening of the "Palace" of Monte Cristo	July 1847
Second Republic: Dumas a Candidate for the Chamber of Deputies	1848
Coup d'état: Dumas leaves Paris for Brussels	1851
Return to Paris: the "Mousquetaire" founded, with Dumas as Editor and Chief Contributor	Nov. 12, 1853
Visit to England.	May-June, 1857
Travels in Russia and the Caucasus	1858-9
Joins Garibaldi's Sicilian Expedition	May 1860
Stay in Naples	1860-64
Return to Paris	1864
Travels in Germany (Frankfort), etc.: after the Prusso-Austrian War	1866
Lectures at the Havre Exhibition	1868
Seized with illness	1869
Taken to Puys, near Dieppe, by his Son	1870
Death there	December 5, 1870
Body removed to Villers-Cotterets by his Son	May 1872
Unveiling of the Statue to Dumas, in the Place Malesherbes, Paris	November 4, 1883

APPENDIX C

LIST OF BOOKS BY DUMAS OR ATTRIBUTED TO HIM, WITH THEIR APPROXIMATE DATES OF PUBLICATION AND REMARKS ON THEIR AUTHENTICITY.

IT is almost impossible for any student of Dumas to compile a perfectly exhaustive and accurate bibliographical list of his works. They were published, some in Paris, some in Brussels, in varying forms and with different titles, and the works of reference available for our purpose are incomplete. Even the Bibliothèque Nationale, Paris, has not a complete set of his works. But for the use of the ordinary reader the following table will be found adequate. It is based on the list of Dumas's works as given by Calmann-Lévy, the authorised publishers, with one or two additions,[1] and is prepared from the notes afforded by Glinel, Parran and Quérard, supplemented by the information supplied in Dumas's various autobiographical writings and in the biographical sketches on Dumas, etc., and by our own researches and information privately supplied to us. For the comments respecting the genuineness or otherwise of the books the writer is, of course, solely responsible, although in most cases his opinion is that of the majority of the impartial critics who have dealt with the subject. For the convenience of readers those books *not* ordinarily accessible in English are printed *in italics*, and to facilitate reference the works are given in alphabetical rather than chronological order.

Several of the dates have been kindly supplied by M.M. Calmann-Lévy.

[1] Those books starred thus * are the only ones not included in the Calmann-Lévy series.

APPENDIX C

Romances and Autobiographical Works.

Name of Book.	Year of Publication.	Remarks re Authenticity, etc.
Acté	1839	Mainly Dumas's, but probably finished by an assistant.
Amaury	1844	(?) *Written* by P. Meurice, probably under Dumas's supervision.
Ange Pitou (or "Taking the Bastille")	1853	For explanation of the abrupt end see Part III. We believe that this book is solely Dumas's.
Ascanio	1843	Dumas, in collaboration with Meurice.
Une Aventure d'Amour	1862	Dumas. This volume also contains "Herminie" or "Une Amazone."
Les Aventures de John Davys	1840	Stated by Thackeray to be half original, half derived from an anonymous work.
Aventures de Lyderic	1842	The story of Siegfried. See "La Bouillie," etc.
Le Bâtard de Mauléon	1846	In collaboration with Maquet, who finished the romance.
Black	1858	
Les Blancs et les Bleus	1867-8-9?	Dumas's last work. Contains "The Eighth Crusade."
La Bouillie de la Comtesse Berthe	1844	A fairy-tale for children. Followed, in Calmann-Lévy, by "Aventures de Lyderic."
La Boule de Neige ("The Snowball")	1853	Written by Dumas from Marlinsky.
Bric-à-Brac	1861	Fugitive papers and autobiographical "mems."
Un Cadet de Famille	1860	A translation, at the direction of Dumas, of Trelawney's "Adventures of à Younger Son."

APPENDIX C

Name of Book.	Year of Publication.	Remarks re Authenticity, etc.
Le Capitaine Pamphile	1840	Written by Dumas for a children's journal.
Le Capitaine Paul (Jones)	1832	Dumas's sequel to Fenimore Cooper's "Pilot."
Le Capitaine Richard	1858	Undoubtedly Dumas.
Catherine Blum	1854	Said to have been suggested by Iffland's "Gardes Forestiers." Dumas. Translation out of print.
Causeries	1860	A collection of autobiographia, *jeux d'esprit* and sporting sketches. Contains also D.'s impressions of England.
Cecile, or Le Robe de Noce	1843	Probably mainly by a collaborator.
La Chasse au Chastre	1841	Dumas. Included in the "Impressions de Voyage" ("Le Midi de la France").
Le Chasseur de Sauvagine	1859	Probably written by Dumas from a story supplied by the Comte de Cherville.
Le Chateau D'Eppstein	1844	According to Dumas, narrated to him in 1841. Probably not his.
Le Chevalier D'Harmenthal (or "The Conspirators")	1843	Dumas, with the assistance of Maquet.
Le Chevalier de Maison-Rouge	1846	Ditto. See "Mémoires d'un Médecin."
Le Collier de la Reine	1849-50	Ditto.
La Colombe	1851	Dumas. Bound with "Maître Adam le Calabrais" (C.L.).
Les Compagnons de Jehu	1857	Dumas. Probably with Paul Bocage's assistance.
Le Comte de Monte Cristo	1844	Dumas, with the assistance of Maquet.

Name of Book.	Year of Publication.	Remarks re Authenticity, etc.
*_Le Comte de Moret_	1866	Dumas. Not available either in French or English.
La Comtesse de Charny	1853-5	Dumas alone. See "Mémories d'un Médecin."
La Comtesse de Salisbury	1839	First chapter fiction; the rest a mere _chronique_ of history.
Les Confessions de la Marquise	1857	Part of a version of the "Mémoires de Madame du Deffand." Not by Dumas.
Conscience l'Innocent "or l'Enfant"	1853	Written by Dumas on the basis of some chapters in Hendrik Conscience's "Conscrit."
*Crimes Célèbres	1839-40	Under the editorship of Dumas, and most of the articles written by him. (See Part III.).
La Dame de Monsoreau ("Chicot the Jester")	1846	Dumas, with the assistance of Maquet. See "Les Quarante-Cinq." _Not_ a sequel to "La Reine Margot."
La Dame de Volupté	1863	From the "Mémoires de Mdlle. de Luynes." Unlikely to be by Dumas.
Les Deux Diane	1846-7	It is said that Dumas, in a letter written to Meurice in 1865, gives that ex-collaborator the entire "honours" of this historical romance. He probably dictated the plot, however. The same no doubt applies to "Le Page du Duc de Savoie."
Les Deux Reines	1864	Sequel to "La Dame de Volupté."
Dieu dispose	1852	Dumas. Sequel to "Le Trou de l'Enfer."

APPENDIX C

Name of Book.	Year of Publication.	Remarks re Authenticity, etc.
Le Docteur Mystérieux	1872	Dumas. Published in book form posthumously. See "La Fille du Marquis."
Emma Lyonna	1865	Sequel to "La San Felice. "Emma" is Lady Hamilton, on whose reputed Memoirs Dumas is said to have based the work.
La Femme au Collier de Velours	1851	Dumas. "After" Hoffmann.
Fernande	1844	Not Dumas. Claimed by H. Auger.
La Fille du Marquis	1872	Sequel to "Le Docteur Mystérieux."
Une Fille du Régent	1845	Dumas with Maquet's assistance.
Le Fils du Forçat	1860	Dumas in collaboration with an anonymous assistant.
Les Frères Corses	1845	Undoubtedly Dumas. With this (in C.-L.) is bound "Otho l'Archer."
Gabriel Lambert	1844	Either based on fact as alleged, or on a story supplied to Dumas.
Georges	1843	Attributed by some to Mallefille. Much more probably by Dumas with Mallefille's assistance.
La Guerre des Femmes (Nanon)	1845-6	Dumas with Maquet's assistance.
Histoire de mes Bêtes	1868	Dumas chatting on pets, servants, etc.: with some autobiographical episodes.
Histoire d'un Casse-Noisette	1844	Translated and adapted from Hoffmann's book of that name.

APPENDIX C

Name of Book.	Year of Publication.	Remarks re Authenticity, etc.
L'Homme aux Contes	1858	Collection of translations of fairy-tales from other languages.
L'Horoscope	1858	Little more than a fragment, but undisputably Dumas.
L'Ile de Feu	1870	Dumas, probably in collaboration with an "assistant" who knew Java.
Ingénue	1854	Dumas. Said to have been written with Maquet, but this is unlikely.
Isaac Laquedem	1853	Little more than a fragment. Stopped by the Censor. Dumas's own work.
Isabel de Bavière	1836	A series of scenes selected, dramatised and vitalised with dialogue from Barante's "Histoire des Ducs de Bourgoyne." Translation out of print.
Jacques Ortis	1839	A translation, said to be by Fiorentino, of a work by Ugo Foscolo.
Jacquot sans Oreilles	1859-60	Said to have been "given" to Dumas: certainly not by him.
Jane	1863	From the Russian of Marlinsky. Contains also "Un coup de feu" and "Le faiseur de cerceuils" (both also from the Russian).
Les Louves de Machecoul	1859	Dumas. Probably with an assistant.
Madame de Chamblay	1863	Doubtful. Attributed to Octave Feuillet.
La Maison de Glace	1860	Translated from the Russian.

APPENDIX C

Name of Book.	Year of Publication.	Remarks re Authenticity, etc.
Maître Adam le Calabrais[1]	1840	Unquestionably Dumas. Bound with "La Colombe." Collaborator: Fiorentino.
Les Mariages de Père Olifus	1850	Dumas. From materials obtained during a visit to Holland.
Le Marquis d'Escoman (Drames Galantes)	1861	Not by Dumas.
Mémoires d'un Aveugle	1856-7	A version of the "Mémoires de Madame du Deffand." See "Les Confessions de la Marquise." Not by Dumas.
Les Mémoires d'un Médecin ("The Memoirs of a Physician")	1847	Dumas, with Maquet's assistance. (Sequels: "Le Collier de la Reine," "Ange Pitou," "La Comtesse de Charny" and "Chevalier de Maison-Rouge."
Le Meneur de Loups	1857	Dumas. A tale of Villers-Cotterets.
Mes Mémoires	1852-4	The story of his life, 1802-32.
* Mémoires d'Horace	1860	Not now accessible.
Les Milles-et-un Fantômes	1849	Said to have been in collaboration with Paul Bocage. A treatise on the horrible, rather than a story.
Les Mohicans de Paris	1854-5	Dumas in collaboration with Bocage. Translation now out of print. Followed by "Salvator."
Les Morts vont vite	1861	"Appreciations" of Chateaubriand, le Duc et Duchesse D'Orléans, Béranger, Sue, De Musset, etc., by Dumas.
Une Nuit à Florence	1861	Dumas.

[1] A translation by the writer will shortly be published.

Name of Book.	Year of Publication.	Remarks re Authenticity, etc.
Olympe de Clèves	1852	It is asserted that Maquet was a collaborator with Dumas in this work. If so, his share was small.
Le Page du Duc de Savoie	1855	See "Les Deux Diane."
Parisiens et Provinciaux	1864	Dumas, in collaboration with the Comte de Cherville.
Pascal Bruno	1838	Dumas. Bound with "Pauline" (C. L.).
Le Pasteur d'Ashbourn	1853	Not by Dumas. At most, rewritten by him from an English story, or a German story with an English *locale*.
Pauline	1838	Dumas. First indications appeared in his Swiss "Impressions de Voyage."
Le Père Gigogne	1860	Chiefly, if not entirely, translations of fairy tales from foreign authors, introduced by "Le Lièvre de mon grandpère," told to Dumas by de Cherville. One story which bears the undoubted stamp of our author's style is "La Jeunesse de Pierrot."
Le Père la Ruine	1860	Probably written with de Cherville.
Le Prince des Voleurs and Robin Hood le Proscrit	1872 1873	Not Dumas. Probably translations of some English stories.
La Princesse de Monaco	1854	Not by Dumas. The title-page announces the book as "recueilli" par Alexandre Dumas.
La Princesse Flora	1863	Translated from Marlinsky.

APPENDIX C

Name of Book.	Year of Publication.	Remarks re Authenticity, tc.
Les Quarante - Cinq ("The Forty - Five Guardsmen")	1848	Dumas, with Maquet's assistance. The concluding portion dictated to his son.
La Reine Margot ("Marguerite of Valois")	1845	Dumas, with Maquet. This book has no sequel.
El Saltéador (In Dent's edition "The Brigand").	1854	In a prefatory note to this romance in the "Mousquetaire," Dumas disavows the authorship. Nevertheless it is probably by him and one of his 'prentices.
Salvator	1855-9	Dumas, with Bocage. See "Les Mohicans de Paris."
La San Felice	1864-5	Proved to be by Dumas. His only long untranslated romance. Followed by "Emma Lyonna" and "Souvenirs d'un Favorite."
Souvenirs d'Antony	1835	A collection of short stories by Dumas, previously published—called after the hero of the famous play, Antony figuring in one of them, "*Le Bal Masqué.*" The others are "*Le Cocher de Cabriolet,*" "Blanche de Beaulieu" (or "Le Rose Rouge"), "*Cherubino et Celestini,*" "*Bernard,*" "*Dom Martyns de Freytas,*" and "*Le Curl Chambard.*" Of the untranslated ones "*Cherubino et Celestini*" is the most important.

Name of Book.	Year Publication.	Remarks re Authenticity, etc.
Souvenirs Dramatiques	1868	Collection of articles by Dumas: dramatic criticisms, essays on the theatre and the State, etc., including "William Shakespeare," "Mon Odyssée à la Comédie Française," and a report of the "special commission" of 1849 (of which Dumas was a member) on the question of the censorship.
Souvenirs d'un Favorite	1865	See "La San Felice" and "Emma Lyonna."
Sultanetta	1859	Dumas's version of a Russian story by Marlinsky.
Sylvandire	1844	Dumas with Maquet's assistance.
La Terreur Prussienne	1867	The thread of fiction is only slight. Dumas treats chiefly of Frankfort during the Prusso-Austrian War of 1866.
Le Testament de M. Chauvelin	1861	Dumas, and partly autobiographical. This volume in C.-L. also contains "Don Bernardo de Zuniga."
Les Trois Mousquetaires	1844	Dumas, with Maquet's assistance. Founded on Courtils de Sandraz's "Mémoires de D'Artagnan." Sequels: "Vingt Ans Après" and "Le Vicomte de Bragelonne."
Le Trou de l'Enfer	1850-1	Dumas, possibly with Gérard de Nerval or some other 'prentice acquainted with Germany. Sequel, "Dieu dispose," probably Dumas's alone.

APPENDIX C

Name of Book.	Year of Publication.	Remarks re Authenticity, etc.
La Tulipe Noire	1850	Dumas, with Maquet's assistance.
Le Vicomte de Bragelonne	1848-50	Dumas, with Maquet. Based on material taken from Madame de la Fayette's "Histoire d'Henriette d'Angleterre." See "Les Trois Mousquetaires."
Une Vie d'Artiste	1854	Dumas's account of the early struggles of the comedian, Mélingue, the creator of the stage "D'Artagnan."
Vingt Ans Après ("Twenty Years After")	1845	Dumas, with Maquet. See "Les Trois Mousquetaires."

History, Biography, etc.

Charles le Téméraire	1859	Historical sketch of Charles the Bold of Burgundy.
Les Drame de '93	1851-2	See "Louis XIV. et Son Siècle."
Les Drames de la Mer	1852	Includes "Boutikoë," "Le Capitaine Marion," "La Junon" and "Le Kent." Stories of shipwreck and other sea-adventures.
Filles, Lorettes et Courtisanes	1873	"Les Serpents" is included in this volume.
Les Garibaldiens	1861	Dumas's "despatches from the seat of war" during Garibaldi's progress from Sicily to Naples, 1860.
Gaule et France	1853	A rapid survey of French history from the earliest time, ending with a remarkable prophecy as to the future.

Name of Book.	Year of Publication.	Remarks re Authenticity, etc.
Les Grands Hommes en Robe-de-chambre:		Part of a scheme for a series biographies of great men from the earliest to the latest period, written from a new point of view.
César	1857-8	
Henri IV.	1866	
Louis XIII., et Richelieu	1866	
* *Histoire des Bourbons*	1863	Originally written in Italian, "I Borboni di Napoli."
Histoire de Louis Philippe	1852	or "Histoire de Dix-Huit Ans" (1830-48), published in 1853, and again, "Le Dernier Roi."
Les Hommes de Fer	1867	A republished collection of "studies" of Pépin, Charlemagne, etc.
Italiens et Flamands	1846	Appreciative sketches of painters—Andrea del Sarto, Botticelli, Holbein, Dürer, etc., etc.
Jehanne la Pucelle	1842	A "chronique" of Joan of Arc.
Louis XIV. et Son Siècle	1844-5	The first of a series of "historical eras" which ended with the "Drame de '93." Dumas's most important historical work.
Louis XV. et sa Cour	1849	The series continued ("La Régence" intervening).
Louis XVI. et la Révolution	1850-1	Ditto: followed by the last of the series, "'93."
Les Medicis	1845	Should be read in connection with "Trois Maîtres" and "Italiens et Flamands."
Mémoires de Garibaldi	1860	An account of Garibaldi's exploits in S. America, written by Dumas from materials afforded by Garibaldi himself.
* *Mémoires de Talma*	1850	Written by Dumas from materials left by Talma.

Name of Book.	Year of Publication.	Remarks re Authenticity, etc.
Mémoires d'Horace	1860	Not now accessible in English or French.
Napoléon	1839	A picturesque biography.
La Régence	1849	See "Louis XIV. et son Siècle."
La Route de Varennes	1860	Story of Louis XVI.'s flight in 1791.
Les Stuarts	1840	Not a trustworthy work. Contains lengthy extracts from Scott's "Abbot," etc.
Trois Maîtres	1862	The three masters are Michael Angelo, Titian and Raphael. See "Italiens et Flamands" and "Les Medicis."

Travels

Une Année à Florence	1841	See "Le Midi de la France."
L'Arabie Heureuse	1860	By Haji 'abd el Hamid Bey. Published by Dumas's assistance.
Les Baleiniers	1861	The travels of Dr Felix Maynard, published by Dumas.
Le Capitaine Arena	1842	Account of a voyage round Sicily, etc. See "Le Speronare."
Le Caucase	1859	Sequel to the Russian "Impressions."
Le Corricolo	1843	Impressions of Naples. Written with Fiorentino.
De Paris à Cadix	1848	Letters from Spain, describing Dumas's tour in 1846. See "Le Véloce."
Excursions sur les Bords du Rhin	1841	Belgium and the Rhine. Possibly with Gérard de Nerval, Dumas's companion.

APPENDIX C

Name of Book.	Year of Publication.	Remarks re Authenticity, etc.
Un Gil Blas en Californie	1852	Published by Dumas, with an introduction by him.
Impressions de Voyage en Russie	1860 and '65	Followed by "Le Caucase."
Impressions de Voyage en Suisse	1833	Dumas's first book of travel, thought by many to be his best.
Mémoires d'un Maître d'Armes	1840	Classified by Calmann-Lévy as "travels." Dumas edited his friend Grisier's impressions of St Petersburg, etc. There is a slight element of narrative.
Le Midi de la France	1841	Followed by "Une Année à Florence" and "La Villa Palmieri." This book concludes with "La Chasse au Chastre."
Un Pays Inconnu	1865	Not Dumas. Notes on Brazilian travel by another hand.
Quinze Jours au Sinai	1839	Written by Dumas from notes by Baron Taylor, and drawings by Dauzats.
Le Speronare	1842	Impressions of Sicily. Written with the help of Fiorentino. Followed by "Capitaine Arena" and "Le Corricolo."
Le Véloce	1848	Account of Dumas's visit to Tangiers, Algiers and Tunis, etc. Sequel to "De Paris à Cadix."
La Vie au Désert	1860	Simply a translation of R. G. Gordon-Cumming's book on the adventures of a lion hunter in Africa.

NAME OF BOOK.	YEAR OF PUBLICATION.	REMARKS re AUTHENTICITY, ETC.
La Villa Palmieri	1843	Souvenirs of Florence. See "Une Année à Florence." Contains "Un Alchimiste du Dix-Neuvième Siècle."

The sixty-six plays are issued in twenty-five one-franc volumes, or fifteen volumes at 3 f. 50 c., by MM. Calmann-Lévy, as follows:—

Tome Ier.—Comment je devins auteur dramatique.—La Chasse et l'Amour.—La Noce et l'Enterrement.—Henri III. et sa Cour.—Christine.

Tome II.—Napoléon Bonaparte.—Antony.—Charles VII. chez ses grands vassaux.

Tome III.—Richard Darlington.—Teresa.—Le Mari de la Veuve.

Tome IV.—La Tour de Nesle.—Angèle.—Catherine Howard.

Tome V.—Don Juan de Marana.—Kean.—Piquillo.

Tome VI.—Caligula.—Paul Jones.—L'Alchimiste.

Tome VII.—Mademoiselle de Belle-Isle.—Un Mariage sous Louis XV.—Lorenzino.

Tome VIII.—Halifax.—Les Demoiselles de Saint-Cyr.—Louise Bernard.

Tome IX.—Le Laird de Dumbiki.—Une Fille du Régent.

Tome X.—La Reine Margot.—Intrigue et Amour.

Tome XI.—Le Chevalier de Maison-Rouge.—Hamlet.—Le Cachemire vert.

Tome XII.—Monte-Cristo (1re partie).—Monte-Cristo (2e partie).

Tome XIII.—Le Comte de Morcerf (3e partie de Monte-Cristo). —Villefort (4e partie de Monte-Cristo).

Tome XIV.—La Jeunesse des Mousquetaires.—Les Mousquetaires.

Tome XV.—Catilina.—Le Chevalier d'Harmental.

Tome XVI.—La Guerre des Femmes.—Le Comte Hermann.—Trois Entr'actes pour *l'Amour médecin*.

Tome XVII.—Urbain Grandier.—Le Vingt-Quatre Février.—La Chasse au chastre.

Tome XVIII.—La Barrière de Clichy.—Le Vampire.

Tome XIX.—Romulus.—La Jeunesse de Louis XIV.—Le Marbrier.

Tome XX.— La Conscience.—L'Orestie. — La Tour Saint-Jacques.

Tome XXI.—Le Verrou de la Reine.—L'Invitation à la valse.—Les Forestiers.

Tome XXII.—L'Honneur est satisfait.—Le Roman d'Elvire.—L'Envers d'une conspiration.

Tome XXIII.—Le Gentilhomme de la Montagne.—La Dame de Monsoreau.

Tome XXIV.—Les Mohicans de Paris.—Gabriel Lambert.

Tome XXV.—Madame de Chamblay.—Les Blancs et les Bleus.—Simples lettres sur l'Art dramatique.

(Maurel adds: "Les Frères Corses," and "Pauline," but there is no record of their public production.)

APPENDIX D.

List of Books Consulted in the Preparation of this Work

The following list gives only the names of those authorities from whom information has been obtained, *i.e.* represents about half the books actually consulted:—

About, Edmond (see "Monument à A. Dumas").
Asseline, A., "Courrier d'autrefois" (*L'Independance Belge*, Nov. 20, 1870).
Audebrand, P., "A. Dumas à la Maison D'Or."
Banville, Theodore de, "Mes Souvenirs."
    "Odes Funambulesques."
Beauvoir, Roger de, "Soupeurs de Mon Temps," with preface by A. Dumas.
Blackwood's Magazine, 1835-72 inclusive.
"Brown, Oliver Madox," by J. H. Ingram.
Bury, Henry Blaze de, "A. Dumas, sa vie, son temps, son œuvre."
Carpenter, G. C., *Forum*, June 1899, on "Will Dumas's novels last?"
Castelar, Emilio, "Byron and other Essays" ("Alexandre Dumas."
"Chambers's Encyclopædia," edition of 1868.
    New edition (article on Dumas *père* by W. E. Henley).
Chasles, Philarète, Portrait d'A. Dumas.
Cherbuliez, Joel, *Revue Critique des Livres Nouvelles*, 1830-50.
Chincholle, C., "Dumas aujourd'hui."
Claretie, J. (see "Monument à A. Dumas").
Conscience, H., "Le Conscrit."
"D'Artagnan, Memoirs of," Courtils de Sandraz.
"D'Artagnan": E. D'Auriac. Comparison of the romance with the Mémoires.

APPENDIX D

"D'Artagnan, The Real," Sir H. Maxwell, Bart. (*Blackwood's Magazine*, June 1897).
Dash, Comtesse, "Mémoires d'autres."
Deschanel, E., "À pied et en Wagon."
Dowden, Prof. E., "French Literature."
Du Camp, Maxime, "Souvenirs Littéraires."
Dumas *fils*, "Le Fils Naturel" (preface); Introductory letter to "Les Trois Mousquetaires," edition de luxe, 1894; (see also "Monument à A. Dumas").
Dumas *père*, Autobiographical works—"Mes Mémoires," "Souvenirs Dramatiques," "Causeries," "Bric-à-Brac," "Les Morts vont vite," "Les Garibaldiens," etc.
    Romances.
    Travels.
    Historical Studies.
    Plays.
Ferry, Gabriel, "Les Dernières Années d'Alexandre Dumas."
Fiorentino, P. A., "Comédies et Comédiens."
Fitzgerald, P., "Life and Adventures of Alexander Dumas."
Garnett, Dr Richard, Introduction to "The Black Tulip."
Gautier, Théophile, "Histoire de l'art Dramatique"; "Histoire du Romantisme"; "Belles Femmes de Paris."
Glinel, C., "A. Dumas: Notes biographique et bibliographique."
Goncourt, Edmund and Jules, "Journal."
Gordon-Cumming, R. C., "The Adventures of a Lion Hunter in South Africa."
Gozlan L., "Almanach Comique," 1848: article on the Chateau "Monte Cristo."
Grisier, "Les Armes et le Duel." (Preface by A. Dumas.)
Hayward, Abraham, "Biographical Essays." ("A. Dumas.")
Heine, H., "Letters on the French Stage."
Henley, W. E., "Views and Reviews."
Hugo, C., "Les hommes de l'Exil."
"Hugo V. au Témoins."
Hugo, V., "Les Contemplations."
L'Illustration, 1846-7.
Janin, J., "Alexandre Dumas."

Karr, Alphonse, "Les Guêpes" (periodical).
Lang, Andrew, "Essays in Little"; "Letters to Dead Authors." Communication to the writer.
Lanson, G., "Histoire de la Littéraire Française."
Larousse, P., "Grand Dictionnaire Français."
Matthews, Prof., Brander "French Dramatists."
Maurel, A., "Les Trois Dumas."
"Monument à Alexandre Dumas." Speeches by MM. About, Claretie, etc.: Introduction by Dumas *fils*.
Mousquetaire, Le, Journal edited by Dumas.
Nisard, D., "Histoire de l'École Romantique."
Nodier, Marie Mennessier, "Charles Nodier."
Parigot, H., "Dumas Père" ("Les Grands Ecrivains"); "Le Drame d'Alexandre Dumas."
Parran, A., "Les Romantiques" (Bibliographical notes).
Pellissier, G., "Le Mouvement Littéraire au XIXe Siècle."
Pifteau, B., "Dumas en manches de Chemises."
Pollock, W. H., "Alex. Dumas" (*Nineteenth Century*, Oct. 1880).
Quarterly Review, 1890.
Quérard, J. M., "Supercheries Littéraires."
Reade, Charles, "The Eighth Commandment."
Romand, H., "A. Dumas" (*Revue des Deux Mondes*, Jan. 15, 1834).
Rossetti, W. M. Communication to the writer.
Sainte-Beuve, C. A., "Causeries du Lundi."
Saintsbury, Geo., Prof., "Essays"; "History of French Literature."
Sand, George: Correspondence.
Séchan, "Souvenirs d'un Homme de Théâtre."
Spectator, December 17th, 1870.
Stevenson, R. L., "Memories and Portraits"; "Letters to his family and friends."
[1] "Stones of Paris," B. E. and C. M. Martin.

[1] This book gives interesting details respecting Dumas's various residences in Paris, and the localities mentioned in connection with the leading romances—the scene of the quadruple duel in "Les Trois Mousquetaires," etc.

Swinburne, A. C., Essays ("Charles Reade"). Communication to the writer.
Thackeray, W. M., "Paris Sketch-Book"; "Roundabout Papers" ("A Peal of Bells"); Letters to the *Revue Britannique*, 1847.
Trelawney, "Adventures of a Younger Son."
Vandam, A., "An Englishman in Paris."
Villemessant, "Mémoires d'un Journaliste.
Walkley, A. B., "Playhouse Impressions."
Weiss, J. J "Le Théâtre et les Mœurs."

INDEX

(*For Dumas's dramatic Works see " Plays ;" for his other Writings see " Works."*)

A

ABOUT, E., 101, 147, 199, 247, 291, 305, 342
L'Amiral (Emilie Cordier), 108-10
Asseline, A., 137
Audebrand, P., 97
Auger, H., 198

B

BALZAC, 147, 157-8, 161, 219, 274, 296, 305, 316
Banville, T. de, 82, 135
Barante, 61, 186, 188
Belgium, Dumas's tour in, 71
Béranger, 17, 129, 162, 265, 313
Berri, Duchesse de, 46-7
Bocage, P., 231, 233, 245, 247
Brandès, G., 278
Bret Harte, 326
Brohan (Mdlle. A.), 112, 164
Brussels (Dumas's stay in), 94-5
Bryce, Prof., 333
Buloz, 25, 158-9
Bury, B. de, 92, 98, 141, 143, 146, 149, 153-5, 157, 224-5, 243, 261, 275-6, 300, 310, 337, 340
Byron, 23, 26, 60, 104

C

CARPENTER, G. C., 206, 211, 241, 296, 322, 334
Cassagnac, G. de, 163, 282, vii
Castelar, E., 200, 286, 291, 313, 341
Chaffault, du, 92-3, 134, 167
Chambers's Encyclopædia, 275-6, viii
Charles X., 26, 34, 40, 42, 46, 69

Chateaubriand, 66, 162, 190, 265
Cherbuliez, J., 191, 266
Cherville, Comte de, 249, 251, 254
Chincholle, C., 242
Cholera, visitation, 62
Claretie, J., 331
Comédie Française, 28-9, 31, 37, 52, 55, 69, 71, 86, 98-9, 118, 127, 151, 154, 158, 165
Conscience, H. ("Le Conscrit "), 239
Cooper, Fenimore, 24, 157, 191
Corneille, 19, 27-8, 76, 127, 131, 156

D

DAME AUX CAMÉLIAS, LA, 144-5, 154, 314
D'Artagnan, Maxwell on, 201
" D'Artagnan, Mémoires de," 201-5
Dash, Comtesse, 72
Davy de la Pailleterie, Marquis A., 4, 6
Delacroix, 23, 59, 119
Delavigne, C., 17, 23, 25, 36, 75, 313
De Leuven, A., 16-7, 19, 24, 112
De Musset, A., 35, 56, 59, 142, 159, 162, 252, 265
Deschanel, E., 95
Dickens, C., 157, 330
Dorval, Marie, 50, 52, 54*n*, 94, 170, 244, 265
Dowden, Prof. E., 278
Doyle, Sir A. C, 227, 326
Du Camp, M., 114-5, 126, 132-4, 140, 263, 301
Dumas :—
Fils, 35, 39, 57, 72, 76, 83, 109, 112, 121-3, 132-3, 142-6, 152-4, 165, 173, 177-80, 208, 210, 247, 312, 315, 331, 340, 347-8

INDEX

Dumas—*continued*
  General, 4, 6-9, 20, 169, 178, 185, 247, 340
  Louise-Cessette, 4, 6
  Madame (*née* Labouret), 4, 13, 21, 32, 39, 69-70, 163, 185
  Madame (*née* Ferrier), 72-3, 159
  Madame (*fils*), 145, and *ded.*
  Marie-Alexandre, 50, 72, 109, 121, 123
  Père, his parentage, 4; birth, 4, 8; boyhood, 9-15; youth, 15-21; goes to Paris, 21; early dramatic successes, 32-8; first love-affair, 38-9; marriage, 72-3; "Trois Mousquetaires" and "Monte Cristo," 76-8; his theatre, 86, 93-4; his chateau, 80, 87, 93-4; exile in Brussels, 94-5; "Le Mousquetaire," 96, 97; visit to England, 101-5; with Garibaldi, 113-15; illness, 120-3; death, 123; burial at Villiers-Cotterêts, 123. Statue to, 342*n*

F

Ferry, G., 90, 106, 116, 171, 173, 255-6
Feuillet, O., 252
Fiorentino, P. A., 77, 161, 192, 215, 259, 266, 292, 310
Fitzgerald, P., 6, 81, 87, 115, 169, 223, 259, 282, viii, ix
Florence (visit to), 73, 76
Foy, General, 22, 267
France, travels in the south of, 67
Frankfort (visit to), 120

G

Gaillardet, 63-4
Garibaldi, 113-15, 251
Garnett, Dr, 263, 274, 279*n*, 332, 336, 338-9, 340
Gautier, T., 76, 194, 291
Girardin, Madame de, 85, 116, 142, 300
Glinel, C., 108, 155*n*, 266-7, 277, x
Goethe, 27, 60, 157, 295, 312-13
Goncourts, The, 202, 330
Gorki, M., 327

Grisier, 147, 192
Guizot, 84, 171

H

Harel, 48, 62-5
Hayward, A., 99, 273, 296, 329, 338
Heine, H., 68, 162, 310, 332
Henley, W. E., 146, 236, 243, 276, 282, 312, 317, 343, viii
Homer, 156, 335
Hugo, C., 112, 165
Hugo, V., 23, 35, 38, 52, 62, 69, 75, 94-5, 98, 112, 135, 156, 162-5, 170, 172, 180, 183, 202, 267, 283, 310-12, 318, 339-40

I

"Indipendant" (Journal), 115
Italy, travels in, 67

J

Jacquot ("E. de Mirecourt"), 81-3, 125, 194, 215, 276, 341, vii, viii
Janin, J., 63, 78, 111-2, 162, 331

K

Karr, A. ("Les Guêpes"), 191
Kean, E., 26

L

Lafayette, Gen., 41-2, 47, 59, 162
La Fayette (Madame de), 205, 210-11
Lamartine, 23, 120, 162, 184, 283, 339
Lang, A., 88, 101, 131, 133, 156, 166, 199, 201, 215, 221, 227, 291-2, 296, 302-3, 320, 335, ix
Lanson, G., 278
Lassagne, 25, 183
Lebay, Madame, 38-9
Lecomte, J., 159-60
Lectures (Dumas's), 119-20
Legion of Honour, Dumas's, 68
Lemaître 59, 68
Letters (from Dumas), 109-12, 145-6
Louis XVIII., 14, 26

INDEX

Louis Philippe (at first Duc d'Orléans), 22, 31, 33, 36, 40, 46-7, 68, 83, 86, 89, 90, 93, ix

M

MAISON D'OR (Dumas at), 97
Malletille, 134, 197, 266
Maquet, A., 85, 95-6, 135-6, 195, 205, 215-7, 222, 226-9, 231, 236-8, 245*n*, 290, 292, viii
"Marion Delorme," 52, 56, 163
Marlinsky, 244, 248
Mars, Mdlle., 16, 32, 52, 59
Matthews, Brander, 287, 289, 305, 312, 328-9, 338, ix
Maurel, A., 250
Mélingue, 112, 136, 245
Merimée, P., 162, 221*n*
Méry, L., 112, 193, 200
Meurice, P., 89, 112, 198, 220, 228, 246
Michelet, J., 241, 315, 340
"Mirecourt, E. de" (*see* Jacquot)
"Mois, le" (Journal), 90
Molière, 27, 76, 288-9, 295
"Monte Cristo and his wife," 214*n*
Monte Cristo, Chateau of, 80-1, 87-9, 93, 94, 140, 265
"Monte Cristo" (Journal), 101
Monte Cristo (Visit to Isle of), 73
Montpensier, Duke of, 78, 83, 85-6-7, 90
"Mourir pour la patrie" (song), 91
"Mousquetaire, Le," 96, 101, 137, 164, 214*n*

N

NAPLES (Dumas at), 114-16, 140
Napoleon, 7, 9, 14, 103, 240, 248, 262
Napoleon III., 66, 73, 90, 118, 122, 295
Nisard, D., 281, 298, 305
Nodier, C., 23, 34-5, 65, 111, 162, 235, 246, 256
Nodier, Marie, 34-5
Norval, G. de, 258

O

ORLÉANS, Duke of (at first Duke of Chartres), 68, 70, 75, 90, 171, 251

P

PARIGOT, H., 6, 41, 49, 190, 202, 210, 211, 221, 225, 236, 243, 258, 259, 267, 275-6, 278, 305, 315, x
Parran, A., 244
Pellissier, G., 278
Pifteau, B., 128, 176*n*, 253
Plays :—
L'Alchimiste, 267
Antony, 23, 32, 49-57, 60, 74, 94, 172, 176, 185, 284-5, 316, 317*n*
Angèle, 59, 74, 185
Caligula, 68-9, 72, 158, 189, 267, 284, 317*n*
Catherine Howard, 68, 103, 298
Charles VII. et ses Grands Vassaux, 56-7, 267
La Chasse et l'Amour, 24, 151
Chevalier de Maison-Rouge, 91
Christine, 28-30, 37-8, 49, 68, 176*n*, 313
Le Comte Hermann, 94, 153, 171, 235, 286-7
La Conscience, 98, 164, 287
Les Demoiselles de St Cyr, 71, 99, 162
Don Juan de Marana, 68, 284, 286, 317*n*
Halifax, 153, 226
Hamlet (translation of), 89
Henri III. et sa Cour, 30-34, 36, 163, 184, 217, 220, 284-5
L'Invitation à la Valse, 101
Kean, 68, 103, 298, 317*n*
Mademoiselle de Belle-Isle, 71, 151, 170, 229
Une Mariage sous Louis Quinze, 71
Le Marbrier, 98, 287
Le Mari de la Veuve, 62
Monte-Cristo, 94, 218
La Noce et L'Enterrement, 25
Napoléon, 48
Richard Darlington, 56-9, 74, 94, 103, 176, 220

Plays—*continued*
  Romulus, 98, 154
  Teresa, 59
  La Tour de Nesle, 63-4, 74, 184, 284, 286, 290, 316
  Les Trois Mousquetaires, 136, 152
  (*For full list of plays see Appendix C.*)
Pollock, W. H., 63-4, 127, 132, 275, 295, ix
Poetry by Dumas, 50-1, 56-7, 70, 267-8
Porcher, 139, 159
"Psyche, Le," 25, 267
Puys, 121-3

Q

"Quarterly Review," 277
Quérard, 228, viii, ix

R

RACINE, 28, 36, 156, 295
Reade, C., 96, 195, 215, 273, 294, 339
"Revue des deux Mondes," 25, 61, 158, 288
Rhine, Dumas's travels on, 71
Romand, H. (on Dumas), 176
Rossetti, D. G., 233, 316-17
Rossetti, W. M., 233, 317
Rossini, 59, 153, 162
Rostand, 315
Rousseau, 129
Russia (Dumas's tour in), 106-8

S

SAINTE-BEUVE, C. A., 35, 267, 280
St Germain, 89
Saintsbury, Prof., 188, 192, 196, 206, 219, 227, 250, 252, 280, 291, 306, 321, 328, 333
Sale of Dumas's work, 122
Sand, George, 142, 158, 162, 230, 274, 314
Sardou, V., 313, 315
Schiller, 17, 19, 27, 28, 153, 157, 285, 311, 313
Schlegel, A. W., 248

Scott, Sir W., 23, 26, 28, 61, 104, 133, 157, 186, 189, 190, 222, 254, 261, 293-4-5, 313, 317-26, 327, 334
Scribe, E., 73-5, 133, 162
Shakespeare, 16, 19, 26, 27-8, 104, 153, 156-7, 209, 223, 265, 285, 287-8-9, 295, 311, 312, 315, 334, 336, 340
Sicily (Dumas in), 114
Sienkiewicz, H., 191, 322
Soissons (Dumas's exploit at), 42-6
"Son of Porthos, The," 214*n*
Soulié, F., 28, 37, 162
Spain, Dumas's visit to, 83-4
Stevenson, R. L., 125, 168, 207-8, 213, 276, 296, 303, 306, 327, 340, 345
"Stones of Paris," 116 and *app. D*
Sue, E., 59, 216
Swinburne, A. C., 162, 184, 234, 307, 316, 340
Switzerland, Dumas's travels in, 66
"Sylphe, La" (poem), 268

T

TALMA, 16, 19, 32
Taylor, Baron, 29, 260
Tennyson, 186
Thackeray, W. M., 68, 157, 191, 196, 201, 207, 293, 316, 326
Theatre (Dumas's), 86-7, 93-4, 119, 218
Thierry, A., 62, 184, 186

U

United States, Dumas and, 116-7

V

Vandam, A., 89*n*, 100, 141, 148, 176*n*
Vendée, La, 46-7
Victoria (Queen), 99
Victor Emmanuel, 115
Villemessant, 76-8, 99, 132, 140, 144, 344
Villers-Cotterêts, 123, 167, 170, 237, 239, 240, 243, 247, 254
Virgil, 157

INDEX

W

"Waverley," 323-4
W———, Mélanie, 49
Works by Dumas, or attributed to him:—
  Acté, 190, 194
  Amaury, 198
  Ange Pitou, 10, 236-8
  Ascanio, 219
  Une Amazone, 252
  Une Aventure d'amour, 142, 252
  Aventures de Lyderic, 194
  Aventures de John Davys, 191
  Le Bâtard de Mauléon, 227
  Black, 248
  Les Blancs et les Bleus, 256
  La Bouillie de la Comtesse Berthe, 257
  La Boule de Neige, 244
  Bric-à-Brac, 154, 228, 265
  Un Cadet de famille, 251
  Le Capitaine Pamphile, 193
  Le Capitaine Paul, 191
  Le Capitaine Richard, 247
  Catherine Blum, 238, 240
  Causeries, 101, 109, 167, 215, 220, 265
  Cécile, 197
  La Chasse au Chastre, 193, 258
  Le Chasseur de Sauvagine, 249
  Le Château d'Eppstein, 194
  Le Chevalier d'Harmental, 195, 335
  Le Chevalier de Maison-Rouge, 224
  Le Collier de la Reine, 231
  La Colombe, 255
  Les Compagnons de Jéhu, 103, 147, 217, 246
  Le Comte de Monte-Cristo, 76-8, 214-9, 233, 245, 274
  Le Comte de Moret, 255
  La Comtesse de Charny, 237-8, 241
  La Comtesse de Salisbury, 188
  Conscience l'Innocent, 10, 238-40
  Création et Rédemption (Le Docteur mystérieux et La Fille du Marquis), 242
  Crimes Célèbres, 266
  La Dame de Monsoreau, 226
  Les Deux Diane, 228
  Dieu dispose, 234
  Le Drame de '93, 261
  Emma Lyonna, 254

Works—*continued*
  La Femme au collier de velours, 235
  Fernande, 197
  Une Fille du Régent, 196
  Le Fils du Forçat, 249
  Les Frères Corses, 220, 223
  Gabriel Lambert, 220
  Les Garibaldiens, 263
  Gaule et France, 261
  Georges, 197
  Un Gil-Blas en Californie, 108
  Les Grands Hommes en robe de Chambre:—
    César, 261
    Henri IV., 261
    Louis XIII. et Richelieu, 261
  La Guerre des Femmes, 220, 222
  Histoire des Bourbons, 253
  Histoire de Louis Philippe, 261
  Histoire d'un casse-noisette, 258
  Histoire de mes Bêtes, 227, 265, 319
  L'Homme aux contes, 258
  L'Horoscope, 248
  L'Ile de Feu, 250
  Impressions de Voyage:—
    En Suisse, 189, 258
    Une Année à Florence, 259
    Les Bords du Rhin, 258
    Le Capitaine Arèna, 259
    Le Caucase, 260
    Le Corricolo, 253, 259
    Le Midi de la France, 193, 258
    De Paris à Cadix, 84, 259
    Quinze jours au Sinaï, 260
    En Russie, 260
    Le Speronare, 259
    Le Véloce, 84, 259
    La Villa Palmieri, 259
  Ingénue, 233, 245
  Isaac Laquedem, 238, 243
  Isabel de Bavière, 61, 158, 186, 188, 288, 289
  Jacquot sans Oreilles, 194
  Jehanne la Pucelle, 261
  Louis XIV. et son Siècle, 261
  Louis XV. et sa Cour, 261
  Louis XVI. et la Révolution, 261
  Les Louves de Machecoul, 249
  Madame de Chamblay, 251
  La Maison de Glace, 250
  Maître Adam, le Calabrais, 192-3
  Le Maître d'armes, 192
  Les Mariages du Père Olifus, 233

Works—*continued*
  Les Médicis, 261
  Mes Mémoires, 10, 41, 48, 51, 58, 63, 85, 129, 131, 157, 172, 234, 238, 263, 285, 288, 318
  Mémoires de Garibaldi, 251
  Mémoires de Talma, 266
  Mémoires d'Horace, 265
  Mémoires d'un Médecin, 85, 228
  Le Meneur de loups, 247
  Les Mille-et-un Fantômes, 231, 242
  Les Mohicans de Paris, 245
  Monte-Cristo (*see* Comte de)
  Les Morts vont vite, 265
  Napoléon, 261
  Nouvelles Contemporaines, 24, 184
  Une Nuit à Florence, 252
  Olympe de Clèves, 236
  Le Page du Duc de Savoie, 246
  Parisiens et Provinciaux, 254
  Le Pasteur d'Ashbourne, 238, 244
  Pauline, 189
  Pascal Bruno, 189
  Un Pays inconnu, 260
  Le Père Gigogne, 238, 257
  Le Père La Ruine, 251
  La Princesse de Monaco, 245
  Les Quarante-Cinq, 166, 230, 233
  La Régence, 261
  La Reine Margot, 220-2, 304
  La Route de Varennes, 262
  Le Saltéador, 244
  Salvator, 245
  La San Felice, 103, 253, 294

Works—*continued*
  Souvenirs d'Antony, 184-5
  Souvenirs d'une Favorite, 254
  Souvenirs dramatiques, 86, 161, 265, 314
  Les Stuarts, 261
  Sultanetta, 248
  Sylvandire, 198
  La Terreur Prussienne, 20, 256*n*, 262
  Le Testament de M. Chauvelin, 50 235
  Les Trois Mousquetaires, 76-8, 122, 173, 184, 199-208, 212, 214, 217, 233, 274, 323-4, 326, 333
  Le Trou de l'Enfer, 234, 248
  La Tulipe Noire, 231, 234, 276
  Le Vicomte de Bragelonne, 207-8, 211-13, 233, 298
  La Vie au Désert, 251
  Une Vie d'Artiste, 245
  Vingt Ans Après, 208, 212, 298
  (*For other works, see Appendix C*)
Weyman, 221, 326

Y

Yonne (Dumas's candidature in the), 91-3

Z

Zola, 297, 330, 340

Printed in the United States
1045300001B/7